Approximat

The early modern period was an age of anatomical exploration and revelation, with new discoveries capturing the imagination not only of scientists but also of playwrights and poets. *Approximate Bodies* examines, in fascinating detail, the changing representation of the body in early modern drama and in the period's anatomical and gynaecological treatises.

Maurizio Calbi traces a number of emblematic figurations of the body, which he sees as dramatized and rearticulated in the period's texts: the eroticized, deformed body of the outsider, for example, or the effeminate body of the desiring male and the disfigured body parts of the desiring female. Drawing on the theories of Foucault, Derrida and Lacan and working through close readings of key plays and treatises, the study examines the way in which social and psychic domains are involved in the early modern construction of the body. Crucially, Calbi argues that the early modern body is obsessively construed in terms of differentiating markers of power such as gender, race, status and eroticism. At the same time, bodies are presented as unstable and unfinished entities, uncannily proximate to one another.

Compelling and impeccably researched, this is a sophisticated account of the fantasies and anxieties that play a role in constructing the early modern body. *Approximate Bodies* makes a major contribution to the field of early modern studies and to debates around the body.

Maurizio Calbi is Associate Professor of English Literature and History of English Culture at the University of Salerno, Italy. He has published on literary theory, early modern drama and culture, contemporary rewritings of Shakespeare and post-colonial literature.

Approximate Bodies

Gender and power in early modern drama and anatomy

Maurizio Calbi

LONDON AND NEW YORK

First published 2005
by Routledge
2 Park Square, Milton Park, Abingdon, Oxon, OX14 4RN

Simultaneously published in the USA and Canada
by Routledge
270 Madison Ave, New York, NY 10016

Routledge is an imprint of the Taylor & Francis Group

Typeset in Baskerville by Bookcraft Ltd, Stroud, Gloucestershire
Printed and bound in Great Britain by TJ International, Padstow, Cornwall

British Library Cataloguing in Publication Data
A catalogue record for this book is available from the British Library

Library of Congress Cataloging in Publication Data
Calbi, Maurizio
Approximate bodies : gender and power in early modern drama and anatomy / Maurizio Calbi.
p. cm.
Includes bibliographical references and index.
1. English drama – Early modern and Elizabethan, 1500–1600 – History and criticism.
2. Body, Human, in literature. 3. English drama – 17th century – History and criticism.
4. Power (Social sciences) in literature. 5. Sex role in literatature. I. Title.
PR658.B63C353 2005
822'.3093561–dc22

2004021082

ISBN 0-415-34560-X (hbk)
ISBN 0-415-34561-8 (pbk)

To the memory of my father and to my mother

Contents

List of illustrations

Acknowledgements

I wish to thank, first of all, Marina Vitale, who initially encouraged me to carry on researching in the area of early modern literature and culture. She has continued to give advice and support by reading the work in progress and making relevant comments throughout. Her work on cultural dynamics has been an inspiration to me. I owe her a lot, much more than she would be keen to admit.

Some of the ideas developed in the book were prompted by memorable discussions around the time of the Essex Early Modern Research Group. I would like to thank the members of the group: Francis Barker, Jerry Brotton, Al Constantine, Tracey Hill, Paula Hutchings, John Joughin, Angelica Michelis and Stephen Speed. John read part of the work, and I have profited much from the serious and semi-serious conversations we have had over the years. Jerry made detailed and incisive comments on the first chapter, and I thank him also for having helped me overcome my scepticism about eating out in Britain. I value very much their intellectual acumen and their ability to look ahead as well as their friendship. Francis Barker, apart from being my friend, acted as my PhD supervisor for the thesis that forms the basis of this book. I have often imagined the pleasure he would have had in receiving this book as a gift. Unfortunately, the gift, like the letter, will never reach its destination. He is no longer with us, and mourning for him will be almost interminable.

I presented sections of the work in progress at the University of Essex, Loughborough University, Bath Spa University College, University of Seville, University of Cádiz, the 2001 World Shakespeare Congress (University of Valencia), the 2001 Conference 'Incontrare i mostri' (University of Salerno), and the 2002 SEDERI conference (University of Vigo). I want to express my gratitude to the people who were involved with these events: Peter Hulme, Jonathan White and Elaine Jordan (University of Essex), also for their long-term friendship, Elaine Hobby and Bill Overton (Loughborough University), Carolina Sánchez-Palencia and Manuel José Gómez Lara (University of Seville), Rafael Núñez Vélez (University of Cádiz), Bruce Smith (Georgetown University), Martin Orkin (University of Haifa), Maria Teresa Chialant (University of Salerno) and Laura Di Michele (University of L'Aquila), also for her encouragement since the days of my MA at Essex. A special mention to Bruce Smith and Martin Orkin, the convenors of the workshop on masculinity at the 2001 World Shakespeare Congress in Valencia, for their astute feedback and comments. Martin has since continued being generous towards to my work, and has made me look at it in new ways. Over the years, I have also incurred intellectual debts with Catherine Belsey, John Drakakis, Gerald MacLean and Patricia Parker.

After a long period in Britain, I took up a position at the University of Salerno (Italy), where I met new and old friends and colleagues. I want to thank Maria Teresa Chialant (also for being always discreetly present), Antonella D'Amelia, Maria Rosaria De Bueriis, Flora De Giovanni (with whom I share a lot), Bruna Di Sabato, Giuseppe Gentile, Antonella Piazza, Eleonora Rao, and others, for having made me feel at home and offered support in different but equally important ways. I also want to mention the scholarship and friendship of colleagues I have come to know since I have been back in Italy: Daniela Corona, Elio Di Piazza, Alessandra Di Maio, Alessandra Marzola, Clara Mucci and Carlo Pagetti.

I owe a special thanks to the members of the PhD programme at the University of Naples 'L'Orientale' for providing another stimulating research environment: Silvana Carotenuto, Iain Chambers, Anna Maria Cimitile, Rossella Ciocca, Lidia Curti, Marina De Chiara, Daniela De Filippis, Simonetta De Filippis, Patrizia Fusella, Marie-Hélène La Forest, Marina Vitale, Jane Wilkinson, and others, including PhD students with a rare ability to engage in intellectual matters. I must single out the coordinator of the programme, Lidia Curti, for her own inimitable way of being a lecturer, a researcher, and a person who cares. Silvana Carotenuto has contributed to the development of most of the ideas presented in this book in ways of which she is probably not fully aware, and has marked it throughout with her intelligence and friendship.

David Ainscough, Cathy Raven, Josie and Lorenzo offered me a place to stay in Coton at a crucial stage in the completion of the project. I am grateful for this. Lastly, I wish to thank Sue for having been the first reader of the book and for having shared with me what matters most. Quite simply, without her, I could not have done this.

Note on texts

When citing from early printed books in original or facsimile editions, I have retained the original orthography, except for normalizing to modern usage the forms of the letters *i* and *j*, *u* and *v*, the long *s*, the tilde, superior letters in contractions, and other abbreviations. I have also substituted 'than' for 'then' whenever necessary. I have corrected a few clear misprints. Punctuation is kept as it appears in the original.

Figure 1 Jacopo Zucchi, *Amore e Psiche* (1589)

Introduction

Thinking about the body

> Car où donc, et quand, y a-t-il du corps quelque chose qui ne soit pas écrit, refait, cultivé, identifié par les outils d'une symbolique sociale?
>
> (Michel de Certeau, 'Des outils pour écrire le corps')

> Thinking the body as constructed demands a rethinking of the meaning of construction itself.
>
> (Judith Butler, *Bodies That Matter*)

> La question du reste, dirions-nous qu'elle est secrètement liée à quelque mort du roi?
>
> (Jacques Derrida, *Donner le temps*)

Keir Elam has recently commented on 'the *corporeal* turn' in the field of Renaissance studies. This is a shift of attention 'from the word to the flesh, from the semantic to the somatic'[1] that has already produced a number of critical works focusing on bodies as disparate as 'bodies tremulous', 'bodies single-sexed', 'bodies enclosed', 'bodies intestinal', 'bodies consumed', 'bodies carnivalized', 'bodies effeminized', 'bodies embarrassed', 'bodies sodomized', 'bodies emblazoned or dissected', 'bodies castrated', or simply 'in parts'.[2] According to Elam, this 'body boom' owes much to the work of Michel Foucault, and is also a reaction-formation against the inability on the part of various kinds of formalist and high structuralist approaches 'to come to terms with [the body's] sheer untidy, asyntactic, pre-semantic *bodiliness*', with 'its irreducible and unrationalizable materiality'.[3]

This book situates itself within, and hopes to be a critical contribution to, this ever-expanding body of body criticism. It principally focuses on Jacobean tragedies and sixteenth- and seventeenth-century anatomical and gynaecological treatises, arguing that these texts are sites of inscription, dramatization and rearticulation of emblematic and complex constructions of the early modern body, of its parts and fluids, as well as of its contours. The constructions of the body the book explores range from the masculine homosocial body operating across boundaries of status to the privatized body of the emerging 'bourgeois' couple; from the scrutinized body of the aristocratic female to the eroticized and deformed body of the outsider; from the effeminate body of the desiring male to the disfigured body parts of the desiring female. The book is structured as a theoretical and historical investigation of these constructions, of their fantasmatic dimension, as well as of the anxieties they engender. It maintains that they take place within historically specific coordinates of power such as gender, eroticism, 'race' and status. Additionally, it suggests that the intersection of two or more of these coordinates results in the destabilization of the coherence of each, and that this not only affects the fashioning of the body, but also activates a series of processes of displacement, projection and substitution.

I speak of 'construction' and 'coordinates of power' in order to underline a few points that are implicitly or explicitly argued in many of the studies of specific representations of the body Keir Elam enumerates. First of all, the body is not a transhistorical entity. Second, it is directly involved in asymmetrical relations of power. To refer to the critical study at the top of Elam's list, Francis Barker's, the body is not 'an extra-historical residue, invariant and mute'.[4] It is 'a relation in a system of liaisons which are material, discursive, psychic, sexual, but without stop or centre'. Precisely because it is 'a relation', Barker proceeds, 'it would be better to speak of a certain "bodiliness" than of "the body"'.[5]

The title of this book attempts to register some of these notions. One of the senses of 'approximate bodies' is that bodies are never self-identical and indivisible. They are unfinished and malleable constructs. The body is one of those 'concepts', to paraphrase from Nietzsche's *On the Genealogy of Morals*, 'in which an entire process is semiotically concentrated'. As such, it 'elude[s] definition'. Indeed, as Nietzsche adds, 'only that which has no history is definable'.[6] Yet, it is worth specifying that the history Nietzsche has in mind, and the one I mostly abide by in the following pages, is not an infinite, uncomplicated and unbroken progression. Nietzsche argues as follows, in a passage that was clearly to influence Foucault:

> The entire history of a 'thing', an organ, a custom ... is ... by no means its *progressus* toward a goal, even less a logical *progressus* by the shortest route and with the smallest expenditure of force – but a succession of more or less profound, more or less mutually independent processes of subduing, plus the resistances they encounter, the attempts at transformation for the purposes of defense and reaction, and the results of successful counteractions.[7]

Thus, there is no such a thing as *the* body. Or, rather, as especially suggested in the analysis of *The Duchess of Malfi* and coeval anatomical and gynaecological discourses in Chapter 1, the body as an entity that is given in its immediacy, substantially identical to itself and agitated by 'natural' heterosexual desires, is itself a historical entity. It flickers into existence in the early modern period at the point of intersection between the science of anatomy and its 'ocular economy' and the emerging ideology of 'companionate marriages', marking its distance from, as well as its complicity with, other historical formations of the body.

In *Gender Trouble* Judith Butler asks: 'Does sex have a history ...? Is there a history of how the duality of sex was established, a genealogy that might expose the binary options as a variable construction?'[8] In his groundbreaking work, significantly entitled *Making Sex*, Thomas Laqueur provides part of this history and genealogy. He describes in great detail how 'we' came to be coherently and dichotomously 'sexed', the historical and epistemological shift from a one-sex model in which male and female bodies were 'arrayed according to their degree of metaphysical perfection, their vital heat, along an axis whose telos was male' to a two-sex model that insisted – and perhaps still insists – on a 'radical dimorphism' and 'biological divergence' between the sexes.[9] He also maintains that it is only within the latter model of incommensurability, which was firmly in place by the end of the eighteenth century, that the body, equated with 'sex', began to be conceptualized as foundational, as the matter-of-fact 'ground' for a variety of claims about the socio-political order. In pre-Enlightenment texts, instead, '*sex*, or the body, must be understood as the epiphenomenon, while *gender*, what we would take to be a cultural category, was primary or "real"'. Laqueur continues as follows:

> At the very least, what we call sex and gender were in the 'one-sex model' explicitly bound up in a circle of meanings from which escape to a supposed biological substrate – the strategy of the Enlightenment – was impossible.[10]

In a sense, then, 'gender' historically precedes 'sex'.[11] This does not mean, of course, that the notion of sex proper to the two-sex model (in other words, sex as an ontological category and the fulcrum of identity) is gender-neutral. Laqueur clarifies:

> Almost everything one wants to *say* about sex – however sex is understood – already has in it a claim about gender. Sex, in both the one-sex and the two-sex worlds, is situational; it is explicable only within the context of battles over gender and power.[12]

In Laqueur's work, therefore, 'sex' is not to 'gender' as nature is to history and culture. 'Sex' *does* have a history, and the very possibility of speaking of 'opposite sexes' or of 'sexual difference' as based upon anatomical, biological or chromosomal difference is the result of a historical transformation in the way in which we conceptualize bodies, pleasures and desires. Relatedly, 'sex' is always-already gendered, inexorably imprinted with power relations. Yet, although Laqueur's is clearly a constructivist approach to the body, he repeatedly lays stress on the importance of holding on to 'a distinction between the body and the body as discursively constituted, between seeing and seeing-as'.[13] In fact, he sees his project in the following terms, as

> poised between the body as that extraordinarily fragile, feeling and transient mass of flesh with which we are all familiar – too familiar – and the body that is so hopelessly bound to its cultural meanings as to elude unmediated access.[14]

Like the body in *Hamlet*, this 'fragile, feeling and transient mass of flesh' does not seem to want to 'melt / Thaw, and resolve itself into a dew' (I.ii.129–30).[15] At the end of his introductory chapter to *Making Sex*, Laqueur goes as far as to express his regret at not having been able to offer 'a sustained account of experience in the body'.[16]

I often refer to Laqueur's work in the course of this book, mostly to raise doubts about the predominance, coherence or stability of the one-sex model, but retaining his important emphasis on the historicity of bodies, pleasures and desires.[17] In the first chapter I argue that Laqueur may be underestimating the significance of the ocular drive structuring both early modern anatomy and the literary representation of the body. Does the desire to bring forth to view, inspect and control a body that comes to be gendered in the 'feminine' merely reinscribe the one-sex body/flesh, as well as the system of resemblances that functions as its epistemological prop? In the third chapter, starting from the marginal example of moles and/or false conceptions, abject products of the womb attributed to female self-insemination or to a conception in which a defective male seed is overwhelmed by the overabundance of female seed and/or menstrual blood, I underline the ideological effort involved in the reassertion of the hierarchy of reproductive fluids inhering in the one-sex model. I also stress the discrepancy between the anatomist's allegiance to textual authorities and the performative aspect of his 'art', and I read this 'art' in terms of a *mise-en-scène* of the dichotomization of the body along gender lines. Moreover, I begin to suggest that medical literature often displays ambivalence towards female sexual pleasure. It simultaneously acknowledges and problematizes this pleasure, and this has considerable repercussions on the figuration of female sexual organs as colder, less perfect and inverted versions of those of the male. I return to these points in the fifth chapter, showing that the 'newly discovered' clitoris is not, as Laqueur asserts, yet another reassuring analogue of the male penis, an instance of the one-sex model's ability to re-present itself in new guises. It is, rather, an uncanny, 'supplementary' double that disrupts the reflection of like to like and insinuates doubts about the originality of the 'sex which is one' and its reproductive and heterosexualized pleasures.[18] In short, I contest a certain tendency on Laqueur's part to homogenize a discursive field that is complex and contradictory; a field, in fact, that is a combination of dominant, residual and emergent elements.[19] Therefore, as I argue in the third chapter, I entirely agree with Patricia Parker's stress on the necessity 'to interrogate the sheer repetition of the [one-sex model] … as symptomatic and ideological rather than as a descriptive discourse, to focus … on the rhetoric of insistence'.[20]

To clarify a little further the theoretical position I develop in the book, I want to underline that my understanding of issues such as 'constructedness' and the materiality of the body is rather different from that of Laqueur. To Laqueur, there is something of the body that somehow escapes its constitution within discourse(s): its materiality, which he consistently *signifies* as the 'flesh', the 'extraordinarily fragile, feeling and transient mass of flesh', or 'the flesh in its simplicity'.[21] Yet, is this extra-discursive 'flesh' – the flesh in its immediacy – anything other than a historically specific formation of the body? Echoing Judith Butler's work, I argue that any and every reference to a certain materiality of the body that eludes construction is a construction and re-deployment of specific forms of materiality. It is intrinsically, even if inadvertently, violent, in that it *decides* what counts and what does not count as the 'matter' of the body.[22] As my reference to the work of Butler should make clear, this is not to advance some version or other of a somatophobic discursive idealism – quite the contrary. It is to suggest, that the relation between the 'body as constructed' and the 'body as unconstructed' is not a relation between an inside and an outside that are clearly distinct from one another. As Butler puts it, 'there is an "outside" to what is constructed by discourse, but this is not an absolute "outside", an ontological thereness that exceeds or counters the boundaries of discourse'. It is, rather, a *constitutive* outside, a notion that 'can only be thought – when it can – in relation to that discourse, at and as its most tenuous borders'.[23]

Butler's notion of the constitutive outside enables one to register, at one and the same time, the force of exclusion and abjection that constitutes the 'outside' as an 'outside' *and* the persistent possibility of its disruptive return, often within the very terms of this exclusion and abjection.[24] To relate this more specifically to the question of constructedness and the materiality of the body, one needs to emphasize that the body is not only *involved* in relations of power. The body does not *pre-exist* such an involvement. Relations of power are formative of the body's very materiality. This is somehow occluded when one speaks, as one inevitably must, of power acting *on* bodies or bodies as *sites* of power, which are expressions implying that the body and its materiality are in a position of exteriority in relation to power, and that power is a 'substance' or a 'subject'. Butler explains as follows:

> The body is not an independent materiality that is invested by power relations external to it, but it is that for which materialization and investiture are coextensive … . 'Materiality' designates a certain effect of power or, rather, *is* power in its formative or constituting effects.[25]

Thus, one major modality of power's hold over the body – another expression that unwittingly reinscribes a metaphysics of substance – is the process whereby bodies are materialized as bodies that matter/mean. Yet, one must add that this materialization is by definition a *reiterative* process, not an act carried out once and for all by a 'subject' or by 'power': 'There is no power that acts, but only a reiterated acting that is power in its persistence and instability.'[26] Moreover, this materialization is simultaneous with the violent institution of 'a domain of radical *unintelligibility* that resists materialization altogether or that remains radically dematerialized'.[27] This is a 'domain of abjected bodies', 'a field of deformation' that not only provides 'the necessary support … for the bodies which … qualify as bodies that matter', but also comes to haunt, as a constitutive outside, these 'meaningful' and 'intelligible' bodies.[28] It endlessly poses the threat of a terrifying return.

From a theoretical point of view, the influence of Judith Butler's work is pervasive in the following pages, especially her assertion that it is 'as important to think about how and to what end bodies are constructed as is it … to think about how and to what end bodies are *not* constructed'.[29] Also crucial is her claim that the construction of the body is in fact a reiterated and reiterable process of 'regulatory production', and that the dynamics of production, regulation, exclusion and abjection have both a social and a psychic dimension.[30] More specifically, Butler's theoretical insights inform the third chapter of the book, where I reconsider Laqueur's one-sex/flesh model to stress how the womb figures as a constitutive outside, as the site of de-formation of a phallomorphic 'regulatory production' of bodies as mirror images of one another, unceasingly posing threats to its coherence. They also permeate the fourth chapter, where I analyse the rhetoric of hypermasculine bodies that present themselves as 'dis-embodied' but nonetheless reveal a troubling kinship with the feminine abject body they continually endeavour to turn away from. Butler's work also has some bearing on the section of the fifth chapter dedicated to the 'discovery' of the clitoris qua female penis. In this section I argue that this 'discovery' is a bringing into being, as well as a regulation of, the clitoris; and that this 'constraining production' is in turn predicated upon a prior resolve about what counts and what does not count as bodily form. I suggest that it is nothing but the *excessive* reiteration of a homosocial specular economy that makes visible the latter's constitutive instabilities. This reiteration raises the suspicion that the 'original' (in other words, the bodily part that matters) may be a rather poor copy of its copy.

To recall the article by Keir Elam with which I started, this book's concern with the body and its literary figuration is not, in any simple sense, equivalent to a turning towards, or a return to, the body's 'irreducible and unrationalizable materiality'.[31] The book *does* deal with some kind of 'pre-semantic *bodiliness*',[32] but not to oppose it to an irremediably 'semanticized' body or to a dis-embodied and 'castrating' logic of the signifier. Instead, it attempts to reassess and displace the terms in which the question is posed. It does so both theoretically and historically. It draws attention to historically specific processes of fashioning of bodies, bodily parts, fluids and contours, arguing that these processes work not only through discursive articulations (by producing and regulating the body and thus, in a sense, by 'semanticizing' it), but also through mechanisms of exclusion and abjection that are social as well as psychic. In other words, it shows not only how bodies are constructed but also the intrinsically violent dynamics whereby bodies are constructed as 'unconstructed', as that which remains, to use Elam's expression, in a state of a 'pre-semantic bodiliness'. It adds that these unconstructed, excluded and abjected bodies are far from occupying a position of absolute exteriority in relation to the bodies that are made into 'bodies that matter'. They are simultaneously internal and external to these bodies, a kind of margin marking its interior, not least because they are the result of a violent process of repudiation that is somehow *dependent* upon that which it repudiates for its articulation.

This is why, I surmise, there is no exclusion and abjection without the excluded and abjected eventually returning, sometimes in a slightly different form, and not simply from an outside or an inside. This is also why haunting can only occur in a field of power relations that are by definition asymmetrically constituted. In effect, I continually underline the interimplication of the 'social' and the 'psychic'.

Partially in the first chapter and throughout the second chapter, I associate haunting with the Lacanian 'ex-timate object', an object at the very centre of psychic economies as the threatening excluded term that can only appear retrospectively, through substitutive objects. This is an uncanny object that exists only *through*, *in* and *as* the process of its coming back to haunt and 'counter-sign' – in more senses than one – intelligible and meaningful bodies.[33] Yet, I insist, at one and the same time, that the vicissitudes of this object are structured by historically specific configurations of vectors of power such as status and gender.

'What is closest *must* be avoided, by virtue of its very proximity', Jacques Derrida argues.[34] The early modern texts I consider incessantly stage bodies that are threateningly *proximate* to one another. The production and regulation of bodies excludes and abjects but is nonetheless unable to rule out haunting. Put differently, what is excluded and abjected never seems to be at a safe distance from the bodies that embody and re-enact the hegemonic discourses by which they are invested and through which they are constituted. It is often *too close* to these bodies, intolerably so, and unceasingly turning into their uncanny 'other'. Moreover, as I show in the analysis of fantasmatic scenarios of male sexual jealousy in the first and second chapter, it is always susceptible to a 'cryptic incorporation' on the part of the bodies that posture as 'bodies that matter'. This is a process that problematizes the relation to itself of an inside and makes the excluded and abjected into a site of dreaded identifications and desires.[35] Whether cryptically incorporated or dangerously proximate, what is excluded and abjected, as I also argue in relation to the representation of masculinity in the fourth chapter, induces anxiety, as well as complex processes of displacement, projection and substitution. Anxiety, in turn, often activates or reactivates violence. On the one hand, this is symptomatic of the destabilizing effect it has on the fabrication of legitimate bodies. On the other, it indicates that the bodies that fail to count as bodies can become sites of further exclusions and abjections. To paraphrase Jonathan Dollimore, there is never safety in exclusion and abjection.[36] As far as the texts under examination are concerned, violence regularly resurfaces when an alleged opposition or a reassuring resemblance between bodies transmutes itself into an *uncanny* similarity.

The regulatory production of the body thus entails a series of complex cultural dynamics. It is an ongoing cultural process, and one that is fragmentary, contradictory and contested. In the course of this book, I read early modern texts as sites of inscription, dramatization and rearticulation of historically specific forms of this process. I am mostly interested in the intersections of these forms within individual texts and across texts; in the way in which these forms contest each other; in the permutations resulting from their being deployed in a variety of contexts; in the fantasmatic scenarios they give rise to, the anxieties they engender, the 'actual' or fantasmatic violence they occasion.

As I have begun to point out, the complexity of these processes is somewhat silenced in Laqueur's account of sixteenth- and seventeenth-century medical literature, in so far as it propounds a fundamentally homogeneous one-sex body reflecting an essentially uniform socio-politic configuration.[37] To move on to the other textual area with which the book is concerned, the nostalgia for unified totalities also seems to affect allegedly Foucaultian re-readings of the representation of the body in Jacobean tragedy such as Leonard Tennenhouse's *Power on Display*. To Tennenhouse, the Jacobean scaffold is the site of the unequivocal reassertion of the 'metaphysics of blood'. It is the *locus* of an endless reaffirmation of 'blood in its purest form', the blood of the patriarch-king, as well as of the enclosure of an 'aristocratic community' centred upon this pure form of blood.[38] This re-legitimizing of blood is achieved through the *public* display of elaborate scenes of punishment of the agent of pollution, most often a transgressive 'aristocratic female' who functions as a conduit for the incorporation of an outsider, and thus obfuscates the distinction between the inside and the outside of the 'aristocratic community'.

Several objections can be made to this interpretation, on both historical and theoretical grounds.[39] In the first chapter I underline, in a reading of John Webster's *The Duchess of Malfi*, that the spectacular display of the body and blood of the sovereign is most notable in its absence; that the 'visibilising'[40] of the body inhering in the deployment of a newly emerging ocular drive is largely inconsistent with the form of visibility proper to this spectacular display, not least because this drive is predicated upon, and perpetuates, something like a distinction between 'public' and 'private'. Moreover, I emphasize that the display of violence is symbolically 'privatized', and that the demonization of the pollution resulting from the 'mismatch' between the Duchess and Antonio is part of the play but is not *the* play. In the second chapter, in a study of Middleton and Rowley's *The Changeling*, I argue that the 'aristocratic community' – *concesso non dato* that there is such a thing and that it is one – is internally divided even prior to pollution, and that the evacuation of contaminated blood is effected not by some patriarchal representative of the King but by a 'surgeon' who is himself a vehicle of contamination.[41] More generally, I maintain that the interplay of status and gender complicates any successful purification in the play. In the fourth chapter I return to the question of the intersection of two or more vectors of power, showing that the interweaving of gender and 'race' in *Othello* problematizes any sense of binarism or closure. Moreover, in this chapter I depart from Tennenhouse's anthropological – and monolithic – model to introduce the elaborate production of abject and deformed bodies in the discourses that take the Levant and Northern Africa as their target.[42] These are discourses that clearly inform Shakespeare's play.

Unlike Tennenhouse, therefore, I read Jacobean tragedy as a cultural form that is scarcely dependent upon the spectacular display of the body and blood of the king qua *pater familias*.[43] In this respect, my analysis is indebted to Francis Barker's argument that the 'metaphysics of presence', signified by the visible body of the sovereign, is not fully in place in Jacobean tragedy.[44] It also owes much to Franco Moretti's hypothesis that Jacobean tragedy re-marks and exacerbates the de-legitimation of the king qua 'fundamental paradigm of the dominant culture', the centre around and through which a whole socio-symbolic system is ordered.[45] This is a king Shakespearean tragedy has already dramatized as the 'impossible being … in whose person the meaning (or rather the loss of meaning) … is concentrated'.[46] To Moretti, desire emblematizes this re-marking and exacerbation of the deconsecration of the sovereign. It is a force of negation or antithesis that inexorably exceeds and suspends any attempt at recuperation or synthesis. It is a principle 'to which everyone … equally succumbs'. 'This very fact', Moretti adds, 'makes it an agent of destruction in a social hierarchy based on the diametrically opposed principle of *inequality*.'[47]

Yet Moretti may be overestimating the significance of the *absence* of the sovereign for an understanding of some of the peculiar features of Jacobean tragedy. I agree that desire is most often represented as a 'spectral obsession', a 'repetition compulsion',[48] and that it is to be read in its intimate and intricate relation with the socio-political realm, in terms of the deleterious effects it has on 'a social hierarchy based on the … principle of *inequality*'.[49] Nonetheless, I often choose to speak of the disruption of the 'deployment of alliance', the *ensemble* of social and political relations implemented and secured through the exchange of women. Michel Foucault defines it as 'a system of marriage, of fixation and development of kinship ties, of transmission of names and possessions', which is built around 'a system of rules defining the permitted and the forbidden, the licit and the illicit', and is 'attuned to a homeostasis of the social body'.[50] Or, alternatively, I speak of the undermining of the 'male homosocial structure', which Eve Kosofsky Sedgwick characterizes as the structure 'whereby men's "heterosexual desire" for women serves as a more or less perfunctory detour on the way to a closer, but homophobically proscribed, bonding with another man'.[51] I underline, especially in the second and fifth chapters of the book, the repercussions of a desire that is 'spectral' and 'compulsive' (in other words, a desire whose object is, to some extent, nothing but desire) on these two interconnected *dispositifs* of constraining production of bodies and identities. But I also pursue, more or less overtly, some of the implications of Moretti's interpretation. If desire is a force 'to which everyone … *equally* succumbs',[52] its material correlative, as well as its space of inscription, is a 'naturalized' and 'pre-symbolic' body that is *potentially* and threateningly unstructured by signifiers of the differential distribution of power – the effect of some kind of *reductio ad absurdum*.[53] From the point of view of the dominant, this body, informed by 'natural' drives, is monstrous and unnatural *because* it is 'natural'. In an important sense, it is part of a nature that no longer unproblematically underwrites a dominant socio-political and ideological formation.[54] But it is worth adding, first of all, that the point of view of the dominant, as represented in this drama, is often labile, contradictory and/or fully involved in this process of reduction whereby bodies tendentially become almost the same as one another (in other words, proximate entities).[55] Secondly, this pre-symbolic and 'factual' body is also sometimes re-deployed as a kind of substratum of the emerging ideology of companionate marriages. It is subjected to, and becomes an essential part of, a 'project' Catherine Belsey illustrates as the attempt 'to ground desire in true love, its moralized, domesticated version, based on partnership, companionship, the fitness of mind and disposition'; a project, she adds, that is fraught with difficulties and anxieties.[56] The body of the Duchess of Malfi in Webster's eponymous play is a case in point. As I argue in the first chapter, the Duchess's departure from the deployment of alliance – her choice of a husband, which is a 'going into a wilderness, where [she] shall find nor path, nor friendly clew to be [her] guide' (I.i.359–61) – goes hand in hand with a laying bare of a 'flesh-and-blood' body unmarked by differentials of status and 'vain ceremony' (I.i.456).[57] This body is monstrous and unnatural only if one equates Webster's play with Ferdinand's or the Cardinal's or Bosola's. It is a body that desires but immediately submits itself to a lack of desire: 'Lay a naked sword between us, keep us chaste' (I.i.501); a body that 'enjoys' and is reproductive off-stage, in-between the acts; a body whose desires, because of external threats and the internal tensions afflicting the emerging 'conjugal couple', cannot but be subordinated to precise rhythms.

Thus, to argue that early seventeenth-century English tragedy dramatizes *either* the irremediable subversion *or* the irreversible perpetuation of aspects of the dominant socio-political and ideological formation such as the 'deployment of alliance', the 'male homosocial structure' or 'sovereignty' would be to disregard crucial aspects of the complex and contradictory negotiations involving bodies, pleasures and identities, as well as the 'deconstructive dynamics' in which the dominant is often implicated.[58] To rephrase Stephen Greenblatt's notorious finale to one of the most contested essays written in recent years, and connect it with this drama's representation of the body, there is subversion, no end of subversion, but this subversion is juxtaposed to ongoing processes of re-fashioning of *dispositifs* of regulatory production of bodies, pleasures and identities.[59] Indeed, whether I explore the constructions of the body in early seventeenth-century tragedy or early modern medical treatises, or investigate the interconnection of these constructions, I continuously lay emphasis on 'the part played by contradiction and dislocation in the mutually reactive process of transgression and its control',[60] as well as on the displacements and disavowals through which potentially disruptive contradictions and conflicts 'may be reconstituted as, and in, new forces of repression'.[61]

1 'That body of hers'

The secret, the specular, the spectacular in *The Duchess of Malfi* and anatomical discourses

There is nothing so highe in the heavens above, nothing so low in the earth beneath, nothing so profound in the bowels of Arte, nor any thing so hid in the secretes of nature, as that good will dare not enterprise, search, unclose or discover.

(John Banister, *Historie of Man*)

'Looking' where there is 'nothing to see'; as if the site of origin, as if one's 'history' was written up in capital letters in the site one has elected as the fantasmatic theatre of one's own 'origin': the inside of the uterus; as if on the scene of desire there was *something* to see.

(Rosi Braidotti, 'Organs Without Bodies')

'Cover her face'

In John Webster's *The Duchess of Malfi*, as he gazes on the strangled body of his sister, Ferdinand addresses his accomplice Bosola as follows: 'Cover her face: mine eyes dazzle' (IV.ii.264). The 'general eclipse' of the Duchess's body, threatened earlier in the play (II.v.79) and understood by Ferdinand as the necessary outcome of her being 'too much i' th' light' (IV.i.42), seems not to occur without the uncanny emergence of the intolerable gaze of the abject corpse.[1] Nonetheless, the apotropaic gesture of covering the Duchess's face is followed by Ferdinand's request to uncover it once more: 'Let me see her face again' (IV.ii.272). This request is also intimately, if obliquely, connected with Ferdinand's envisioning of another – more gruesome – scene of uncovering: 'The wolf shall find her grave, and scrape it up: / Not to devour the corpse, but to discover / The horrid murder' (IV.ii.309–11). In these lines the Calabrian Duke presents himself as other than himself, as a less-than-human hybrid entity moving uneasily in the liminal zone where the Duchess's corpse has already been situated. He will continue to exercise his keen sight, but the fantasmatic reiteration of his visual mastery over the 'object' disquietingly comes to coincide with the undoing of the 'human'.

The double injunction to veil and unveil the female body is not confined to this scene in which the Duchess of Malfi is strangled. It is part of the contradictory and unstable desire to see and not to see that pervades Webster's play. In the course of this chapter, I want to explore the gender and class dynamics of this desire, and show some of the ways in which it intersects with the equally ambiguous 'ocular drive' governing coeval anatomical and gynaecological discourses. By following the textual movement of a play I regard as emblematic of a multi-layered crisis in the constraining production of bodies, pleasures and identities, I also want to develop further some of the theoretical questions I started addressing in the 'Introduction'.

The female body and the body politic

Within the 'ocular economy' of Webster's tragedy the female body is construed as an entity that is at once entirely visible and threateningly opaque. It simultaneously upholds and undermines the 'body proper' of the social.[2] One of the initial constructions of the female body is Antonio's 'picture' (I.i.207) of the Duchess as the 'normative' and inaccessible Lady of courtly love, a high-born virginal being whose 'countenance' is liable to be misinterpreted as erotic provocation and yet remains, fundamentally, nothing but the embodiment of 'continence' and denial:

Ant. For her discourse, it is so full of rapture
You only will begin then to be sorry
When she doth end her speech ...: whilst she speaks,
She throws upon a man so sweet a look,
That it were able raise one to a galliard
That lay in a dead palsy, and dote
On that sweet countenance: but in that look,
There speaketh so divine a continence
As cuts off all lascivious, and vain hope.

(I.i.190–2; 194–200)

It is worth adding that the Duchess is presented not only as a woman – or, rather, to use Lacanian language, as 'Woman' or '*The* woman', the fantasmatic support of masculine identity[3] – but also as a way of making statements about the body politic. More specifically, she is the yardstick against which the 'political' activities of her two brothers can be gauged.[4] In this sense, Antonio's praise of the Duchess relates back to the panegyric of the 'judicious' French king he offers only a few lines into the start of the play:

Delio. How do you like the French court?
Ant. I admire it –
In seeking to reduce both state and people
To a fix'd order, their judicious king

Begins at home: quits first his royal palace
Of flatt'ring sycophants, of dissolute
And infamous persons …
Consid'ring duly, that a prince's court
Is like a common fountain, whence should flow
Pure silver drops in general: but if 't chance
Some curs'd example poison 't near the head,
Death and diseases through the whole land spread.

(I.i.4–9; 11–15)

Antonio's commendation of the Duchess also links with, and is in fact the last of, a series of arresting tableaux through which various members of the Malfi court are introduced, from Bosola[5] to the Cardinal and Ferdinand. Unlike the Duchess, they are characterized in such a way that they come to stand for the lethal 'curs'd example' of Antonio's initial speech. They contaminate the court qua fountain 'near the head'.[6]

Therefore, as Franco Moretti points out in his study of Jacobean tragedy, the court is signified as 'the exemplary site of an unrestrained conflict of private interests', as the new 'collective protagonist' replacing the centre previously provided by the tragic hero and king.[7] Sovereignty is a receding formation in Webster's play, not only because it is located elsewhere, but also because this 'elsewhere' is already internally split when it begins to function as a term of comparison for the Malfi court. Strictly speaking, it is the French king's reiterated endeavour to *re-establish* a 'fix'd order' that prevails over the undivided presence of the king qua foundation of a hierarchically organized body politic.[8] Yet, in spite of, or because of, this twofold 'deconsecration' of sovereignty, the Duchess's body is somewhat reinvested – and not only by Antonio – with the principle of 'fix'd order', so as to sustain the 'proper' boundaries of class, gender and eroticism.

This is not to suggest that the attempt to supplement the – double – absence of the sovereign through the regulatory production of the body of the Duchess is successful. Antonio is the most outright champion of this substitutive process. Yet the play's 'wooing scene' implicates him in the Duchess's re-marking of her body away from 'the figure cut in alabaster kneel[ing] at [her] husband's tomb' (I.i.454–5), thus revealing his unreliability as a spokesperson for rigid demarcations. Moreover, one could argue, with Lacan, that Antonio's 'picture' of the Duchess is not in itself entirely unambiguous. Behind the Lady as a narcissistic projection filling in the potentially castrating lack in the Other, there seems to show through the spectre of a distanced and inhuman 'partner', indicative of the traumatic Thing that cannot be specularized or symbolized.[9] It is perhaps as a form of anticipatory defence against this trauma that Antonio brings forward a sense of quietude so uncannily similar to death as the ultimate sign of the *propriété* and lack of desire of the Duchess's body:

Ant. Her days are practis'd in such noble virtue
That sure her nights – nay more, her very sleeps –
Are more *in heaven* than other ladies' shrifts.

(I.i.201–03)[10]

Bodily discoveries, eroticism and mimicry

The finale to Antonio's eulogy of the Duchess shows that we are not too far away from the 'eclipse' of the female body with which I began. Still, Antonio's depiction of the Duchess's modest self-display and proper withdrawal, for all its ambiguity, does not quite match Ferdinand's construction of his sister's body and identity as potentially opaque and ominously predicated upon the discrepancy between a public façade and a secret inner part:

> *Ferd.* [B]e not cunning:
> For they whose faces do belie their hearts
> Are witches, ere they arrive at twenty years –
> Ay: and give the devil suck.
>
> (I.i.308–11)

The overlapping of 'countenance' and 'continence' in Antonio's 'picture' is thus replaced by a split identity. The emergence of this identity is, in turn, the *conditio sine qua non* for the implementation of an almost endless process of disclosure, whose ostensible aim is that of bringing – or bringing *back* – to light what is hidden and private, so as to reinforce visibility as a modality of power over the body of the Duchess:

> *Ferd.* Hypocrisy is woven of a fine small thread,
> Subtler than Vulcan's engine: yet, believe't,
> Your darkest actions – nay, your privat'st thoughts –
> Will come to light.
>
> (I.i.313–16)

Earlier in the play Ferdinand disdainfully rejects the suggestion that a prince might act through a third person, 'by a deputy' (I.i.100). Yet it is Bosola who is charged with the task of inspecting and controlling the 'young widow' (I.i.255). He is to 'observe the duchess, / To note all the particulars of her 'haviour' (I.i.252–3). To the Calabrian Duke, Bosola's 'old garb of melancholy' (I.i.278) should be able to give him 'access to private lodgings' (I.i.281), one of which is of course the Duchess's.[11]

In an article that attempts to contextualize some of *Othello* and *Hamlet*'s key words, Patricia Parker refers to the proliferation of spies and secret informers in the early modern period as compensating for the lack of a fully developed policing apparatus.[12] 'Their number', as Monticelso observes in *The White Devil*, 'rises strangely and some of them you'd take for honest men' (IV.i.45–7).[13] Parker also points out the close relation between the delator's activity of bringing something hidden before the eye and the 'voyeuristic' drive of early modern anatomical and gynaecological discourses that seeks to *expose*, in all senses of the word, the 'secret place' of women. This 'secret place', she adds, is most often interpreted as something folded, closed or concealed.[14] Some of Bosola's speeches in *The Duchess of Malfi* situate themselves at the point of conjunction between these two discourses.

One of the many masks he puts on in his role of 'intelligencer' is that of the physician detecting the signs of the transformation of the Duchess's body:

> *Bos.* I observe our duchess
> Is sick o' days, she pukes, her stomach seethes,
> The fins of her eyelids look most teeming blue,
> She wanes i'th' cheek, and waxes fat i'th' flank.
>
> (II.i.63–6)

After tempting her with some 'dainties' (II.i.143), he concludes as follows: 'her tetchiness and most vulturous eating of the apricocks are apparent signs of breeding' (II.ii.1–3). But it is in the following speech that Bosola's scrutiny of the body reveals even more its embeddedness in the anatomical and gynaecological discourse's ocular impulse to see and know, to lay bare and exhibit the secrets of the female body:

> *Bos.* A whirlwind strike off these bawd farthingales,
> For, but for that, and the loose-body'd gown,
> I should have discover'd apparently
> The young springal cutting a caper in her belly.
>
> (II.i.148–51)

The Duchess's pregnant body does not fully pre-exist the act of examination and discovery. Bringing before the eye the 'secrets' of the female body is a bringing into being of that which one claims merely to uncover. It is a *production* as well as a *regulation* of the body. Bosola's reading of the body and subsequent diagnosis, as well as his fascination with the hidden scene taking place in the Duchess's 'belly', inscribe a knowledge of the reproductive body that has less to do with a gradual understanding of its status than with the implementation of relations of domination. The perusal of the signs of pregnancy is only the *incipit* of Bosola's 'work' (II.i.63) as a would-be man-midwife. Still, it plays an important role in what a 1612 midwifery treatise not uncommonly calls 'the government and ordering' of the pregnant woman.[15]

As Michel Foucault has persuasively argued, in the context of a discussion of the body's involvement in the exercise of power, 'there is no power relation without the correlative constitution of a field of knowledge, nor any knowledge that does not presuppose and constitute at the same time power relations'.[16] In this sense, the 'objective' status of the pregnant body of the Duchess emerging from Bosola's inspection is symptomatic of a far more 'realistic' knowledge of the body, especially when compared to the misogynistic loathing of the flesh articulated in Bosola's virulent tirades against his 'rival', the Old Lady-midwife whose appearance immediately precedes and follows his 'observation' of the Duchess. Yet this 'realism' needs to be understood as one of the effects of the anatomical and gynaecological discourses in which the play participates. These are discourses that invest and take hold of the body to 'en-gender' it as a quasi-empirical object subjected to the male gaze.

However, the relations of power thus activated do not go uncontested. As Foucault also points out, the intricate mutual implication of power/knowledge cannot be grasped outside 'the processes and the struggles that traverse it and of which it is made up'.[17] The Duchess of Malfi shows her inevitable entanglement in a discourse driven by the impetus to uncover the secret behind the 'rich tissue' (II.i.57). Nevertheless, the 'dis-covery' is also in her case a self-discovery, a wilful stripping of her prerogatives as a political ruler and public persona that is in turn the precondition for a recasting of her body as the 'private' locus of authenticity and self-determination.[18] Here is the Duchess addressing Antonio in the 'wooing scene':

Duch. What is't distracts you? This is flesh, and blood, sir;
'Tis not the figure cut in alabaster
Kneels at my husband's tomb. Awake, awake, man!
I do here put off all vain ceremony,
And only do appear to you a young widow
That claims you for her husband, and like a widow,
I use but half a blush in't.

(I.i.453–9)

The Duchess's departure from the 'deployment of alliance' – her choice of a husband, which is equivalent to 'going into a wilderness, where [she] shall find nor path, nor friendly clew to be [her] guide' (I.i.359–61) – goes hand in hand with her laying bare of a body that is made of 'flesh … and blood'.[19] This is a 'flesh' that refuses to stand for lust or the corruption of 'a dead and rotten body' (II.i.75), and a 'blood' that has little to do with lineage and rank. The Duchess's is a 'palpable' body that acts as a self-evident and essential entity. Heterosexual desire seems to flow spontaneously from this body, breaking down, at least in theory, any and every social boundary and magically dispelling class and gender tensions. Yet this is also a body whose desire rapidly changes into a deferral of desire: 'Lay a naked sword between us, keep us chaste' (I.i.501). It is sanitized as soon as it is brought to light. Reproductive only in-between the acts, it finds its proper meaning within the emerging ideology of companionate marriages.[20] As Catherine Belsey points out, Webster's play 'stands as a perfect fable of emergent liberalism', representing marriage as 'a transcendent union based on romantic love' and connoting the family as 'a private realm of warmth and fruitfulness separate from the turbulent world of politics':[21]

Duch. Bless, heaven, this sacred Gordian, which let violence
Never untwine.
Ant. And may our sweet affections, like the spheres,
Be still in motion.
Duch. Quickening, and make
The like soft music.
Ant. That we may imitate the loving palms,

Best emblem of a peaceful marriage,
That ne'er bore fruit, divided.

(I.i.480–7)[22]

Yet the 'violence' and division mentioned by the bridal pair are never far away. In fact, to paraphrase one of the Duchess's lines, 'discord' is not simply '*without* this circumference' (I.i.469) traced by the Duchess and Antonio's embracing bodies, in the form of sinister incarnations of the dynastic version of marriage such as the Duchess's brothers;[23] it is also *within*, as the old and the new order, the dynastic and the 'liberal' version of marriage, impinge upon each other, inducing those class, gender and erotic anxieties supposedly alien to this 'private realm'.

Antonio's immediate response to the Duchess's metaphoric 'unveiling' and marriage proposal is an example of these tensions, in that it does not swerve from the language of 'vain ceremony' (I.i.456) the Duchess has just rejected: 'Truth speak for me: / I will remain the constant sanctuary / Of your good name' (I.i.460–1). As Frank Whigham observes, Antonio is torn between 'the traditional hierarchy of rank, which enjoins his submission, and ... the traditional gender hierarchy, which enjoins him to dominate'.[24] This goes some way towards explaining why he seems to be rather reluctant to model himself on the picture of the 'complete man' the Duchess outlines:

Duch. You were ill to sell yourself –
This dark'ning of your worth is not like that
Which tradesmen use i'th' city; their false lights
Are to rid bad wares off: and I must tell you
If you will know where breathes a complete man –
I speak without flattery – turn your eyes
And progress through yourself.

(I.i.431–7)

In her redefinition of the 'complete man', a construction that is meant to couple that of the 'complete' woman she postures as being, the Duchess invites Antonio to 'turn [his] eyes' and explore the depth of his inner self. Yet her emphasis on personal merit and interiority can only be couched in terms that are indebted to the language of *both* the spectacular body of the old regime *and* the expanding market economy. She asks Antonio to '*progress* through [himself]' in order to discover a self whose inner 'worth' is inevitably associated with a market place where merchandises are bought and sold.[25] The 'complete man' may be a sample of good rather than 'bad wares'. Yet he is still a commodity to be sold dearly.[26]

The survey of the realm of the self the Duchess advocates is consistent with the path she herself follows in her voyage of discovery – and production – of a 'true' self and bodily identity lying behind the doubling, equivocations, riddles and dreams of those 'that are born great' (I.i.441). However, the 'bourgeois' authenticity she adumbrates is only one of the subject-positions she speaks from. Antonio underlines this multiplicity as he articulates his regret about not having played an active role in the wooing: 'These words should be mine, / And all the parts you have spoke' (I.i.472–3). If Antonio is caught in the double bind of gender and rank, some of the Duchess's 'parts' are not necessarily empowering. Rather, they seem to register a partial incorporation of the patriarchal values of the old and new regime she is simultaneously challenging.[27]

Antonio suggests near the beginning of the 'wooing scene' that the Duchess should 'provide for a good husband' and 'give him *all*' (I.i.387–8).[28] Complying with this advice, she offers herself as a prize and material asset: 'So now the ground's broke, / You may discover what a wealthy mine / I make you lord of' (I.i.428–30). In short, she presents herself within the parameters of the wealthy widow. On the one hand, by calling Antonio her 'lord', the Duchess paves the way for a re-inscription of the asymmetry of gender. On the other, it is she who makes Antonio 'lord' of the 'wealthy mine' she sees herself as being, and this suggests an active position in the disposal of her body. Both her 'active' and 'passive' positions are nonetheless at odds with the attempt to create a private sphere in which they possess an equal share. The word 'mine' gives a further twist to the ambiguity of the Duchess's speech. As with Antonio's inner and material 'worth' to be discovered by means of a thorough exploration of the self, the Duchess's 'mine' situates itself at the point of intersection of seemingly conflicting discourses, where the discovery of her material belongings uneasily superimposes upon the discovery of her most prized 'private' possession: her *self* as a highly individualized body and being.

To some extent, the Duchess's impersonation of the wealthy widow overlaps with her brothers' stereotype of the lecherous widow in search of a new lover, whose paradigmatic example in Jacobean tragedy is perhaps Livia in Middleton's *Women Beware Women*. As many critics have noted, this stereotype is the effect of the displacement onto sexuality of male anxiety regarding the widow's liminal position *vis-à-vis* the marital paradigm, and her relative economic independence in early modern society.[29] The widow's active pursuit of a new subjugation only partially assuages male anxieties. In fact, there never seems to be a satisfactory re-positioning of the widow's body or her properties in early modern drama. A widow's remarriage takes place by definition too soon and/or is frowned upon because of the inappropriateness of the partner, as plays such as *Hamlet*, *The Insatiate Countess* and *The Duchess of Malfi* show. Even in *Women Beware Women*, where remarriage is not on the agenda, Hippolito's first response to the news of his sister Livia's involvement with Leantio is: 'He is a factor!' (IV.i.162).[30] In *The Duchess of Malfi*, where a socially acceptable partner for the Duchess is seemingly available in the form of the 'great Count Malateste' (III.i.39–44), the latter's name is clearly brought up by Ferdinand only to scrutinize the Duchess's reaction. Indeed, Ferdinand's suggestion can scarcely be said to dissipate his previous solemn proclamation: 'Marry! they are most luxurious / Will wed twice …. / Their livers are more spotted than Laban's sheep' (I.i.297–9).

The stereotype of the wealthy and 'luxurious' widow remains threatening. The Duchess of Malfi repeatedly *approximates* this position. She undermines the habitual correlation between lusty widow and immoderate desire without entirely subscribing to the ideological construction of the chaste woman.[31] To borrow from

Homi Bhabha's discussion of colonial mimicry, she is almost the same as a 'luxurious' widow but not quite.[32] A significant example of this is when the Duchess states that, '*like* a widow', she 'use[s] but half a blush' in 'claim[ing]' Antonio 'for her husband' (I.i.457–9).[33] The emphasis here is on the *citation* of a subject-position, whose original is at any rate a male projection, as well as on the mimicry of one of the languages of desire available to her to articulate the heterosexually oriented flesh-and-blood body she uncovers.[34] Moreover, the other half of the Duchess's 'half a blush' can be interpreted as the sign of her impersonation of 'feminine' coyness, as a masquerade. After the marriage *per verba de presenti* (I.i.479), and following the Duchess's proposal that they should 'lay a naked sword between [them]' to 'keep [them] chaste' (I.i.501), the Duchess's 'blush' reappears to disappear, but not without having first permeated the 'private' realm of affection newly established by the conjugal couple: 'O, let me shroud my *blushes* in your bosom, / Since 'tis the treasury of all my secrets' (I.i.502–3).[35] It must be added that the Duchess has already converted Antonio's 'bosom' into the repository of her heart: 'You have left me heartless – mine is in your bosom' (I.i. 449). This is a heart, she hopes, that 'will multiply love there' (I.i.450). If one takes this 'multiplication' in Antonio's 'bosom' as an allusion to the biblical command to 'increase and multiply', the Duchess's last speech in the first act becomes even more ambiguous. It begins to sow the seeds of confusion between the presence and absence of desire, between desire and its fulfilment, thus forming a kind of Derridean 'hymen'.[36] This to-and-fro movement will soon be brought to an end with the consummation of the marriage. But this 'fulfillment' can only take place offstage, in another 'secret' place that is by definition absent and unrepresentable.

Mimicry is the strategy the Duchess most frequently adopts. In the soliloquy that takes place just before the 'wooing scene', she takes on the position of the male hero:

Duch. If all my royal kindred
Lay in my way unto this marriage,
I'd make them my low footsteps: and even now,
Even in this hate, as men in some great battles,
By apprehending danger, have achiev'd
Almost impossible actions – I have heard soldiers say so –
So I, through frights, and threat'nings, will assay
This dangerous venture.

(I.i.341–48)[37]

Yet this is only *one* of her positions, and, more importantly, she marks her distance from it even as she occupies it: 'I have heard soldiers say so.' Once again, the Duchess's is an approximation, but her falling short of the original does not so much reveal *her* inadequacy as the fact that there is only mimicry without any original. Indeed, there are no 'men in some great battles … achiev[ing] almost impossible actions' in the play.[38] Thus, the Duchess interrogates the regulation of gender and sexuality implemented through the exchange of women's bodies under the 'dynastic' version of patriarchy, including the correlation between her upward movement (in terms of gender) and lust, without situating herself fully outside this regulation. Enabled to do so mostly because of her social status, she traverses masculine and feminine sites. She combines the erotic and the martial. In short, she occupies a number of contradictory positions that *supplement* each other, even as she envisages her body as some kind of 'ground' of this *différance*.[39]

I want to return now to the question of the Duchess's 'secrets'. This is her last word in the 'wooing scene', before her female servant Cariola takes centre-stage to deliver some – bathetical – comments on the Duchess's 'fearful madness' (I.i.506).[40]

Secret places, abject bodies and the politics of violence

In *Bodies That Matter* Judith Butler highlights the performative process of 'constraining production' as a strategy of materialization of bodies as sites and signs of power. She adds that there are bodies that 'are *not* constructed ...; bodies that fail to materialise' and thus 'provide the necessary "outside", if not the necessary support, for the bodies which ... qualify as bodies that matter'.[41] This *constitutive* 'outside' is characterized as a 'domain of abjected bodies, a field of deformation'.[42] It is utterly marginal – and marginalized – and yet symbolically central. It is this domain of abject bodies, I would argue, that Patricia Parker implicitly takes up in her discussion of early modern texts' obsession with the female body as a secret. She points out that both drama and anatomical discourses articulate 'a desire to see and not to see, to display to the eye and to discourage or refrain from looking'.[43] To Parker, Helkiah Crooke's 1615 anatomical treatise *Microcosmographia* somehow exemplifies this contradictory impulse. For Crooke, the 'bigger cleft' divides into two the female 'lap', which is also called 'vulva' or 'valva' or 'pudendum' and likened to a 'floodgate' that opens and shuts. He proceeds in his description of the female 'lap or privities' as follows:

> It bendeth backward to the fundament from the share-bones [i.e. pubic bones] ... and the more it bendeth backward the deeper and broader it is, and so degenerateth into a trench or valley, representing the figure of a boate. In the middle of this trenche is placed the orifice of the necke, and this is the fissure that admitteth the yard, and it is a part thought too obscene to look upon.[44]

Thus, in the anatomical journey the desires to see and to avert the eye are inextricably related to each other. Moreover, when an anatomist such as Crooke *does* 'look upon' a woman's 'lap', he discovers that the latter is still 'too obscene' and with no definite form of its own. It does not cease to partake of the confusing features of the abject or lack thereof, which forces the proliferation of resemblances trying to reduce the 'unknown' to the – male – 'known'.

Crooke's particularized descriptions complement his argument that it is not 'so uncouth in Nature that those parts which in some creatures [i.e. men] are prominent and apparent, should in others [i.e. women] be veyled and covered' (216). These 'veyled and covered' parts are assimilated to 'captives', by which Crooke means 'not those which are not at all, but which are in restraint or in bonds' (216). It seems that it is only by visually unfolding and penetrating a woman's 'secrets' that what is 'veyled by nature' (197) finally reaches an adequate shape and actualizes its potential status. It is only by 'reveyl[ing]' and 'prophan[ing]' (197) that the female 'captives' are set free to be newly subjugated to the power of a form that is homologous to that of the male organ.[45] Helkiah Crooke, who is often sceptical of the age-old Galenic model, repeats the following 'truth':

> The necke of the womb is in stead of the yard, for they are both of a length, and by friction and refriction the seed is called out of the like parts into the same passage (216).[46]

A woman's 'privy' thus remains a bodily excess that cannot be properly categorized within anatomical discourse's ocular production of bodies that matter; a discourse in which it is nonetheless inserted as an 'object' and in the form of a 'masculinized' morphology.

Patricia Parker associates this paradoxical bodily part 'too obscene to look upon', or *not* to look upon, with the hidden place of Desdemona's sexuality in *Othello*.[47] This is a place, as Iago warns Othello, that it is impossible to see (III.iii.408), an 'ob-scene' offstage locus 'too hideous to be shown' (III.iii.111–12) and yet situated at the centre of the play.[48] It cannot be brought to light and yet it is endlessly displayed in part, or shown to be soon re-hidden, as in the bedroom scene at the end of the play. In *The Duchess of Malfi* it is mainly the position of Ferdinand that is fraught with this contradictory desire to see and not to see; a desire that finds an emblematic articulation, as argued earlier, in relation to the Duchess's corpse. At the beginning of Webster's play it is the desire to see that prevails. Yet the dialogue between the Duchess and her two brothers in I.i., which can be referred to as the 'examination scene', as well as Ferdinand's hiring of Bosola to 'observe the duchess' (I.i.252), already complicate this impulse. They show that the Duchess's 'place' is construed not only potentially, but also inherently, as the site of inscrutable secrets impervious to the male gaze, even prior to the possibility of transgression.

In the 'examination scene' the Duchess is defined as a credulous widow[49] and the likely bodily recipient of what Ferdinand calls 'a kind of honey-dew that's deadly', circulating in the 'rank pasture' of the court (I.i.306–7). She is also fabricated as the 'infection' rather than the 'infected', as the assertive widow playing an active role in what her two brothers vehemently interpret as transgression:

> *Card.* You may flatter yourself,
> And take your own choice: privately be married
> Under the eaves of night.
> *Ferd.* Think't the best voyage
> That e'er you made; like the irregular crab,
> Which though 't goes backward, thinks that it goes right,
> Because it goes its own way.
>
> (I.i.316–21)[50]

As the dialogue progresses, the possibility that the Duchess may act out the role of the 'luxurious' widow (I.i.297) her two brothers so scrupulously lay out for her gradually becomes a near certainty.[51] Likewise, the emphasis on the discrepancy between the Duchess's 'outside' and 'inside', which is epitomized by the figure of the witch (one of those 'cunning' women 'whose faces do belie their heart' [I.i.308–10]), seems to take second place. Needless to say, the obfuscation of the distinction between 'outside' and 'inside' is far from signifying the re-creation of the lost transparency. Rather, it indicates its opposite, as the Duchess is shown to be wholly absorbed, to use Bakhtinian terms, in the 'grotesque' undermining of her 'classical' body and public persona, and so much so that she *essentially* becomes one with the mask she wears.[52] The mask, in turn, comes to coincide with the negatively marked secret inner locus concealed behind it. One of the last of Ferdinand's 'terrible good counsel[s]' (I.i.312) to the Duchess, which exemplifies the shift of tone towards the end of the 'examination scene', is that he 'would have [her] to give o'er these chargeable revels' (I.i.333). By way of explanation, he tells her that 'a visor and a mask are whispering-rooms that were ne'er built for goodness' (I.i.335).[53]

Thus, Ferdinand's harangues in the 'examination scene' not only announce the inevitable detection of the Duchess's 'darkest actions', and even of her 'privat'st thoughts' (I.i.315), but also display to the eye something whose threatening depth is re-presented through a double disguise, 'a visor and a mask') that blurs the lines of sight and emblematizes one of the Duchess's most 'privy' places (the 'whispering-rooms'). Ferdinand predominantly inscribes the point of view of the old regime, in whose system of bodily signification, as Francis Barker remarks, depth is achieved 'not in the figure of interiority by which the concealed inside is of another quality from what is external, but by a *doubling of the surface*'.[54] *Mutatis mutandis*, and given the homology between a woman's secret parts and her intimate private closet or cabinet, Barker's 'doubling' can be related to the anatomical and gynaecological discourses in which Ferdinand's position, and the play more generally, participates.[55] According to these discourses, as Thomas Laqueur points out, there is only one body: a one-sex or one-flesh teleologically male body whose colder, less perfect and inverted mirror image is gendered female.[56] The 'concealed inside' represented by the female sex-organs is thus not 'of another quality' or *essentially* different from the exterior surface signified by the male sex-organs. Rather, to return to Crooke, it is its double as well as doubled-over counterpart, a folded 'lap or privitie' (212) which unfolds in 'coition' so as to become 'rigid and straight' and 'straightly embrace' (234) the male member. It extends, then, *not* to reveal its difference but to reinscribe its similarity with the externalized male organ, which is often called the 'yard'. This doubled-over 'lap' also doubles, as in the previous quotation from Helkiah Crooke, where the 'bigger cleft' of the 'lap' (237) is spread out to exhibit another 'lap' ('a trench or a valley') (239), whilst the 'orifice of the necke [of the womb] … that admitteth the yard' [i.e. the vagina] finds its duplicate in the orifice of the bottom of the womb (i.e. the cervix) (232). This latter 'orifice' similarly opens and shuts like a door first to release the female seed and then to keep the two mingled seeds, and is compared by Crooke to the 'hole in the nut of the yard' (233).

Helkiah Crooke's *Microcosmographia*, like most sixteenth- and seventeenth-century anatomical and gynaecological treatises, is marked by anxiety towards this ambivalent interior fold of the one-sex/flesh body. This fold is veiled and covered by nature to register a woman's proper place but is potentially suspect, like anything that is concealed or secret.[57] In other words, the construction of a woman's 'cabinet' within the parameters of the Galenic introverted homology does not make it less menacing. Doubling repeatedly tends to re-present itself as uncanniness. In a discussion of early modern conceptions of sexual difference, Jonathan Dollimore argues as follows: 'The woman was … feared in a way in which the homosexual now is – feared, that is, not so much, or only, because of a radical otherness, as because of an inferior resemblance presupposing a certain proximity.'[58]

In *The Duchess of Malfi* this proximity induces anxiety; anxiety easily turns into violence. Ferdinand, echoing Jacobean characters such as Othello and Corvino, does not fail to promise that he will 'hew' his sister 'to pieces' (II.v.31), after threatening to dispense mixed doses of cure and punishment:[59]

> *Ferd.* Apply desperate physic:
> We must not now use balsamum, but fire,
> The smarting cupping-glass, for that's the mean
> To purge infected blood, such blood as hers.
> (II.v.23–6)[60]

However, this is not to argue that Ferdinand's perspective, forcefully implemented by the end of the fourth act, coincides with Webster's play, or that the latter provides the scaffold where 'the monarch … demonstrated his ability to penetrate and control the natural body of the subject at the micro level of its parts'.[61] Much as Ferdinand's pledge recalls the violence unleashed on the king's enemy in the spectacle of punishment,[62] the Duchess's murder is carried out in a *private* space – her 'lodging' (IV.ii.3) – by a number of nameless executioners who use strangling rather than dismemberment as a mode of re-inscription of power over her body. Moreover, her prolonged torture, which reaches its apogee when Ferdinand decides to 'remove forth the common hospital / All the mad-folk, and place them near her lodging' (IV.i.127–8), does not seem to achieve the desired effect.[63] The Duchess ironically comments as follows: 'Indeed, I thank him: nothing but noise and folly / Can keep me in my right wits' (IV.ii.5–6). There is also no confession to seal the violence of execution. The Duchess's 'last dying speeches' repeatedly focus on the monotony of the spectacular display that requires her subjection; or, alternatively, they mark her difference from this display, whether it be the 'sad spectacle' (IV.i.57) of the wax statues of Antonio and the children, the masque of madmen or Bosola's multifarious disguises: 'Who must despatch me? / I account this world a tedious theatre, / For I do play a part in't'gainst my will' (IV.i.83–5).[64] Most significantly, just before her execution, not only does she temporarily step out of a set speech on death to reassert the tediousness of the spectacle; she also associates this spectacle with the 'whispering' and clandestine manoeuvrings of Ferdinand and his acolytes. This reverses the connotation of 'whispering' as *her* secret and illicit sexuality:

Duch. I know death hath ten thousand several doors
For men to take their exits; and 'tis found
They go on such strange geometrical hinges,
You may open them both ways: – any way, for heaven-sake,
So I were out of your whispering.

(IV.ii.219–23)

In short, 'whispering', like the revolving doors of death, goes 'both ways'.

Violence thus inexorably marks this newer and 'de-theatricalized' sense of identity of the Duchess. Yet, the system of resemblances, which provides the epistemological foundation for the spectacle of punishment described by Michel Foucault, does not map the whole space of being.[65] As Francis Barker suggests, in relation to the representation of the body in Jacobean tragedy, one cannot ignore the emergence of contradictions within the metaphysics of presence prevalently emblematized by the spectacular body of the king.[66] To argue, therefore, that some version or other of an organic socio-political and cultural totality fully and unproblematically informs Webster's tragedy and anatomical treatises is to imply that the hegemonic is singular, uniform or static. It is to disregard the way in which the interplay of dominant, emergent and residual elements affects the construction of the body in both early modern tragedies and anatomical and gynaecological discourses.[67] As for medical discourses, one needs to point out that 'anatomy' as the prominent emerging figure for organizing knowledge is a performative discourse that constructs, abjects and atomizes bodies – bodies that then become the source of its authority. It does not necessarily coincide with a sense of 'anatomy' as the description of bodily parts and sex-organs that may or may not re-inscribe the dominant Galenic model.[68] As Valerie Traub succinctly puts it, anatomy is not 'any self-evident structure of the body, but a discipline of knowledge that inscribes a bodily schema'.[69]

Yet, even in a crucial study such as Thomas Laqueur's *Making Sex*, theoretically indebted to Foucault's analysis of the order of resemblances, there seems to be a coalescence of these two senses of anatomy.[70] More specifically, the idea that early modern anatomy and gynaecology articulate 'an assertion of male power to know the female body and hence to know and control a feminine Nature', in support of which Laqueur invokes a number of texts and drawings appealing to truth, ocularity and the empirical status of the opened body, is put forward only to be rejected.[71] The main reason for this rejection is that most of the bodies appearing in frontispieces of anatomical books, or actually anatomized, are male. This is contradictory, to say the least, within Laqueur's own terms of analysis, as he stresses throughout the book the historical priority of gender over 'sex' and the later historical appearance of 'sex' as an ontological bodily feature that matters. He ironically asserts that anatomists, in spite of their rhetoric of truth based on ocularity, could only '*see* … that women were inverted men'.[72] Yet, this does not invalidate the fact that they *were* seeing, 'en-gendering' and creating a domain of abject bodies, irrespective of their 'sex'. In this sense, the reiteration of the inveterate structural similarity between the male and female body may well be read as a reaction-formation against the implications of the implementation of the relatively new *dispositifs* of power embodied by anatomical and gynaecological discourses. To sum up a complex matter that has been the object of much attention in Renaissance studies, and to which I shall return, in anatomy 'the desire for analysis confronts an older love of resemblance'.[73] By way of brief illustration, I shall stay with Helkiah Crooke's text, which is a hotchpotch of contradictory and sometimes incompatible discourses. In this text an emergent discourse insisting on the profanation of the mysteries of nature – a discourse that sees itself as an attack on 'false modesty' (197) – uncomfortably mixes with a Galenic model that is patently rejected (270–2), whilst the emphasis often shifts from physiology to moral judgements and easily re-deployable misogynistic tropes. For instance, in one of the 'Controversies' appended to the fifth book on 'The History of the Infant', Crooke explains the fact that women are more wanton than men in spite of their being 'colder' by nature by arguing that 'the imaginations of lustfull women are like the imaginations of bruite beasts which have no repugnancie or contradiction of reason to restrain them' (276). To Crooke, they are more lascivious than men not because they are hotter but because of the 'impotencie of their minds' (276).

The 'publishing' of bodies and the *mise-en-scène* of jealousy

The historical and epistemological 'in-betweenness' of anatomical and gynaecological discourses is shared by Webster's play. I have shown this to be the case especially by considering the Duchess's position(s) in relation to the regulation of bodies and identities inhering in the 'deployment of alliance' as dramatized by the play. This 'in-betweenness' has also surfaced in the analysis of the Duchess's self-discovery, a process that is not only highly ambiguous in itself, but is also linked, in complex and contradictory ways, to Bosola's detection of her hidden teeming body, as well as to Ferdinand's exposure of the essential opacity of a woman's secret place. I now want to illustrate the extent to which the strategies of power activated in the course of the process of 'dis-covery' of the body problematize the class, gender and erotic status of the male discoverer.

Ferdinand and his acolyte Bosola come up against a dilemma that similarly agitates a number of anatomical and gynaecological treatises, and in many ways exacerbate it. In these treatises discovery is envisaged, on the one hand, as a necessary task to save women from themselves. As the anonymous translator of Jacques Guillemau's *Child-Birth* writes in 1612, 'women … must be content to have their infirmities detected, if they will have helpe for them'.[74] Likewise, John Sadler, when considering 'the manifold distempers of body, which … Women are subject unto', attributes them to women's 'ignorance & modestie'. He insists on disclosing that which women are by definition 'loth to divulge and publish … unto the Physitian to implore his aide'.[75] On the other hand, there is always a danger 'in prostituting and divulging that, which [for women] would not have come to open light', or in 'export[ing] and [making] common a commoditie, which the learned would have had private to themselves'.[76] This is the reason why Guillemeau's translator wishes that this unfolding 'might not come to any eare or eye, but to those which they themselves would have acquainted therewith' (in other words, (B18.3) the 'Chirurgions & Midwives, who are called to this kind of employment').[77]

Guillemeau's treatise moves within the parameters set by Eucharius Roesslin's *The Birth of Man-Kinde* (1540), the first gynaecological treatise published in English, in whose 'augmented' edition re-translated by Thomas Raynalde in 1545, the impulse to lay bare the 'inwards parts of women' is even more pronounced because of the inclusion of 'lively and expresse figures, by the which every part before in the Booke described, may in a manner bee as exactly and clearely perceived, as though yee [i.e. women] were present at the cutting open of Anatomy of a dead woman'.[78] The risk involved in this display seems to increase accordingly. This can be gathered from the objections Raynalde anticipates – objections that range from the fact that women may be 'moved ... the more to abhore and loath the company of women', to the fact that the publication of a treatise in the 'vulgar tongue' may be improperly used by 'every boy and knave'.[79] Therefore, Raynalde ends his 'Prologue' by requiring 'the gentle readers thereof, that if they finde any thing therein interpretable to divers senses, to accept onely that which may make to the best, according to my meaning'.[80] In Jakob Rueff's *The Expert Midwife* (1637), the criticism that the treatise may in fact be designed 'for young heads to prie into' is countered by inviting 'young and raw heads, idle serving-men, prophane fiddlers, scoffers, jesters, rogues' to 'pack hence'.[81] Moreover, in the first chapter of the second book, whose heading reads 'On the Necessity of the Anatomy of the Womb', the author states that it is only because of his 'being moved' by the plight of 'ignorant midwives' that he is 'willing to put forth to view this figure of womans body with the Matrix and other parts of the wombe'.[82] In fact, the whole chapter 'might easily be omitted'.[83]

In anatomical and gynaecological treatises there is only a fine line between the denunciation of 'modestie' as a form of conduct that would obstruct the examination of women's 'private parts' and the allegation that modesty is but false modesty, a cover for the misuse of the body. This is a line Ferdinand and Bosola unceasingly cross. The logic of suspicion towards that which he sees as merely an 'outward form' (II.i.45) prompts, for instance, Bosola's tirades against the Old Lady's 'painting'. It makes him 'acquainted' with her 'closet' (II.i.34), which is likened to 'a shop of witchcraft' and is said to contain 'the fat of serpents, spawn of snakes, Jews' spittle, and their young children's ordure' (II.i.35–7). Unlike the treatises I have cited, whose rhetorical amplification *vis-à-vis* a woman's 'closet' he shares in many respects,[84] Bosola seems to believe that it is not women who benefit from the detection of their 'infirmities' but the physician himself, who 'renew[s] his footcloth with the spring and change[s] his high-prized courtezan with the fall of the leaf' (II.i.41–3). Yet, being cast for the most part of the first and second scene of the second act as a man-midwife facing a rival practitioner such as the Old Lady, Bosola would probably agree with the definition of midwives as 'cunning women' who 'desire to excell men, or at least to seeme to go beyond them' in Guillemeau's *Child-Birth*.[85]

The conversation between Antonio and Delio (II.i.160–5) clarifies that the Old Lady plays the part of a midwife. This allows one to read Bosola's diatribe against her and her cortège of 'foster-daughters' (II.ii.24) within the context of the increasingly negative re-fashioning of the body of the 'sage woman', which is instrumental to her marginalization and to the parallel rise of the man-midwife.[86] It also corroborates Peter Stallybrass's suggestion that there is a hidden similarity between the under-privileged status of the Old Lady qua woman and that of Bosola qua malcontent desperately seeking preferment.[87] This similarity is, paradoxically, directly proportional to the violence of Bosola's harangues. They both offer 'entertainment' and service in exchange of a 'precious reward' (II.ii.16). Moreover, it is not only the Lady with her 'painting', but also the malcontent with his disparate masks that adulterates and endlessly defers the highly mystified 'truth' of the body he simultaneously upholds.

Bosola's 'dis-covery' of the Old Lady is thus bittersweet. To employ some of the terms of the gynaecological treatises I cited, it 'divulges' the parallelism between his position and that of the lady, making 'common' the fact that he partakes of the characteristics of the 'commoditie' he 'exports'. As for Ferdinand, the exposure of the Duchess's 'whispering-rooms' as something remote from a private reservoir of chastity undoubtedly intensifies the voyeuristic pleasure of discovery. Yet it also exacerbates the anxiety linked to a display that might transform the Duchess's 'private' place into a 'common' place, and thus undermine the control over her body that motivates the process of discovery in the first instance. When the Duchess's illicit use of her body comes to light, in the form of a letter by Bosola relating the 'happy discovery' (II.iii.60) of the Duchess's delivery, one of Ferdinand's first reactions is, paradoxically, to align himself with the 'rogues' who 'publish' his sister's behaviour. At his brother's request to 'speak lower' (II.v.4), Ferdinand replies:

Ferd. Lower?
Rogues do not whisper 't now, but seek to publish 't …
Aloud; and with a covetous searching eye
To mark who note them: – O confusion seize her!
(II.v.4–5; 7–8)[88]

On the one hand, the 'publishing' stance Ferdinand adopts is only temporary. He soon decides to keep Bosola's 'parcel of intelligency' (II.iii.67) secret and 'study to seem the thing [he is] not' (II.v.62–3), at least 'till [he] know[s] who leaps [his] sister' (II.v.77).[89] On the other, this linear unfolding of exhibition and concealment is fractured by a compulsive staging of what can *not*, or must *not*, be seen: a *mise-en-scène* of jealousy that, like any 'phantasy scene', is simultaneously the articulation of desire *and* a defence against it, both in its content and in the way in which it is introduced:[90]

Ferd. Methinks I see her laughing –
Excellent hyena! – talk to me somewhat, quickly,
Or my imagination will carry me
To see her, in the shameful act of sin.
Card. With whom?
Ferd. Happily with some strong thigh'd bargeman;
Or one o'th' wood-yard, that can quoit the sledge,

Or toss the bar, *or else* some lovely squire
That carries coals up to her privy lodgings.
(II.v.38–45) (my emphasis)

The question arises, of course, as to whose desire and what kind of desire this *mise-en-scène* delineates.

Jacques Lacan concisely remarks that 'the phantasy is the support of desire, it is not the object that is the support of desire'.[91] Moreover, for Lacan, the subject in the phantasy scenario is 'more or less recognisable ..., split, divided, generally double'.[92] In their classical study of phantasy, Jean Laplanche and Jean-Bertrand Pontalis develop these suggestions. They stress that what counts in phantasy is not so much the object or the fulfilment of a wish as its setting, which provides the framework for the subject to articulate and re-articulate its desire.[93] The subject, in turn, although inevitably present in the *mise-en-scène* of desire, cannot at times 'be assigned any fixed place in it'.[94] In fact, it may appear 'in a desubjectivised form, that is to say, in the very syntax of the sequence in question'.[95]

In the 'syntax' of Ferdinand's 'sequence' the subject undoubtedly surfaces 'in a desubjectivised form'. It is not present as such but, rather, present *and* absent. It is re-presented in, as well as subjected to, the shifting of the signifier 'or', which is a signifier marking the site where the imagined lovers of the Duchess and their sexual performances alternate. Indeed, the conjunction 'or', which also inaugurates the fantasy scene,[96] paves the way for a potentially infinite series of fantasmatic permutations, one of which may therefore furtively accommodate Ferdinand's desire and identification. I speak of desire *and* identification because the conjunction 'or' not only positions Ferdinand as one of the Duchess's potential lovers in the phantasy scenario. By bringing the Calabrian Duke into close contact with his male antagonists, it also signifies the forging of a fantasmatic bond of identification – and rivalry – between men, a homosocial bond over and against the body of the Duchess, once more reduced to her 'privy lodgings'. Furthermore, that the chain of male substitutes occupies almost the whole scenario suggests that the fantasy of identification is not merely the necessary but unproblematic detour one must take in order fantasmatically to inscribe heterosexual desire.[97] If it is a detour, then it is one that does not guarantee a return to a heterosexual 'object'.

In a theoretically related context, Mikkel Borch-Jacobsen speaks of the fantasy of identification as 'a stratagem aimed at wish fulfilment', a 'particularly oblique' stratagem, though, in that 'instead of representing the object of the wish directly, it represents [the subject itself] taking the place of another person who is positioned so as to enjoy the object'.[98] He continues as follows:

> The subject will derive pleasure from the fantasmatic scene only if he or she identifies with one or another of the drama's protagonists, by enjoying as the protagonist does, in the protagonist's place. In this sense, saying that wishes are fulfilled phantasmatically and that enjoyment is based on identification amounts to saying the same thing.[99]

One can immediately see the relevance of this argument to the interpretation of Ferdinand's identification(s) with the 'protagonists' of the 'drama' he stages. But before returning to Ferdinand's *mise-en-scène*, I want to stress that, as Borch-Jacobsen's analysis develops, what may seem at first a relatively innocuous statement on how obliquely to fulfil one's desire turns into a complex and rigorous deconstruction of some of the major polarities in Freud's work, most of all of the opposition between identification and object-oriented desire. To sum up, 'desire ... does not come first, to be *followed* by an identification that would allow the desire to be fulfilled'.[100] Identification is redefined as a quasi-transcendental condition of possibility *and* impossibility of object-oriented desire, which is the reason why it is so difficult to determine, except in specific contexts, whether there *is* object-oriented desire, or whether desire is fulfilled or not fulfilled. Indeed, obeying the logic of a quasi-transcendental construct, identification is what gives rise to the process of desire, but, at the same time, it is inextricably implicated in the process it engenders.[101]

This has important consequences for psychoanalytic theory. Suffice it to point out here that Borch-Jacobsen's work aligns itself with recent investigations of the blind spots and paradoxes within the narrative of the normative assumption of 'sex' or 'sexual identity' through the threat of castration and the – paternal – Law of the Symbolic. This is a narrative that is understood as strictly dependent upon the dichotomy identification versus desire. Judith Butler, for instance, who is not entirely unsympathetic to a redescription and mobilization of psychoanalytic categories, sees the mutual opposition between identification and desire as pivotal to the historical and psychic regime of compulsory and hyperbolic heterosexuality, which unceasingly installs the category of 'sex'.[102] Hence, she problematizes the psychoanalytic postulate that the 'coherently heterosexualized deflections' that are produced by the 'primary prohibitions [against incest] ... require that identifications be effected on the basis of similarly sexed bodies and that desire be deflected across the sexual divide to members of the opposite sex.'[103] She reaches the following conclusion:

> To identify is not to oppose desire. Identification is a phantasmatic trajectory and resolution of desire; an assumption of place; a territorializing of an object which enables identity through the temporary resolution of desire, but which remains desire, if only in its repudiated form.[104]

Pursuing a similar line of thought, but specifically commenting on Ferdinand's speech, Jonathan Dollimore underlines that the fantasmatic *mise-en-scène* of male sexual jealousy in Webster's play, and in Jacobean drama more generally, unsettles the logic of a 'heterosexual economy' in which, especially as far as men are concerned, '*identification with* [other men, including one's rivals] should actually preclude *desire for* [them]', just as '*desire for* [women should] preclude *identification with* [women]'.[105] Dollimore's interpretation is worth citing in full:

> For the sexually jealous male [such as Ferdinand], the separate/d objects of identification and desire – the rival man and the faithless woman – have united actually as a distorted counterpart of the forbidden conjunction in the jealous

> subject between identification and desire. Thus his erotic imagining of the usurping male is not the eruption of repressed homosexual desire so much as the fantasized, fearful convergence of identification and desire, precipitated by an actual convergence of their respective objects.[106]

Dollimore's interpretation recalls Freud's reading of male sexual jealousy as 'experienced bisexually'. Freud explains: 'A [jealous] man will not only feel pain about the woman he loves and hatred of the man who is his rival, but also grief about the man, whom he loves unconsciously, and hatred of the woman as his rival.'[107] According to Freud, as jealousy develops into its 'delusional' form, which can never be properly differentiated from 'normal' jealousy, it becomes increasingly marked by the jealous male's projection upon the supposedly faithless woman of his almost exclusive preoccupation with – and unconscious homosexual desire for – his male rival. As is also made clear by his interpretation of Ferdinand's lines, Dollimore acknowledges the importance of Freud's insight but also questions, on historical grounds, the Freudian 'depth-model' that regards male jealousy as a symptom of 'the eruption of *repressed* homosexual desire'.[108] Instead, for Dollimore, the eroticized figurations of the male rival seem to be 'created by rather than repressed by the social bond'.[109] Even outside the scenario of male sexual jealousy, male homosocial bonds remain dependent upon an 'always unstable disjunction between identification and desire'.[110]

That Ferdinand's 'erotic imagining of the usurping male' is, as Dollimore argues, 'the fantasized, fearful convergence of identification and desire' still begs the question as to why this 'imagining' does not involve just *any* male rival or only *one* rival. In fact, although Ferdinand does not yet know 'who leaps [his] sister' (II.v.77), one of the sides of the triangle man–man–woman – that of the male rival – divides itself to stage a number of men of inferior rank, from the 'strong thigh'd bargeman' to the 'one o'th' wood-yard' to the 'lovely squire that carries coals up [the Duchess's] privy lodgings' (II.v.42–5). As argued earlier, the potentially infinite proliferation of male rivals inscribes the presence *and* absence of Ferdinand. This argument can be slightly reformulated here by saying that this proliferation is not casual but structured as an ascending gradation of men of lower ranks that should lead *up* – hierarchically – to Ferdinand but does *not* in fact fully include him. In other words, social status is implicated in the articulation of, as well as in the defence against, the vacillation of the mutual opposition between desire and identification. One can thus conclude that the fantasmatic inscription of Ferdinand's prohibited heterosexual desire is haunted by the spectre of the identification with the woman not only because of the gender of the 'object', but also because this 'object' is a woman who collapses the class distinction between men, which also results in the intensification of misogynistic attacks. Conversely, the fantasy of identification with one's male rivals seems to be inextricably linked to male homoerotic desire, but the reverse side of this 'fantasized … convergence' is a quasi-homophobic defence, not because the conjunction of identification and desire is 'fearful' in itself but mostly because its 'objects' are members of the lower classes.[111]

Male bonds, social status and laughing matters

It is not only in the staging of male sexual jealousy that questions of social status complicate the play of identification and desire. The concluding lines of the 'examination scene' similarly rehearse a triangular situation in which class affects the homosocial line-up of 'masculine attributes'. These are attributes that seem regularly to surface as highly fetishized in the context of an apparently obsessive and compulsory heterosexuality:

Ferd. And women like that part which, like the lamprey,
Hath ne'er a bone in't.
Duch. Fie sir!
Ferd. Nay,
I mean the tongue: variety of courtship; –
What cannot a neat knave with a smooth tale
Make a woman believe? Farewell, lusty widow.

(I.i.336–40)[112]

I showed earlier that this scene moves from the articulation of the threatening discrepancy between the Duchess's outside and inside to the near certainty that the Duchess's 'private' place is in fact a 'common' place. Here Ferdinand, by indulging in the unfolding of a woman's subjection to multiple penetrations, transmutes this near certainty into an indubitable truth. At the same time, the rhetorical and phallic power of the 'neat knave with a smooth tale' – a 'neat knave' who also possesses an obscene 'tail' – cannot but recall the force of persuasion Ferdinand himself has just exercised throughout the 'examination scene'. He speaks *of* the position *from which* he has just been speaking. In this sense, Ferdinand's lines are a strategy of control by means of which he analeptically and proleptically seeks to thwart any threat for his, or his sister's, B18.3) status. The endeavour to 'make a woman believe' is, of course, ineffective, as clearly shown by the Duchess's reaction to Ferdinand's rhetorical question, which takes the form of another rhetorical question: 'Shall this move me? If all my royal kindred lay in my way unto this marriage, I'd make them my low footsteps' (I.i.341–3). For my purposes here, the failure of this strategy is far less important than the fact that Ferdinand's identification with a *generic* smooth-talking 'knave' and his appropriation of a misogynistic 'tongue' – a 'tongue' commonly spoken by a stage malcontent such as his 'creature' Bosola (I.i.287) – are hardly congruent with the *singular* status, in class terms, he repeatedly claims for himself.

Peter Stallybrass argues, in a related context, that the Jacobean malcontent's misogynistic stigmatization of the signifiers of the privileges of the court lady is inextricably bound with an attack on *men's* class privileges, since women in the dominant social classes are allocated privileges that, in the early modern *dispositif* of alliance, 'can only be conferred back on *men*'.[113] This indirectly suggests that Ferdinand's position is caught in a double bind. He 'em-bodies', as a strategy of control of the Duchess, a misogynistic tongue–phallus that also articulates a fantasized interruption, as well as a redirection, of the class-bound and unilateral exchange of women. This tongue–phallus is thus at odds with his rank as well as with his jealous preservation of class boundaries, dependent as the latter are upon *either* a restricted and endogamous circulation of the Duchess's body *or* the blocking of any form of exchange within the *dispositif* of alliance.

This double bind indicates that Ferdinand is implicated, in more senses than one, in the abjection of his sister. Or, put differently, the butt of Ferdinand's joke on the boneless 'part' and the 'tale' qua obscene 'tail' turns out to be not only his sister but also himself. Freud argues that 'smut is like an exposure of the sexually different person to whom it is directed', and that 'the desire to see what is sexual exposed' is its 'original motive'.[114] The 'sexually different person' is, paradigmatically, the woman, who is 'assailed' by the 'utterance of the obscene words'.[115] But, for Freud, the dirty joke can function properly as a joke only if another man is involved as an onlooker or listener, which eventually paves the way for the re-presentation of the woman only as an absence or as a part of her body. Therefore, in this triangle the structural position of the woman is subordinated to that of the man 'to whom the smut is addressed'.[116] As Eve Kosofsky Sedgwick clarifies, the Freudian *Witz* needs to be understood as a 'mechanism for moving from an ostensible object of desire to a true homosocial one'.[117] However, Ferdinand's obscene jokes show that, because of his preoccupation with the hierarchical structure of male homosocial bonding, the path to a 'true homosocial' object of desire is anything but straightforward. This is also borne out when, earlier in the first act, the misogynistic 'truth' of women's sexual promiscuity is applied to Julia, Castruchio's wife, in the context of a number of cuckolding jokes at the expense of Castruchio promoted by Ferdinand himself. Unlike the 'examination scene', there does not seem to be any direct threat to Ferdinand's status. Nonetheless, he takes it upon himself to elucidate that bawdy laughter rests upon social distinctions of degree:

Ferd. Why do you laugh? Methinks you that are courtiers
should be my touch-wood, take fire, when I give fire;
that is, laugh when I laugh, were the subject never so
witty.

(I.i.122–5)

Ferdinand's reprimand is aimed less at laughter as such, or as a means of creating bonds between men, than at inhibiting any further attempt to turn the structure of authority itself into a laughing matter. It is mainly Silvio who triggers off Ferdinand's reaction. It is Silvio, rather than the other courtiers laughing at his joke on Castruchio,[118] who has temporarily taken Ferdinand's place, if only as a jester. Indeed, Ferdinand's concern about hierarchy is often articulated as anxiety about his being replaced as the *origin* of his subjects' actions and, more generally, as the entity 'authorising' their identities.

This is an origin that is erected upon the strict equivalence of masculinity and violence, and it is as such that it is first introduced in this presence-chamber scene. To

Castruchio's advice that a prince 'should not desire to go to war in person' (I.i.93–4), and that 'he were far better do it by a deputy' (I.i.99), Ferdinand replies as follows:

> *Ferd.* Why should he not as well sleep, or eat by a deputy?
> This might take idle, offensive, and base office from him,
> whereas the other deprives him of honour.
>
> (I.i.100–2)

However, as soon as Ferdinand's lewd jokes take over, his presence to himself – his rejection of impersonation 'by a deputy' – comes dangerously close to signifying the stance of a high-rank jester. In a Derridean sense, this is a supplementary position marking a non-presence, a mimesis without an original continuously producing simulacra, including those of a belligerent masculinity. In effect, the princely war is soon metamorphosed into the 'fighting' Castruchio's wife cannot 'endure'; this 'fighting' is in turn transmuted into a 'quarrel' between 'gallants', a 'quarrel' that, Ferdinand implies, Julia would want to suspend only to turn their 'weapons' to other forms of 'fighting' (I.i.105–14). Yet, in spite of, or because of, the undermining of the masculine presence of Ferdinand and the partially self-inflicted adulteration of his role as the origin of authority, violence or the threat of violence remains, traversing from within even this section of the first act, whose atmosphere is seemingly relaxed when compared to the rest of the play. As shown earlier, one symptomatic sign of this violence is Ferdinand's silencing of Silvio qua rival jester and the easily led courtly audience, which follows the Calabrian Duke's anxious repression and substitution of a 'jest' by Julia, as reported by Castruchio (I.i.107–10). Moreover, and perhaps more importantly, violence takes the form of a forceful attempt to 'contain' the woman and thus guarantee the 'masculinization' of the place of reception of bawdy jokes,[119] problematic as this masculinization often turns out to be for Ferdinand's rank:

> *Ferd.* I would … have a mathematical instrument made for
> her [Julia's] face, that she might not laugh out of compass.
>
> (I.i.136–7)

This is the 'therapy' Ferdinand prescribes in order to 'cure' Julia's conviction, as reported by Castruchio, that 'too much laughing, and too much company, fills her too full of the wrinkle' (I.i.134–5). That Julia has already vacated the position of the spectator – she cannot 'endure to be in merry company' (I.i.133) – does not abate Ferdinand's aggressive reaction, which is once more a function of the uncanny convergence between his position and that of his real or alleged antagonist. Julia prefers originating jokes, or is fantasized as doing so, to being a spectator and laughing, or laughing too much, at them. She therefore *approximates* Ferdinand's position, as the latter is one of the few jesters who would go so far as to tell jokes only to himself, so as to bond only with himself – without laughing.

The economy of 'private' pleasures of the conjugal couple

These last remarks re-emphasize a point I made earlier: the instability of gender and sexuality does not coincide with the cessation of violence. However, violence has less to do with the spectacular display of power than with the reduction of the presence of the spectacle to a theatricality that competes, in its turn, with alternative structurations of power and knowledge. Violence is a way of taking into account in advance, as well as a reaction-formation against, the historical incompatibility of different strategies of regulation of bodies, identities and desires.

It is nothing but historical difference that the Duchess traces when she defines her 'battle' as a resolution to go beyond any calculable programme:

> *Duch.* I am going into a wilderness,
> Where I shall find nor path, nor friendly clew
> To be my guide.
>
> (I.i.359–61)

This is so even if her 'venture' (I.i.348) is clearly structured from within by the language of patriarchy, as the use of the word 'wilderness' indicates. But perhaps the contamination of languages is nowhere more explicit than when she tells Cariola: 'I wink'd and chose a husband' (I.i.349). For her to choose 'with her eyes shut' obviously casts a shadow over her decision.[120] Yet, this can alternatively be seen as a 'transgressive reinscription' from within of a system of signification in which vision is inherently complicit with the control of her body.[121] It is also worth pointing out in this context that the historical difference the Duchess delineates is occasionally signified not only as bodily excess but also as something that exceeds the visibility of the body. To use a Foucaultian language, Ferdinand's predominant focus on what is sexually permitted or forbidden in the context of juridical relations of alliance sometimes joins with the attempt to reach out for the impalpable entities haunting the act of sexual transgression, such as the Duchess's 'privat'st thoughts' (I.i.315–16).[122] It is the search for her 'privat'st thoughts' that undoubtedly motivates Ferdinand's approach to her bedchamber to 'force confession from her' (III.i.79). Likewise, once the Duchess' s body is safely 'contained', Ferdinand's excessive concern over how she 'bear[s] herself in her imprisonment' (IV.i.1–2) seems to suggest that the text is marked by a movement towards 'a punishment that acts in depth on the heart, the thoughts, the will, the inclinations'.[123] Her 'silence' (IV.i.9) is quickly transformed into a 'strange disdain' (IV.i.12), whilst her 'restraint' is seen to reproduce those 'pleasures' it is designed to occlude:

> *Bos.* This restraint
> (Like English mastiffs, that grow fierce with tying)
> Makes her too passionately apprehend
> Those pleasures she's kept from.
>
> (IV.i.12–15)

The reading of the Duchess's body as an opaque surface that intermittently raises the spectre of its 'beyond' demonizes, but also implicitly acknowledges, the historical difference in which the Duchess is inscribed. Arguably, this 'beyond' is nothing but the distorted image of a body that flickers into existence to sustain, as mentioned earlier, the ideological effect of reality of an emerging monogamous and 'bourgeois' heterosexuality. In the bedchamber scene it is the private economy of pleasure of this body that articulates itself as much as is historically and theatrically possible:

Duch. Bring me the casket hither, and the glass: –
You get no lodging here tonight, my lord.
Ant. Indeed, I must persuade one: –
Duch. Very good:
I hope in time 'twill grow into a custom
That noblemen shall come with cap and knee,
To purchase a night's lodging of their wives.
Ant. I must lie here ....
Duch. To what use will you put me?
Ant. We'll sleep together: –
Duch. Alas, what pleasure can two lovers find in sleep?

(III.ii.1–10)

The casket and the glass; later on, the kissing, Antonio's reference to the Duchess and Cariola as two 'faces so well form'd' (III.ii.43), the Duchess's concern about her hair and its colour – all these elements contribute to the impression of reality through which the alcove scene attempts to naturalize itself as well as the pleasures it contains. Of course, the publicly displayed 'natural' pleasures and pleasurable teasing of the alcove scene are only precarious. The Duchess has merely to turn her head, whilst delivering what turns out to be the most inappropriate of lines ('Have you lost your tongue?' [III.ii.68]), to face the threat to these 'private' pleasures in the form of Ferdinand looking on, who is defined as an 'apparition' (III.ii.142) and a 'terrible thing' (III.ii.147). However, the 'invasion' of the private enclave of the conjugal couple also comes from within. In the 'wooing scene' the Duchess's bodily self, discovered as the locus of authenticity and desire, finds itself enmeshed in a language of property and propriety that superimposes self-possession (in a subjective sense) upon the possession of a bodily self as a quasi-empirical object, owned as some kind of valuable asset. Likewise, in the 'alcove scene' the bodies of the conjugal couple are invested with an erotic charge that finds its condition of representation in an equally ambiguous language of *propriété*: a 'night's lodging' must be purchased and properly obtained; bodies must be put to use and used properly. Moreover, when the 'strong thigh'd bargeman' of Ferdinand's fantasy scene materializes in the figure of Antonio, he does so as a labouring man who makes good use of his time, and whose pleasure coincides with the anticipation of its end:

Cari. Wherefore still when you lie with my lady
Do you rise so early?
Ant. Labouring men
Count the clock oft'nest Cariola,
Are glad when their task's ended.

(III.ii.17–20)

The emerging heterosexualized pleasures of the Duchess and Antonio are far removed from those of the conjugal pair of a later historical period; a couple that will be awarded, according to Foucault, the right to be 'spoken of less and less' and thus function as a 'stricter' and 'quieter' norm.[124] The conjugal couple of Webster's play *does* speak of itself, albeit only with a tremulous voice, as well as of an earlier regulation of bodies and identities it differentiates itself from. It is, no doubt, vociferously spoken of. Moreover, it does not stand for an erotic norm. The presence of Cariola in the alcove scene not only shows that the private sphere is not fully constructed, but also that the conjugal couple has not yet naturalized or normalized its heterosexual pleasures in such a way as to demonize the staging of other erotic positions. Cariola can still speak of the Duchess in terms that neither exclude nor unequivocally affirm the possibility of female homoeroticism:

Cari. My lord, I lie with her often; and I know
She'll much disquiet you: – …
For she is the sprawling'st bedfellow.

(III.ii.11–13)

This is not to argue that Cariola inhabits a mode of desire that stands opposed to heterosexual desire. As Valerie Traub clarifies in a related context, there is contiguity between female homoeroticism and female heterosexual desire in a culture in which the regime of 'object choice' has not yet been fully established:

> [F]or female characters who did not challenge conventional gender roles – who did *not* cross-dress, who did *not* wear swords, who were *not* anatomically 'excessive', who did *not* use 'illicit devices' … – desire may have been allowed to flow rather more freely if less sensationally between homoerotic and heterosexual modes.[125]

Female homoeroticism *could* therefore be demonized, as well as become the object of male fantasies and fears, when associated with an undermining of gender roles and/or 'when perceived as a threat to the reproductive designs of heterosexual marriage'.[126] The Duchess, of course, being 'an excellent feeder of pedigrees' (III.i.5–6), does not pose an erotic threat to the reproductive imperative of marriage. As far as Cariola is concerned, the possibility that this threat may arise is countered by means of a gentle interpellation:

Ant. When wilt thou marry, Cariola?
Cari. Never, my lord.

Ant. O fie upon this single life! forgo it!

(III.ii.23–4)

This interpellation will again be refused when Cariola glosses as 'vain poetry' (III.ii.33) the emblematic examples Antonio uses to illustrate the benefits of an inclusion in the charmed circle of heterosexual marriage.[127] One can also surmise that once the 'liberal' version of marriage becomes dominant and its furtive pleasures – and violence – normative, the threat to the reproductive designs of heterosexual marriage posed by female homoeroticism as an *exclusive* mode of desire will also be perceived as a threat to the reproduction of essential identities. In other words, at stake in the 'liberal' version of marriage, as can be glimpsed in some of the speeches by Antonio and the Duchess, is not only the physical and ideological work of reproduction of bodies, but also the reproduction of essential constructs such as *being* a father or *being* a mother.[128] These are constructs that certainly overlap with, but are also historically distinct from, being a father or a mother qua performance of a role in the 'dynastic' version of marriage.

Uncanny specular reversals

According to Frank Whigham, Ferdinand's is a 'desire to evade degrading associations with inferiors'. He goes as far as to redefine his 'incestuous inclination toward his sister' as the irredeemably social, if excessively endogamous, 'narrow[ing] [of] his kind from class to family', with the Duchess coming to stand for 'his own radical purity', conceived in class terms.[129] Yet, it is mostly retrospectively, and as a 'lost object', that the Duchess's body fully emerges as containing Ferdinand's 'radical purity'. The following is perhaps one of the most telling instances:

Ferd. Damn her! That body of hers,
While that my blood ran pure in't, was more worth
Than that which thou wouldst comfort, call'd a soul.

(IV.i.121–3)

In fact, what Whigham calls 'preemptive possession' of the Duchess's body is nothing but an imaginary formation.[130] I suggest that 'imaginary' is to be taken in a Lacanian sense, not least to underline that there is more involved in Ferdinand's cathexis of the Duchess's body than the possession of *her* body.

For Lacan, the imaginary centres on the mirror stage. This is understood as the subject's identification 'with the visual *Gestalt* of his own body', or the body of another, which is constitutive of the sense of wholeness of the ego as a bodily ego and essential to the establishing of its contours.[131] Yet, this wholeness is only ever 'fictional'.[132] It is, in fact, temporally and spatially dislocated. The 'total form of the body' with which the subject identifies is only ever an anticipated image, which makes the control of the chaotic reality of the body into a mirage of mastery.[133] Moreover, this 'ideal unity' of the bodily ego emerges only from the outside, as a mirror image.[134] The Duchess's body, construed by Ferdinand as a body in which *his* blood – his rank – flows uncontaminated, similarly functions as a specular image, conferring an 'ideal unity' also on *his* body. Put another way, Ferdinand's possession is simultaneously an appropriation of another body *and* a bodily *propriation*: a making 'proper', a construction of the contours of *his own* body, which is, once more, inseparable from the process of demarcation of class boundaries.[135]

This 'ap-propriation' mostly appears in the form of a nostalgic evocation. It remains, to a large extent, an 'orthopaedic' form of 'ap-propriation'.[136] Articulated retrospectively, it is just as dislocated as the specular identification described by Lacan. Moreover, the instability of the subject's imaginary identification also affects the logic of the signifier. The threat to Ferdinand's 'body proper' is most often signified through a signifier such as 'blood' qua passion and desire. This is a signifier that brings an intolerable effect of sameness to bear on 'blood' as lineage, which is one of the privileged points of identification around which the contours of the 'body proper' attempt to establish themselves. This is perhaps nowhere more apparent than when 'blood' as the cherished signifier of Ferdinand's 'rank' uncannily turns into a 'rank blood': 'Her witchcraft lies in her rank blood' (III.i.70). Moreover, the 'salutary *imago*'[137] of Ferdinand's plenitude often presents itself from without, as an uncanny and lethal *coincidentia oppositorum* that is the distorted counterpart of the Duke's idealized complementarity between two bodies:

Ferd. Methinks her fault and beauty,
Blended together, show like leprosy,
The whiter, the fouler.

(III.iii.62–4)

The ambivalence of the specular image underlined by Lacan corresponds in many ways to the ambivalence of the double described by Freud in his paper on the 'uncanny'. In this paper, Freud argues that in specific circumstances the double as 'insurance against the destruction of the ego' – the double qua *heimlich* – 'reverses its aspect', so as to become 'the uncanny harbinger of death'.[138] For Freud, as is well known, this reversal is a sign of the return of the 'surmounted' stage of 'unbounded self-love', associated with 'primary narcissism'.[139] This is a return that transforms the once *so* familiar interchangeability between the ego and its image into something *too* familiar to be endured.[140] As far as Ferdinand is concerned, the salutary interchangeability between his body and 'that body of hers', which retrospectively appears *so* familiar, re-presents itself as a hostile and *un-heimlich* image, an image whose effect is one of fragmentation. Needless to add, this fragmentation instantaneously makes way for an active will to punish. What Lacan calls 'aggressivity' is in the play a desire on the part of Ferdinand to 'hew … *her* to pieces' (II.v.31) in order to grasp *his* precarious and 'imaginary' sense of unity.[141] Yet, as both Freud and Lacan insist, although in slightly different terms, the estranging and 'foreign' image that keeps on returning from without is nothing but one's own projected image. It therefore makes perfect sense for Ferdinand to declare, speaking to his brother:

Ferd. I could kill her now,
In you, or in myself, for I do think
It is some sin in us, heaven doth revenge
By her.

(II.v.63–6)[142]

The anticipation of the deleterious effect the co-implication of a beneficial *and* lethal specular image may have upon Ferdinand – not to mention his sister – institutes the deferral of that desire which is called aggressivity:

Ferd. Till I know who leaps my sister, I'll not stir:
That known, I'll find scorpions to string my whips,
And fix her in a general eclipse.

(II.v.77–9)[143]

Once Ferdinand comes into close proximity to the rival 'who leaps [his] sister', this deferral is further deferred, apparently *ad infinitum*:

Ferd. Whate'er thou art, that hast enjoy'd my sister,
For I am sure thou hear'st me – for thine own sake
Let me not know thee: I came hither prepar'd
To work thy discovery, yet am now persuaded
It would beget such violent effects
As would damn us both: – *I would not for ten millions*
I had beheld thee; therefore use all means
I never may have knowledge of thy name.

(III.ii.90–7)[144]

These lines immediately follow an exchange between the Duchess and Ferdinand in which the Duke ironically claims that he would accept to 'see [her] husband' only if he 'could change eyes with a basilisk' (III.ii.86–7), a reptile, that is, whose eyes were imagined to strike people dead. Short of this metamorphosis, it is the *antagonist* – an antagonist whose 'discovery' Ferdinand was 'prepar'd to work' – whoseems to embody something that is impossible to look upon: 'I would not for ten millions I had beheld thee'. This is identifiable with the threatening reversibility – the return – of the look. Or, as Lacan would have it, the antagonist seems to body forth an *un-heimlich* specular image that provokes anxiety because it includes the gaze qua *objet petit a*. This is a gaze that usually subtracts itself from the 'geometral' point of vision from which the bodily 'I' qua eye recognizes itself in the mirror.[145]

These remarks are meant to dispute 'classical' interpretations of Ferdinand's lines such as the one put forward by Clifford Leech. He maintains that Ferdinand's 'holding back from identifying her husband' is one amongst the many 'clues' – clues that include 'the grossness of his language to her in Act I, the continued violence of his response to the situation …, his momentary identification of himself with her first husband, his necrophily in Act V' – that 'seem to point in one direction'.[146] This unambiguous 'one direction' is, of course, Ferdinand's incestuous desire for his sister.[147] In other words, Ferdinand abandons, at least momentarily, the 'discovery' of Antonio because this discovery would be tantamount to bringing to light his unconscious identification with the male rival who heterosexually 'enjoys' his sister.

Leech's interpretation is also objectionable on the grounds that it assumes that a man's identification with another man is not a desire but merely a diversion inevitably leading to a heterosexual object of desire. Yet, identification and desire do not necessarily proceed along mutually exclusive lines. As shown earlier, the 'heterosexual matrix' is not historically invariant or fully in place in the early modern period.[148] In answer to run-of-the-mill 'pseudo-psychoanalytic' interpretations such as Leech's, one needs to combine, therefore, the critique of the psychic normativity and historical immutability heterosexuality often claims for itself with a questioning of the reliance of traditional psychoanalytic criticism on a 'humanistic' conception of the character. As for the latter, the idea that a forbidden and incestuous desire agitates the psyche of a character does not so much dismantle the essence and unity of the character qua subject as reconstitute it at a deeper level, at the level of what lies behind its 'manifest' representations. In fact, this *substratum*, according to Borch-Jacobsen's quasi-Heideggerian re-reading of the basic tenets of psychoanalysis, is nothing but the subject, in the sense of *subjectum*.[149] In short, the 'humanism' that is characteristic of traditional psychoanalytic readings reduces the historical play of identification and desire, as well as the 'otherness' of the unconscious. As Borch-Jacobsen usefully summarizes, the question of the unconscious does not concern 'repressed representations so much as ... the ego's identity or, more precisely still, its *identification*. Which is quite a different thing, precisely because an identification with an other comes into play'. In other words, 'the otherness called unconscious ... designates my identity or my very sameness *as that of another*'.[150]

After the murder of the Duchess, typically effected through the intermediary of a multiple double, Ferdinand's confession gives a further twist to the question of the double: 'She and I were twins: / And should I die this instant, I had liv'd / Her time to a minute' (IV.ii.267–9). Once again, Ferdinand's plenitude reappears only as lost. Moreover, by linking the elimination of his double to his own death, he implicitly remarks that his 'proper' being is out there, in the 'other'. But his reaction towards the Duchess's corpse in this scene, as well as subsequent events in the play, also indicates that the erasure of the distance between the two sides of himself results in the emergence of a 'singular entity' – 'singular' in the sense of both 'unique' and 'strange' – that is even more unsettling than the adverse image reflected back to him from the 'other'. The last act of the play bears witness to the materialization of this uncanny ipseity, as Ferdinand presents himself as follows:

Ferd. Leave me.
Mal. Why doth your lordship love this solitariness?
Ferd. Eagles commonly fly alone: they are crows, daws, and
starlings that flock together: – look, what's that follows
me?

Mal. Nothing, my lord.
Ferd. Yes: –
Mal. 'Tis your shadow.
Ferd. Stay it, let it not haunt me.
Mal. Impossible: if you move, and the sun shine: –
Ferd. I will throttle it.[*Throws himself down on his shadow.*]

(V.ii.28–38)

Moreover, he is reported to be affected by lycanthropy and to have been found 'behind Saint Mark's church, with the leg of a man / Upon his shoulder' (V.ii.14–15). The doctor continues:

Doc. He howl'd fearfully;
Said he was a wolf, only the difference
Was, a wolf's skin was hairy on the outside,
His on the inside; bade them take their swords,
Rip up his flesh, and try.

(V.ii.15–19)

Ferdinand re-presents himself as a turned-inward version of himself but this 'introversion', which makes him resemble the folded and hidden places that have been brought to light during the play, is here oddly identified with the constrictive movement that reverses the skin of a ferocious wolf. This is a movement that inevitably induces an intolerable cohabitation. It spurs him on compulsively to return to the same place. In a way, it does not make sense any longer to say that Ferdinand is haunted by the double. By the end of the play the Calabrian Duke *is* – and the copula here must both be stressed and put under erasure – the deformed embodiment of haunting. He is situated at the point where absolute 'singularity' and absolute 'otherness' uncannily coincide with each other without neutralizing each other.[151] As such a disfigured figure of haunting, he cannot but haunt that by which he is haunted: the grave, where the scene of discovery as well as its violence are endlessly re-enacted in an occluded form.

2 'Behind the back of life'

Uncanny bodies and identities in *The Changeling*

He brings salves and balm with him, no doubt; but before he can act as a physician he first has to wound; when he then stills the pain of the wound *he at the same time infects the wound* – for that is what he knows best of all, this sorcerer and animal-tamer, in whose presence everything healthy necessarily grows sick, and everything sick tame.

(Friedrich Nietzsche, *On the Genealogy of Morals*)

What is closest *must* be avoided, by virtue of its very proximity.

(Jacques Derrida, *The Post Card*)

Telling a tale 'behind the back of life'

Towards the end of Middleton and Rowley's *The Changeling*, Beatrice emerges from Alsemero's closet, where De Flores has stabbed her. She delivers the following notorious lines, addressed primarily to her father Vermandero:

Bea. Oh come not near me, sir, I shall defile you:
I am that of your blood was taken from you
For your better health; look no more upon't,
But cast it to the ground regardlessly:
Let the common sewer take it from distinction.

(V.iii.149–53)[1]

In this 'self-debasing' and 'self-expelling' speech,[2] she associates the blood flowing from her wounded body – a theatrical reality – with that part of her father's blood removed in the course of what she sees as a kind of phlebotomy.[3] In fact, she comes to identify herself entirely with this plethoric blood ('I am that of your blood'), whilst signifying it as a contaminating and contaminated remainder that can no longer be approached ('Oh come not near me') or seen ('look no more upon't') without danger. It must simply be thrown to the ground 'regardlessly'. The ultimate proper destination she envisages for this abject fluid is the 'common sewer'. It is in this receptacle that the loss of the distinctive physiological characteristics of blood, as well as the annihilation of her aristocratic prerogatives qua Vermandero's daughter – her 'distinction' – will finally be sealed.

Beatrice's speech suggests not only that there is an intimate connection between her sexual transgression and the pollution of aristocratic blood, but also that the introduction of a socially alien 'poisonous' substance (namely, her servant De Flores) into her body and blood has brought about a fundamental 'change' – a word the play highly fetishizes – to her status. She has turned from a visible bodily vessel in which, to refer to *The Duchess of Malfi* again, male aristocratic blood 'ran pure' (IV.i.122), to an irremediably adulterated body synonymous with waste blood. The violent evacuation of the excrementitious matter she has become seems to be the only appropriate remedy to pollution, and is in fact figured as restorative of the 'better health' of the patriarchal and aristocratic body of her father Vermandero. Can one therefore argue, by extending to *The Changeling* Leonard Tennenhouse's approach to other Jacobean 'tragedies of blood', that Middleton and Rowley's play upholds the political and symbolic necessity of 'blood in its purest form, that is, the blood of the patriarch', in spite of the fact that it stages the signs of its contamination?[4] More specifically, to stay with the play's finale, does the violent subordination or evacuation of Beatrice 'renew ... the symbolic power of the sexual body to authorize patriarchy'?[5]

The cure of the disease that, in the form of corrupted blood, affects the aristocratic body and community is, no doubt, eventually carried out. Yet, the success of this surgical operation is somewhat compromised by the fact that the latter is not performed – and not performed *publicly* – by one of the male members of the aristocratic community, as one might expect following the logic of Tennenhouse's argument.[6] Instead, the evacuation of Beatrice's infected blood is executed, or at least initiated, in the most private of places (Alsemero's closet) by none other than De Flores, a 'surgeon' who uses a 'penknife' (V.iii.173) and who is ambiguously positioned in relation to the aristocratic community: he is 'a gentleman' by birth but has been 'thrust ... out to servitude' (II.i.48–9).[7] Moreover, this is a surgeon who is most often shown, also *because* of his liminal status, to partake of the same lethal characteristics as those of the abject substance he removes. As a matter of fact, the recurrent emphasis on the interchangeability between De Flores and poison is sometimes developed in such a way as to make it clear that the poison he incarnates is equivalent to contaminated and contaminating blood. In the penultimate scene of the play, for instance, the mere appearance of De Flores over the stage induces the following comments by Tomazo de Piracquo, brother to the murdered Alonzo:

Tom. He's so foul ...; so most deadly venomous,
He would go near to poison any weapon
That should draw blood on him.

(V.ii.15; 17–19)

De Flores's blood is 'most deadly venomous' inasmuch as it is plethoric, at least to judge from one additional effect his ghostly reappearance has on Tomazo's aristocratic body: 'What, again? / He walks a' purpose by, sure, *to choke me up*, / To infect my blood' (V.ii.23–5).[8]

That the 'surgeon' employed to expel excrementitious blood is but another embodiment of a socially codified venomous and plethoric fluid indicates that the play's finale, even as it 'violently subordinates the female body to male authority', fails to restore 'blood in its purest form, that is, the blood of the patriarch'.[9] On the one hand, the threat posed by Beatrice's blood is contained. In fact, it is more than *contained*: it flows down the drain, as it were, along with a blood that is reduced to a status of utter undifferentiation. On the other hand, the abjection of Beatrice promotes De Flores to a symbolically central position and thus reinstates the 'distinction' (V.iii.153) only to confound it again. It introduces into the aristocratic body another version of the poison that has just been ejected. In other words, De Flores's bloodletting obeys the logic of the *pharmakon* described by Derrida. It simultaneously decontaminates *and* infects.[10]

In the light of these remarks, one may dispute Tennenhouse's contention that the reassertion of the 'law of patriarchy' in Jacobean tragedies is synonymous with the re-establishing of the 'distinction' of rank and the boundaries of 'a pure community of aristocratic blood'.[11] In the case of *The Changeling*, this reassertion *depends* for its effectiveness upon a 'contaminating' identificatory bond between men across class boundaries. One of the forms of this homosocial bond, feared and yet inescapable, is the essential agreement between Alsemero and De Flores over the meaning of Beatrice's transgression. This is a compact whose binding force is not erased by Alsemero's stress on the equal retribution that lies in wait for the 'twins of mischief' (V.iii.142):

De F. Has she confessed it?
Als. As sure as death to both of you,
And much more than that.
De F. It could not be much more;
'Twas one thing, and that – she's a whore.
Als. It could not choose but follow; oh cunning devils!
How should blind men know you from fair-fac'd saints?
(V.iii.105–9)[12]

Thus, the play's finale activates contaminating substitutions, most notably the substitution of an outsider for a male member of the aristocratic community as the active agent in the performance of the 'deed' (V.iii.129), and uncanny symmetries, such as the cross-class identificatory bond between Alsemero and De Flores. I shall argue that these strange permutations and equivalencies are not specific to the end of the play, or only relevant to an understanding of De Flores and Alsemero's positions. Rather, they are symptomatic of the fact that bodies and identities are constructed throughout the play as sites of contradictory and unstable articulations of different vectors of power such as class, gender and eroticism. In the course of this chapter, I shall explore some of these constructions, focusing on their social, psychic and fantasmatic aspects. I shall also stress that the vicissitudes of the gaze, and, more generally, the multifarious ways in which the ocular and the specular are deployed within the play, are deeply implicated in these constructions. It is not by chance, to stay with some examples from the end of the play, that Beatrice's speech insists that her father avert the gaze from her contaminated blood, thereby linking the restoration of his 'better health' to the distinctness of vision: '*Look no more upon't*, but cast it to the ground *regard*lessly' (V.iii.151–2).[13] Or that Alsemero, in the dialogue with De Flores I have just cited, resolutely, if implicitly, thinks of himself as no longer one of those 'blind men' (V.iii.109) who lack a patriarchally inflected eyesight.[14] Or, finally, that Alsemero's advice to Vermandero regarding the 'wounded' part of the latter's 'name' (V.iii.180), whilst rehearsing the dominant logic of repression and ejection instituted at the end of the play, does not fail to recite that the threat to this logic lies in what is hidden or too close to be looked at:

Als. Let it be blotted out, let your heart lose it,
And it can never *look you in the face*,
Nor tell a tale *behind the back of life*
To your dishonour.

(V.iii.182–5)[15]

The mirror, the gaze and the body 'a(na)morphous'

The play opens with Alsemero meditating outside the church where he has just seen Beatrice for the second time:

Als. The place is holy, so is my intent:
I love her beauties to the holy purpose,
And that, methinks, admits comparison
With man's first creation, the place blest,
And is his right home back, if he achieve it.
The church hath first begun our interview,
And that's the place must join us into one.

(I.i.5–11)

This soliloquy firmly locates Alsemero's courtly love for Beatrice in an erotic economy wherein the male lover's libidinal investment in, and overvaluation of, the Lady is not opposed to but superimposed upon his desire for himself, a narcissistic desire to recover or constitute his own self as a unity.[16] Waiting for the – improbable – fulfilment of the fantasy of oneness and completion, Alsemero is 'forc'd to repetition' (I.i.70). He is forced to reiterate his loving stance and chivalric pose: 'I love you dearly' (I.i.71).[17] As to the Lady, she keeps on acting as his mirror image and fantasmatic counterpart, thus signifying, to use a Lacanian terminology, the conflation of the Other with the *objet petit a* qua support of male fantasies, the reduction of the Other to man's imaginary other.[18] Later in the play, to Beatrice's avowal: 'I have within mine eyes all my desires' (II.ii.8), Alsemero typically responds as follows:

Als. W'are so like
In our expressions, lady, that unless I borrow
The same words, I shall never find their equals.
(II.ii.12–14)

However, the play has already shown that the complementary relation between the two lovers is an unstable imaginary formation. In fact, the precariousness of the sense of wholeness and completion the specular double mirrors back to the subject comes to the fore as soon as Alsemero requests 'the confirmation by the hand royal' (I.i.81–2) of his love, but realizes that this ratification is not, as he assumes, the Lady's 'part' (I.i.82). It belongs, instead, with Beatrice's father, as she emphasizes: 'Oh, there's one above me, sir' (I.i.83).

Because of his rank and the former 'acquaintance' between his father and Vermandero (I.i.167–86), Alsemero could have been a suitable husband to Beatrice and, more to the point, an appropriate son-in-law to Vermandero.[19] Yet, in Beatrice's words, he has 'come so near his time' only to 'miss it' (I.i.85–6), and this *contre-temps* makes his desire irreconcilable with Vermandero's equally ardent 'will' to forge a bond with his daughter's betrothed, Alonzo de Piracquo.[20] The play expands on this homosocial desire in great detail:

Ver. I tell you, sir, the gentleman's complete,
A courtier and a gallant, enrich'd
With many fair and noble ornaments;
I would not change him for a son-in-law
For any he in Spain ….
Als. He's much
Bound to you, sir.
Ver. He shall be bound to me,
As fast as this tie can hold; I'll want
My will else.
Bea. [aside] I shall want mine if you do it.
(I.i.212–16; 217–20)

However, Vermandero's pursuit of an honourable alliance with a man of similar social standing is so intense that he 'unconsciously' keeps his options open. He invites Alsemero to 'see [his] castle, / And *her* best entertainment' (I.i.201–2), and take part in his daughter's wedding.[21] On the one hand, Vermandero's requests 'abject' Beatrice's suitor: 'He means to feast me, and poison me beforehand' (I.i.207). They also seem irremediably to prejudice his return to an ideal Edenic point of origin before the Fall; a return for which the passage through Beatrice's body is still, at this stage of the play, an essential prerequisite:

Als. [aside] How shall I dare to venture in his castle,
When he discharges murderers at the gate?
But I must on, for back I cannot go.

(I.i.222–4)

On the other hand, Vermandero's invitation positions Alsemero as close as possible to the 'homosocial centre' of the play, and so much so that once the sequence of substitutions making up the plot comes to an end, he will be able to present Vermandero with 'a son's duty' (V.iii.216).

Vermandero's 'will' (I.i.220) also finds itself at odds – but this time with no ambiguous or mitigating overtones – with Beatrice's endeavour to renegotiate her position after her encounter with Alsemero. In II.i. Beatrice dilates upon her father's desire in terms that emphasize her little margin for manoeuvre within the homosocial economy of Alicante:

Bea. [W]hat's Piracquo
My father spends his breath for? And his blessing
Is only mine, as I regard his name,
Else it goes from me, and turns head against me,
Transform'd into a curse.

(II.i.19–23)

She concludes by stressing the extent to which her betrothed's over-eagerness contributes to her predicament:

Bea. He's so forward too,
So urgent that way, scarce allows me breath
To speak to my new comforts.

(II.i.23–5)

Interestingly, these concluding lines can also be read as referring to Vermandero's desire (i.e. his impatience to obtain a son-in-law), just as, in the previous citation, the 'name' Beatrice is compelled to 'regard' can alternatively be taken to be Piracquo's. This is a sign of the interchangeability between the discursive position of the father and that of the prospective son-in-law. Both men are 'hot preparing for this day of triumph' (I.i.189), the marriage match that will seal their alliance.

It is this interchangeability that facilitates the substitution, on Beatrice and Alsemero's part, of Alonzo de Piracquo for Vermandero as the primary target of aggression and aversion. This displacement safeguards the position of the father, in practical and, to a certain extent, symbolic terms. Alonzo, for instance, is identified in II.ii. as the 'cause' of Vermandero's 'command', a 'cause' Alsemero offers to 'remove' in the course of an aristocratic duel (II.ii.23–24). He is also defined as 'an enemy, a hateful one, that wishes *poison*' to the 'poor kiss' the two lovers have just exchanged (II.ii.16–18).[22] In short, the roles Vermandero and Alonzo respectively play in the enforcement of marriage are tacitly reinterpreted and reversed, so that the latter comes to embody an active and 'lethal' function that is remarkably similar to the one attributed to the former in I.i.[23] Of course, the father's 'will' does not cease to matter. Yet, by now it significantly – and literally – takes second place:

> *Bea.* [H]ow well were I now
> If there were none such name known as Piracquo,
> Nor no such tie as the commands of parents!
>
> (II.ii.18–20)

Alonzo and Vermandero are not the only male characters that 'scarce allow … [Beatrice] breath' (II.i.25). No sooner does she end her speech on her father and/or betrothed's 'forwardness' in II.i. than De Flores enters to deliver the following aside:

> *De F.* I can as well be hang'd as refrain seeing her;
> Some twenty times a day, nay, not so little,
> Do I force errands, frame ways and excuses
> To come into her sight.
>
> (II.i.28–31)

In effect, it is whilst running one of these 'errands' that De Flores comes on to the stage for the first time. In the first scene of the play, he sets himself to announce the arrival of Vermandero but his alacrity is immediately rebuked by Beatrice, who has just alluded to her father – the 'one above [her]' (I.i.83) – in her dialogue with Alsemero:

> *Bea.* What needed then
> Your duteous preface? I had rather
> He had come unexpected; you must stall
> A good presence with unnecessary blabbing.
>
> (I.i.95–98)

'Stall' is a notoriously controversial textual crux.[24] What seems clear is that De Flores impairs Vermandero's 'presence'. He hinders his entrance and makes it largely ineffective with a 'preface' that, according to Beatrice, is as 'duteous' as it is inconsequential; or, alternatively, he surfeits the father's 'good presence' with this insignificant ceremonious introduction, in much the same uncanny way as he 'chokes up' Tomazo with his appearance in V.ii. Yet, Beatrice is not only concerned about De Flores's 'blabbing', a strategy of deferral that is much more pronounced in II.i., where the delivery of a message is protracted for some twenty lines; she is 'displeas'd … on the sudden' (I.i.108) also because De Flores is a 'deadly poison' to her 'eyes …, the same that report speaks of the basilisk' (I.i.112; 114–15). She regards his appearance as the emergence of an adverse and defiling gaze. This gaze punctures the specular reflection of like to like in which Alsemero and

Beatrice engage. This suggests, in turn, that there is some kind of uncanny overlapping, in spite of the opposition established by Beatrice, between the position of De Flores and that of Vermandero, the bearer of the paternal 'hand royal' (I.i.82) who implicitly refuses to countersign the two lovers' specular desire.

Lacan's discussion of the discrepancy between the subject's eye and the gaze qua *objet petit a* can usefully be recalled in this context. In *The Four Fundamental Concepts of Psycho-Analysis*, he argues: 'In our relation to things, in so far as this relation is constituted by the way of vision, ... something slips, passes, is transmitted, from stage to stage, and is always to some degree eluded in it – this is what we call the gaze.'[25] For Lacan, the gaze thus 'escapes the grasp of [the] form of vision' that inheres in 'that order, which is particularly satisfying for the subject, connoted in psycho-analytic experience by the term narcissism'.[26] The gaze is not contained or reflected in the mirror in which one pleasurably 'see[s] oneself seeing oneself' from one 'geometral' single point.[27] In short, as he states, '*You never look at me from the place from which I see you*'.[28] Slavoj Žižek glosses this as follows: 'I can never see properly, i.e., include in the totality of my field of vision the point in the other from which it gazes back at me.'[29] This 'point in the other' – the point of the ever elusive gaze – is, for Lacan, nothing but a blot, a 'stain',[30] standing for lack *and* surplus, undermining the subject's self-mirroring and self-recognition and dividing its desire.

In *The Changeling* De Flores 'em-bodies' this 'stain'. As mentioned earlier, he is assimilated to a 'deadly poison' (I.i.112) and likened to the basilisk, a fabulous reptile with a killing look. The extent to which this look is lethal, 'to [Beatrice's] eyes' (I.i.114) in particular, can be assessed within the context provided by Beatrice and Alsemero's imaginary construction of their bodies and identities in each other's ideal image. This is a construction in the course of which they repeatedly bring into the foreground discerning eyes and 'intellectual eyesight' (II.i.19) as that which is proper to love, thus showing the intimate connection between the form in which each lover likes to be seen by the other and a sense of vision which is clear and all-encompassing.[31] This sense of vision is emblematized by the image of 'plenitude' Beatrice evokes in II.ii. as she sees Alsemero: 'I have within mine eyes all my desires' (II.ii.8).

De Flores's hostile and repugnant look interferes with these 'imaginary' bodies and lines of sight. It begins to hint at something that is 'in the subject more than the subject;'[32] something that is 'strange to me, although it is at the heart of me',[33] 'radically interior and at the same time already exterior'.[34] In other words, De Flores's appearance shifts the focus of Beatrice and Alsemero's dialogue from eyes as 'sentinels unto ... judgements' (I.i.72) to eyes caught off guard; from a love that is synonymous with 'certain judgement' (I.i.73) to a dislike for which Beatrice cannot 'render reason' (I.i.110); and, most importantly, from the opposition between love and aversion to that which subtends and haunts this opposition.

Alsemero chivalrously attempts to justify Beatrice's inexplicable aversion for De Flores by attributing this 'infirmity' (I.i.109) to 'a frequent frailty in our nature' (I.i.116), whereby 'one distastes / The scent of roses, which to infinites most pleasing is, and odoriferous; / One oil, the enemy of poison; / Another wine, the cheerer of the heart' (I.i.118–22). Yet, the line that summarizes this eulogy of diversity suggests that repulsion and attraction may be uncannily interchangeable: 'There's scarce a thing but is both lov'd and loath'd' (I.i.125).[35] Moreover, the exchange following Alsemero's admission that he is not immune to 'irrational' loathing only stretches the paradox,[36] since it registers the surreptitious inclusion in the *speculum* of courtly love of a substance whose exclusion is the essential prerequisite for imaginary bodies and identities to establish and sustain themselves:

> *Bea.* And what may be *your poison*, sir? I am bold with you.
> *Als.* What might be *your desire*, perhaps, a cherry.
>
> (I.i.127–8)[37]

It can therefore be argued, in Lacanian terms, that De Flores's look marks the point in the mirror image where the gaze qua *objet a* reappears as a 'foreign body'. In other words, the gaze does *not* re-emerge as a complementary 'object' that brings pleasure or wholeness but, rather, as an 'ex-timate' object that keeps on signifying the uncanny reverse side of the subject, its intimate alterity to itself.[38] As far as Beatrice is concerned, this is an 'object' that compulsively 'come[s] into [her] sight' (II.i.31) in the first two acts of the play, and 'more disturbs [her] than all [her] other passions' (II.i.53–4). She expands on this as follows:

> *Bea.* I never see this fellow, but I think
> Of some harm towards me, danger's in my mind still;
> I scarce leave trembling of an hour after.
>
> (II.i.89–91)

The emergence of the point from which Beatrice's 'fellow' gazes back at her, representing her as 'other' than she is (in other words, other than her ideal image of herself), does not cease to provoke anxiety. But it is worth specifying that it is by virtue of his disfigured and 'a(na)morphous' countenance (as an 'ominous ill-fac'd fellow' [II.i.53]) that De Flores provides the 'material correlative' of a gaze that is too close for comfort: the 'overproximate' gaze qua *objet petit a*.[39] To paraphrase one of Slavoj Žižek's definitions of the *objet petit a*, De Flores's is a 'strange body' that cannot be properly symbolized or specularized and is therefore 'produced as a residue, a remnant, a leftover … embodying horrifying *jouissance*'.[40] As a form of 'surplus enjoyment', it 'simultaneously attracts and repels'.[41] In Alsemero's appropriate words, it '*tempts* [Beatrice's] sight' (I.i.131).[42] It lacks proper and regular features and, by the same token, sticks out. As such, it unbalances Beatrice's position as a viewer and inexorably draws her towards that 'point of otherness' where the *distance* from the image with which she is presented is threatened with annihilation.[43]

De Flores himself repeatedly returns to his unsightly appearance and the detrimental effect it has on Beatrice. The following lines re-emphasize that his body acts as the material support of the gaze, thus becoming 'a body too much':

De F. She … does profess herself
The cruellest enemy to my face in town,
At no hand can abide the sight of me,
As if danger or ill luck hung in my looks.

(II.i.32–6)[44]

As the speech progresses, De Flores's 'looks' reveal themselves to be hideous as a result of a process of abjection that is social as much as psychic. He confesses that his face 'is bad enough' (II.i.37). Nonetheless, he adds, 'far worse ha[ve] *better fortune*, / And not endur'd alone, but doted on' (II.i.38–9).[45] He goes on to describe these 'far worse' faces as follows:

De F. [S]uch pick-hair'd faces, chins like witches',
Here and there five hairs, whispering in a corner,
As if they grew in fear of one another,
Wrinkles like troughs, where swine-deformity swills
The tears of perjury that lie there like wash
Fallen from the slimy and dishonest eye.

(II.i.40–5)

He concludes with lines that may seem to have little to do with the rest of the speech: 'Though my hard fate has *thrust me out to servitude*, / I tumbled into th'world a gentleman' (II.i.48–9).[46] Yet, these are lines that establish an intimate connection between the lesser 'fortune' of his face and the expulsion that forced him to cross a social boundary and turned him into an abject remainder that cannot be looked at straight on. In short, De Flores's deformed 'looks' are anything but 'natural'. They are matter 'in the wrong place' also in social terms.[47] They bear the same lethal traits as those of the 'rejected bits and pieces' Mary Douglas refers to in her notorious study of pollution.[48] They retain a 'half-identity' that constitutes a threat not only 'to good order' and 'the distinctions made', but also to the distinctness of vision, causing 'the clarity of the scene in which they obtrude [to be] impaired by their presence'.[49]

De Flores's speech therefore suggests that the psychoanalytic approach I have been putting forward needs to be supplemented by an emphasis on the interimplication of the 'social' and the 'psychic'. In *The Changeling* the differential distribution of power within the 'social' seems to function as the site of articulation of 'psychic material'. In Beatrice's case, for instance, the play *does* stage the discontinuity or splitting of an identity that is faced with the re-emergence of a traumatic 'object'. However, this *mise-en-scène* takes place within historically contingent coordinates of status, gender and eroticism.[50] As a matter of fact, Beatrice's aversion for De Flores can be re-read as the repetition of the process whereby the latter is 'thrust … out to servitude', as a kind of class abjection that cannot be safely carried out because of *her own* lesser 'fortune' and socially coded 'ill luck' within the patriarchal system of constraints in Alicante. 'Would creation … had form'd me man' (II.ii.107–8), she sighs in the dialogue in which she sets in motion her partially successful plan to employ De Flores to eliminate her betrothed Alonzo. She continues with a speech in which she refers to her powerlessness *vis-à-vis* Alonzo, one of her 'two inveterate loathings' (II.ii.145).[51] Nonetheless, this speech also throws some light on why her aversion for the repulsive 'fallen' gentleman *she is speaking to* is unable to sustain itself:

Bea. Oh, 'tis the soul of freedom!
I should not then be forc'd to marry one
I hate beyond all depths, I should have power
Then to oppose my loathings, nay, remove 'em
For ever from my sight.

(II.ii.109–13)

As suggested earlier, the 'overproximate' gaze clinging to De Flores's 'looks' (II.i.36) brings back into being the uncanny reverse side of Beatrice's body and identity. It can now be argued that the appearance and reappearance of this 'other-than-ideal' side of Beatrice – the 'a(na)morphous' blot in the mirror she can only see by fading as a 'subject' – is inextricably linked to the subjection and abjection in gender terms that make her class position, as well as any process of expulsion and repulsion initiated from this position, dangerously unstable. It is also worth emphasizing that it is her turning away from the object of her father's homosocial desire – her 'making choice of [Alsemero]' (II.i.9) – that exacerbates the precariousness of her already hybrid and split identity within the patriarchal and aristocratic community of Alicante, and thus facilitates the excruciating return of this uncanny lethal double of her self.[52]

Intimate bonds, corporeal 'acts', and bodily contours

In her reading of *The Changeling*, Lisa Jardine associates Beatrice's 'choice' and love for Alsemero with the emerging model of companionate marriage, a marriage-friendship that entails 'the active consent of both parties, and some kind of equal participation', and is based upon 'mutual affection and shared preference'.[53] She points out that this 'newly mutual and personalised love between partners in a marriage love-match' is comparable with the equally emergent model of intimate male friendship as a basis for 'service'.[54] The latter is a new kind of liaison between men similarly predicated upon '"affection" and individualised emotional attachment', escaping 'the terms of recognised kinship relationships' and 'formally unacknowledged in the public sphere'.[55]

This goes some way towards explaining why Beatrice finds herself juxtaposing her 'choice' of Alsemero to the latter's 'choice' of his 'friend' and attendant Jasperino:

Bea. How wise is Alsemero in his friend!
It is a sign he makes his choice with judgement.

Then I appear in nothing more approv'd,
Than making choice of him;
For 'tis a principle, he that can choose
That bosom well, who of his thoughts partakes,
Proves most discreet in every choice he makes.

(II.i.6–14)

Yet, as Jardine observes, 'her assumption that she too can build such intimacy in the form of a friendship-marriage turns out … to underestimate the gendered nature of such relationships'.[56] In early seventeenth-century culture, both male–male and male–female intimate and 'private' love bonds generate anxiety as they 'collide against a backdrop of traditional dynastic and lineal aspiration'.[57] However, in Middleton and Rowley's play this anxiety is predominantly displaced from the former kind of liaison to the latter and, more precisely, to one of the characteristic features of the 'companionate' model of marriage: the stress on 'the active participation of the woman', which 'makes her love equivalently more active'.[58] For instance, just before the speech previously cited, Beatrice praises the 'fair service' (II.i.1) Jasperino performs on behalf of Alsemero (his acting as a go-between). This is a 'service / Which makes *the name of friend* sit glorious on [him]' (II.i.1–2), but nonetheless contributes to the disruption of the 'traditional' marriage alliance arranged by Vermandero just as much as Beatrice's 'love'.[59] Yet, as the play progresses, it is Beatrice who 'is made to bear the burden of an irresolvable conflict between [these] competing social models'.[60] In fact, she 'is driven out into the wilderness like the proverbial scapegoat'.[61] By contrast, not only does the threat posed by male–male 'private' bonds pass into silence, but, by the end of the play, new relationships between men are firmly implemented, most notably those between Alsemero and Vermandero, Alsemero and Tomazo.[62]

Jardine argues that Beatrice's choice of a marriage partner becomes 'the epicentre of blame', and especially inasmuch as it indicates some kind of agency on her part.[63] Paradoxically, however, the character that is mainly entrusted with the indictment of this choice is none other than De Flores, a character, that is, whose erotic prospects are *furthered* by her transgression of her father's command:

De F. [aside] I have watch'd this meeting, and do wonder much
What shall become of t'other [Alonzo]; I'm sure both
Cannot be serv'd unless she transgress; happily
Then I'll put in for one: for if a woman
Fly from one point, from him she makes a husband,
She spreads and mounts then like arithmetic,
One, ten, a hundred, a thousand, ten thousand,
Proves in time sutler to an army royal.

(II.ii.57–64)

The secret rendezvous between the two lovers thus strengthens De Flores's misogynistic conviction that, sooner or later, he will obtain a share of her favours.[64]

He sees her choice as a 'serial' act, an act whose repeatability can only mean that he too will 'have [his] will' (I.i.237) and partake of the horizontal bond of 'alienated brothers' invading her 'castellated' body.[65] In III.iv., as he claims the 'reward' for his 'service' (II.ii.129–30), which he anticipates as being so 'precious' that 'the thought ravishes' (II.ii.132), De Flores associates her 'fly[ing] from one point' with a disreputable 'change' in her 'affection' from her 'first love'. He then interprets this movement and permutation as strictly and literally synonymous with another kind of 'change': the murder of Alonzo.[66] The assumption is that Beatrice's choice is nothing less than a kind of homicidal act:

De F. Though thou writ'st maid, thou whore in thy affection!
'Twas *chang'd* from thy first love, and that's a kind
Of whoredom in thy heart; and he's *changed* now [Alonzo],
To bring thy second on, thy Alsemero,
Whom … if I enjoy thee not, thou ne'er enjoy'st.
(III.iv.142–7)[67]

Jardine notes that 'the strongest lines imputing dangerously disruptive motives to the active woman are all put into the mouth of the arch-villain'.[68] She maintains, however, against a counter-argument that might emphasize that De Flores's voice, precisely because it is the voice of an 'arch-villain', cannot be taken as representative of the 'dominant' drive of the play, that 'the final message the audience carries strongly away from *The Changeling* is that when a woman freely chooses her sexual partner she moves beyond restraint'.[69] Much as I doubt that Middleton and Rowley's play conveys a 'final message', I do not want to dispute the gist of Jardine's argument, or the relevance of her conclusion to the interpretation of the gender and sexual politics of the text. Nonetheless, I want to suggest that the fact that De Flores plays such a crucial role in the demonization of Beatrice's 'fashioning' of a male–female intimate relationship – a fashioning from whose bankruptcy he profits – has more far-reaching implications than Jardine's analysis allows. In particular, it calls for a more extensive investigation of the discursive position(s) De Flores adopts. Furthermore, this peculiar – and recurrent – aspect of the text has intricate effects on the politics of male–male bonds and the re-establishing of these bonds at the end of the play.

For Jardine, De Flores is a Bosola-like 'household servant of the new model, who offers service for material reward', and lives in a world where 'service is costed, and where the "rate" for disposing of a suitor is sexual intimacy'.[70] Thus, he cannot but rebuff Beatrice's appeal to the distinction of blood as an obstacle to a recompense of a sexual kind. Jardine refers to these often-cited lines to support her point:

Bea. Think but upon the distance that creation
Set 'twixt thy blood and mine, and keep thee there.
De F. Look but into your conscience, read me there.
'Tis a true book, you'll find me there your equal:
Push, fly not to your birth, but settle you

In what the act has made you, y'are no more now;
You must forget your parentage to me:
Y'are the deed's creature; … and I challenge you,
As peace and innocency has turn'd you out,
And made you one with me.

(III.iv.130–7; 138–40)

That form of 'service' which is De Flores's 'act' inevitably implicates Beatrice. It brings about the undermining of the 'distance' signified in the blood and makes her 'one with [him]'. Sign and symptom of a Machiavellian kind of praxis, this is an 'act' that expels them both in a 'private' economy of negotiations and exchanges that is at odds with the fixed ordering of bodies and identities inhering in the *dispositif* of alliance. This is not to argue that the transactions associated with this 'proto-bourgeois' economy are unmarked by inequalities of power – quite the contrary. In the 'reward scene' the most conspicuous amongst these transactions entail some form or other of coercion, such as the 'marriage' De Flores forces upon Beatrice and the ensuing consummation. They constitute a travesty of the mutual exchange and coalescence of bodies and identities typical of the emerging ideology of 'companionate' marriages.[71] After the 'act', De Flores declares that they 'should stick together' (III.iv.84), and that it is not 'fit' that a couple like them, 'engag'd so jointly, should part and live asunder' (III.iv.88–9). He then tries to seal his vows with a kiss, having already presented Beatrice with the ring complete with finger he has cut off from Alonzo's body. Therefore, the undoing of class distinctions is not synonymous with the obliteration of all power demarcations. This has a bearing on the positions De Flores occupies, which are multiple and heterogeneous to one another.

To some extent, the dialogue previously cited re-marks De Flores's career as the uncanny double of Beatrice. It shows once again the socially coded impossibility on Beatrice's part to uphold or re-create the boundaries of her body and identity through the abjection of, or the displacement of her gender abjection onto, De Flores without the latter coming back to haunt her.[72] Yet there are some new elements in the dialogue, as well as in the 'reward scene' as a whole, that re-articulate the dynamics of haunting in quite peculiar ways. In this respect, one needs to specify that De Flores is not only inscribed *in* the 'true book' of 'conscience' as Beatrice's 'equal', as the double that persistently and compulsively designates the intolerable sameness and uncanny interchangeability between allegedly opposed socially marked entities. By enjoining her to 'look', 'read', and 'fly not', he also speaks *with* the voice of conscience. Thus, perhaps more clearly than anywhere else in the play, he puts on the robes of a sadistic and guilt-producing super-ego, a figure that watches Beatrice and measures her against her *class* and *gender* ideal.[73] To put it somewhat differently, the supposedly common 'expulsion' of Beatrice and De Flores into 'equality' is, from the latter's perspective at least, superimposed upon an imaginary process of *reversal* of the movement that has 'thrust [him] out to servitude'.[74] This fantasmatic process of return to, and identification with, his ideal social self is a paradoxical form of class and gender advancement that is indistinguishable from the displacement of his abjection onto Beatrice. It is precisely this fantasmatic process that enables the 'fallen gentleman' to pose as the embodiment of the gaze and voice of a judgemental super-ego. That De Flores also instigates Beatrice's sexual transgression – her insertion in the 'private' bodily economy opened up by the 'act' – whilst speaking from this position does not invalidate his functioning as an agent of psychic and social regulation. On the contrary, it is by coupling this instigation with the injunction to recognize the distance between herself and herself, as opposed to the class 'distance' between them, that he ensures that *her* transgression be a highly regulated kind of *affair*.[75]

De Flores's disdainful rejection of Beatrice's offer of pecuniary remuneration for the murder of Alonzo, which occupies most of the rest of the 'reward scene', also needs to be related to the fantasmatic reversal that culminates with his assumption of the stance of a super-egoic figure. To De Flores, this is an offer that implicitly and explicitly ascribes to him a status that is not properly his:

De F. Do you place me in the rank of verminous fellows,
To destroy things for wages? Offer gold ...? I could ha' hir'd
A journeyman in murder at this rate,
And mine own conscience might have slept at ease,
And have had the work brought home.

(III.iv.64–5; 68–71)

Later on, however, he qualifies these lines by acknowledging his current predicament:

De F. You see I have thrown contempt upon your gold,
Not that I want it not, for I do piteously:
In order I will come unto't, and make use on't.
But 'twas not held so precious to begin with.

(III.iv.111–14)

In fact, he adopts a pragmatic approach to the matter: 'Well, being my fees I'll take it' (III.iv.46), whilst hastening to add: 'Great men have taught me that, or else my merit / Would scorn the way on't' (III.iv.47–8).

It should be clear by now that one cannot merely dismiss De Flores's 'scorn' and 'contempt' for Beatrice's 'gold' as indicative of the fact that he, like Bosola in *The Duchess of Malfi*, 'rails at those things which he wants' (I.i.25). He admits that he wants, and 'piteously'. Yet he wants more, and in direct proportion not only to the quality of the 'service' carried out on Beatrice's behalf, or the risks involved therein, including the deleterious, if calculated, effect on his 'conscience', but also to what he sees as his 'merit' and 'rank'. He does not want 'wages', or even just sexual intercourse with Beatrice. He longs for her 'virginity':

De F. And were I not resolv'd in my belief
That thy virginity were perfect in thee,

I should but take my recompense with grudging,
As if I had but half my hopes I agreed for.

(III.iv.116–19)

In the 'reward scene' Beatrice's body is construed in two overlapping ways. This construction is interwoven with the double coding of De Flores's 'act': an 'act' emblematizing a Machiavellian praxis that is at odds with a sense of identity as the pre-established performance of the role occupied in the hierarchized body politic of Alicante;[76] but also, at one and the same time, an 'act' symptomatizing De Flores's fantasmatic recovery of his ideal self, of the self he once was before the 'expulsion'. First of all, Beatrice's body is identified with, and essentialized as, a 'flesh-and-blood' body whose hymenal membrane is the 'proper' and all too material 'recompense' for an 'act' that is represented not only as erotically charged but also as that which eroticizes the body of the perpetrator.[77] Indeed, as the 'reward scene' progresses, Beatrice is constrained to see her bodily identity, through De Flores's eyes, not only as a 'hymeneal object' of transaction but also as the passive counterpart to De Flores's own body.[78] This is a body that is figured as the quasi-literalized factual site of sexual drives:

De F. I have eas'd you
Of your trouble, think on't, I'm in pain,
And must be eas'd of you; 'tis a charity,
Justice invites your blood to understand me.

(III.iv.97–100)

In other words, the dystopic suspension of the metaphysical and political order of blood distinctions goes hand in hand, from De Flores's point of view, with the emergence of 'natural' and palpable bodies, of entities whose materiality consists in that they are always-already marked by asymmetrical differences of sex and gender. These differences function, in turn, as the primary determinants of erotic desire. Nonetheless, no sooner do these 'natural' and heterosexualized bodies appear, offering a glimpse of a historically different formation of bodies and desires, than they are re-figured as entities that provide the bodily means for De Flores's articulation of his fantasmatic class and gender mobility at the expense of Beatrice. Hence, a second construction of Beatrice's body that is superimposed upon the first. Within the terms of this construction, Beatrice's body once again corresponds to her hymen, but this time this bodily margin is fantasized by De Flores as a class margin, as a partially idealized *limes* that can be re-crossed.[79]

The 'pro(re)gression' of male homosocial desire

De Flores re-presents himself in the 'reward scene' as the same as Beatrice, in a way that is intolerable to her; but also, simultaneously, as not quite the same as her, not least because of the fact that the 'act' is also some kind of cleansing that paves the way for his partial recasting of himself as the super-egoic figure censoring her. It is by appropriating, and speaking from, this super-egoic position that De Flores, in spite of a concomitant rhetoric of sameness and equality, underlines that his desire for Beatrice is not a form of identification.[80] Or, to be more precise, that his 'private' bond with her is structured from within by gender asymmetry *and* mostly subordinated to a fantasmatic bond with an idealized and class-bound former version of himself. But how does this disjunction between desire and identification relate, if at all, to the male homosocial economy governing the play? This is an economy wherein, to borrow from Eve Kosofsky Sedgwick, male heterosexual desire is 'a desire to consolidate partnership with authoritative males in and through the bodies of females'.[81]

Within the male homosocial economy of Alicante, Beatrice's body is equated with her virginity and thus reduced to a detachable bodily element that is not so much a part synecdochically standing for the whole as a fetishistic object to which her body, and even her 'soul', (I.i.193) is attached. More importantly for my argument here, this body part is figured in such a way as to reflect the more general fracture in women's status within a male homosocial economy; a 'schism', as Sedgwick points out, 'between being ostensibly the objects of men's heterosexual desire and being more functionally the conduits of their homosocial desire towards other men'.[82] As the following dialogue suggests, Beatrice's hymen *matters* inasmuch as it is marked in advance by an act of 'legitimate' penetration sealing relations of friendship between men. But in itself, as merely the object of heterosexual desire, Beatrice's hymen is nothing, and nothing but a trifle, a 'toy':

Ver. [Alonzo]'s hot preparing for this day of triumph ....
Bea. Nay, good sir, be not so violent, with speed
I cannot render satisfaction
Unto the dear companion of my soul,
Virginity, whom I thus long have liv'd with,
And part with it so rude and suddenly;
Can such friends divide, never to meet again,
Without a solemn farewell?
Ver. Tush, tush, there's a toy.
(I.i.189; 191–7)[83]

Tomazo, the betrothed's brother, does not share Vermandero's homosocial confidence that the male heterosexual detour through the body of Beatrice is but an insignificant diversion that unproblematically – and teleologically – leads to homosocial gratification.[84] He spots the 'small welcome in [Beatrice's] eye' (II.i.106) and 'the dullness of her parting' (II.i.124). He thus realizes that Alonzo's identification with Vermandero's over-identification with him,[85] by being *de facto* structurally congruent with the lack of proper supervision of Beatrice, is unable effectively to counter and counterbalance the 'effeminizing' threat posed by the heterosexual detour of male desire. Tomazo calls this detour the 'madness' of 'love', whereby 'a man quickly steals into vexation' (II.i.154–55). Indeed, to Tomazo, who takes for granted the male traffic in women, the exchange of a 'property' such as Beatrice from Vermandero to Alonzo in order to create or renew a homosocial alliance between the men does not act as a guarantee for its possession: 'Your faith's cozened in her, strongly cozened; / Unsettle your affection with all speed / Wisdom can bring it to, your peace is ruin'd else' (II.i.128–30). To strengthen his point, he conjures up a scenario that paranoically explores the 'vexation' his brother would have to undergo as a result of the 'movement' of the woman qua property, even if this movement was but minimal and 'imaginary', and strictly taking place within the legitimate confines of marriage:

Tom. Think what a torment 'tis to marry one
Whose heart is leap'd into another's bosom:
If ever pleasure she receive from thee,
It comes not in thy name, or of thy gift;
She lies but with another in thine arms,
He the half-father unto all thy children
In the conception; if he get 'em not,
She helps to get 'em for him.

(II.i.131–8)[86]

In the fantasmatic scenario Tomazo envisages, Beatrice's imaginary transgression inexorably puts Alonzo in an unbearable triangular situation in which he serves as the 'feminized' and 'objectified' conduit for relations of erotic exchange between Beatrice and her lover. Moreover, and perhaps more crucially, it disrupts the reproductive designs that mostly motivate the heterosexual detour of male homosocial desire; designs that, through the transmission of the name, property and rank of the father, ultimately coincide with the reproduction and perpetuation of publicly acknowledged bonds between men. Yet, in spite of the fact that Alonzo is transformed into a vehicle for the – repeated – intercourse between a man and a woman, the woman is not promoted to a position of power comparable to that occupied by the man within the dominant and normative man–man–woman triangulation of desire. She 'receive[s]', 'lies', and, at the most, 'helps to get [children]' for another man. In other words, even as Tomazo dramatizes the threat posed to homosocial gratification by a betrayal that exposes Alonzo to a confusion of identities with Beatrice, the latter is misogynistically turned into some kind of doubly reproductive but still subordinated medium, facilitating relations between a man and further 'narcissistic' versions of himself. Moreover, and relatedly, the usurping male is, from the point of view of the betrayed male, as much the focus of anxiety and desire as the deceitful woman, or more. In this sense, Tomazo's *mise-en-scène* can be said to provide the raw material for a typical early modern scenario of male sexual jealousy. According to Jonathan Dollimore, these scenarios are 'obsessively heterosexual', but do not fail compulsively to exhibit 'eroticized images of the rival male'.[87] Indeed, they show that, for the betrayed male, '*the separate/d objects of identification and desire – the rival man and the faithless woman –* ... *unite* ... as a distorted counterpart of ... the fantasized, fearful convergence of identification and desire'.[88] Hence, in Tomazo's imagining, the erotic contiguity between the rival man and Alonzo – an anxiety-ridden fantasmatic *and* syntactic contiguity, as particularly displayed by the following line: 'She lies but with *another* in *thine arms*' (II.i.135);[89] but also, at one and the same time, the equally anxious proximity between Alonzo and the faithless woman. Because of the intervening male, this proximity is non-reproductive or only half-reproductive. It causes the legitimate husband to become the inverted but symmetrical double of the excessively and improperly reproductive woman. It is thus liable to be connoted, within most early modern discourses on gender and sexuality, as lustful and 'effeminizing', as an identification with, or a regression into, the 'inferior' status of the woman.[90]

To Tomazo, therefore, Alonzo's detour through Beatrice's body threatens to bring into being, or bring *back* into being, the instability of the mutual opposition between identification and desire that is constitutive of masculine identity within the male homosocial economy of the play. But, of course, it is not Alonzo who will undergo this kind of 'torment' (II.i.131). It is, rather, the fantasized rival himself (that is, Alsemero) who will endure something similar to the 'vexation' Tomazo imagines. In this respect, it is worth pointing out that, outside the scenario of male sexual jealousy, Alsemero is not characterized by his sexual exploits.[91] At least initially, he is marked by his feats as a seaman-adventurer. These deeds are mystifyingly connoted as a kind of obligatory and only temporary deferral of an even more masculine enterprise: the revenge upon 'those rebellious Hollanders' (I.i.183) who have killed his father. Given this, as well as the related fact that he is represented as satisfyingly operating within an almost egalitarian homosocial milieu before the start of the play,[92] his 'friend' Jasperino cannot but exclude heterosexual love – that effeminizing 'hidden malady' (I.i.24) – as the reason for his unexpected decision to bring his 'inclinations to travel at a pause' (I.i.27):

Jas. Lover I'm sure y'are none, the stoic was
Found in you long ago; your mother nor
Best friends, who have set snares of beauty (ay,
And choice ones, too), could never trap you that way.
(I.i.36–9)

However, it is precisely the prospect of a love bond with Beatrice that lies behind Alsemero's resolve to protract his stay in Alicante. At this stage in the play, he does not see a male–female bond as effeminizing, or in any way endangering his masculine identity. Nor does he consider it incompatible with his indefatigable peregrinations: 'I'm all this while a-going, man' (I.i.45). Jasperino, whose position in relation to Alsemero is in some respects structurally similar to that which Tomazo occupies in relation to Alonzo, warns him that the 'movement' in which he is engaged may be 'backwards' (I.i.46). Nonetheless, he decides to join forces with his 'friend' and master and become 'a venturer in this voyage' (I.i.90): 'Yonder's another vessel [Diaphanta, the waiting-woman], I'll board her' (I.i.91). However, as far as

Alsemero is concerned, this is not just any kind of 'voyage'. Beatrice's virginal body, as well as the sacred enclosure of the temple with which her body is associated, are 'his right home back' (I.i.9) to a paradisiacal beginning: back, that is, to a lost plenitude and, simultaneously, back to the Father. Beatrice's body should be the proper alternative route enabling Alsemero to seal the gap opened up by his father's death.

As is often the case with the play as a whole, Alsemero uses the language of metaphysics to articulate sexual politics. He emphasizes an even balance between a male–female and a male–male bond, as well as an unproblematic passage from one to the other. However, Beatrice's impending marriage thwarts the arrangement of bodies and identities he contemplates. In particular, it implicitly and explicitly turns his desire, which is ultimately a desire to put an end to desire, into yet another forward motion that threatens endlessly to defer the return – the movement *back* – to the Father: 'But I must on, for back I cannot go' (I.i.224). This compulsive movement forward indicates a loss of masculine self-control. Consequently, it is virtually indistinguishable from that 'going backwards' Jasperino warns Alsemero against, which stands for a frightful identification with, and a regression into, that which he heterosexually desires. Moreover, because of the impossibility on Alsemero's part formally to negotiate reliable bonds with authoritative males inside the body politic of Alicante, this movement forward or backward also threateningly points to a confusion of identities between him and a class outsider such as De Flores. In effect, as he strives to re-cross those class boundaries he fantasizes as embodied by Beatrice, De Flores similarly 'cannot choose but love her' (I.i.235) and is 'enjoin'd / To follow … whilst she flies from [him]' (I.i.101–2).

The effeminizing and class-bound 'pro(re)gression' to which Alsemero is subjected does not come to an end with his marriage to Beatrice, which takes place soon after the disappearance of Alonzo. This is because of the repercussions on the marriage of Beatrice's decision to have one 'poison' (De Flores) 'expel another' (Alonzo) (II.ii.47–8), which is coterminous with her firm refusal of Alsemero's chivalrous offer to dispatch Alonzo. Even if it is made in order to protect Alsemero from the threat of contamination, this decision triggers off a number of defiling substitutions.[93] Crucial amongst these is the substitution of De Flores's 'service, resolution, manhood' (II.ii.93) for Alsemero's 'service' and 'valour' (II.ii.21; 27),[94] which leads up to the 'occupation' by the former of the latter's bed and the replacement by Diaphanta of Beatrice herself as the 'legitimate' bride on the wedding night.[95] These substitutions give a further impetus to the uncanny logic of 'pro(re)gression', as well as to the deleterious class, gender and erotic meanings with which it is associated.

'Re-visions' and cryptic incorporations

The play's finale shows the completion of the movement leading back to the Father: 'Sir, you have yet a son's duty living, please you, accept it' (V.iii.215–16). This coincides with the creation of a fraternal bond between Alsemero and

Tomazo: 'Your change is come too, from an ignorant wrath to knowing friendship' (V.iii.202–3).[96] But to what extent is Alsemero able fully to obliterate, or reverse, that 'pro(re)gression' he has not ceased to inhabit in spite of himself? The first crucial step towards this obliteration is the detection of the secret liaison between De Flores and Beatrice, which echoes De Flores's discovery of the equally clandestine relationship between Alsemero and Beatrice in II.i.:

Jas. Your confidence, I'm sure, is now of proof.
The prospect from the garden has show'd
Enough for deep suspicion.
Als. The black mask
That so continually was worn upon't
Condemns the face for ugly ere't be seen –
Her despite to him, and so seeming-bottomless.

(V.iii.1–6)

This is a discovery that undermines De Flores's control over the 'private' spaces and hidden recesses of Vermandero's castle, including those emblematized by Beatrice's body. De Flores's control over these spaces is repeatedly linked with his mastery of a scrutinizing gaze. It is by appropriating this gaze that Alsemero launches his own visual inspection of Beatrice. Following Jasperino's advice to 'search this ulcer soundly' (V.iii.8), he employs the gaze as a surgical 'probe' (V.iii.7) to explore and bring to light what is concealed or secret: 'I'll ... seek out truth within you, if there be any left' (V.iii.36). Coterminously, he does not fail to vow that '[he]'ll ransack [her heart] and tear out [his] suspicion' (V.iii.38–9).[97] This is a pledge that indicates, once again, how an active will to punish regularly surfaces in a context in which a 'salutary' double – a double erstwhile facilitating relations between oneself and (the other as) oneself – re-presents itself as an opaque,[98] 'deform'd' (V.iii.77) and 'castrating' double: 'Did my fate wait for this unhappy stroke at my first sight of woman?' (V.iii.12–13).[99]

Alsemero implements an aggressive economy of the *speculum* that is inextricably bound up with his attempt to construct – or, rather, *extract* from Beatrice – a consistent and unified narrative aimed at making sense of the traumatic events that have taken place in Alicante. This is a narrative that represses, but does not fully suppress, alternative accounts of the same events such as the one Beatrice offers. She insists on Alsemero's implication in Alonzo's murder ('Your love has made me / A cruel murd'ress' [V.iii.64–5]; 'Forget not, sir, / It for your sake was done' [V.iii.77–8]), as well as on the system of patriarchal constraints that has left her no 'better means than that worst, to assure [Alsemero] to [her]' (V.iii.71–2). Yet, the coherence of Alsemero's narrative is not only based upon the violent proscription of the 'illegitimate' violence of the subordinated – that 'dangerous bridge of blood' (V.iii.81) – and her stories.[100] It is also, and perhaps more crucially, predicated upon two overlapping processes of 'constraining production' of Beatrice. Firstly, she is fashioned as an entity that is subjected to a negatively inflected 'change' from 'beauty' to 'ugly whoredom' (V.iii.197–8); or, alternatively, she is fabricated as a dichotomous identity one of whose sides already harbours its own opposite.[101] Secondly, she is construed as a 'confessant subject' who anxiously views herself as such a 'changed' or inherently changeable identity, incorporating within herself the gaze of that judgemental Other Alsemero comes to embody. In the first scene of the fourth act, she starts attributing this super-egoic gaze to Alsemero. This is soon after being 'undone … endlessly' by De Flores (IV.i.1):

Bea. One that's ennobled both in blood and mind,
So clear in understanding (that's my plague now),
Before whose judgement will my fault appear
Like malefactors' crimes before tribunals –
There is no hiding on't, the more I dive
Into my own distress.

(IV.i.5–10)

By focusing on Beatrice's 'change', and implicitly contrasting it to his masculine stability (that is, his 'true devotion' [V.iii.75]), Alsemero undoubtedly deflects attention from his entanglement in Beatrice's 'giddy turning' (I.i.156) from Alonzo to him, as well as from the fact that this 'turning' remains the precondition for his upward movement in social terms – his transformation from an 'outsider' to Vermandero's next of kin.[102] Yet, by the same token, he draws attention to the uncanny homogeneity between the strategies he adopts and those employed by De Flores towards the end of the 'reward scene'. As argued earlier, it is De Flores – or, at least, one of the De Floreses involved in this scene – who construes any and every form of change on Beatrice's part as 'a kind of whoredom in [her] heart' (III.iv.144), even as he profits from this 'change'. Moreover, it is De Flores who similarly forces her to see herself through the eyes of the Other as a guilty identity inhabiting the difference between herself and her class and gender ideal.

Crucial to Alsemero's discovery of the truth is also a process of re-vision of the trauma, which compulsively drives his narrative towards a 'dramatic' turn.[103] This re-vision reaches its climax when he recasts himself as a dramatist, and incites De Flores to join Beatrice in the closet.[104] He solicits the re-enactment of that 'scene of lust' which takes place offstage at the end of the third act – a potentially iterable 'scene' that will later be shown, for theatrical and ideological reasons, only through its effects, as an evacuation of contaminated fluid:

Als. Nay, you shall to her.
Peace, crying crocodile, your sounds are heard!
Take your prey to you, get you in to her, sir. *Exit* DE FLORES.
I'll be your pander now; rehearse again
Your scene of lust, that you may be perfect
When you shall come to act it to the black audience
Where howls and gnashings shall be music to you.
Clip your adult'ress freely, 'tis the pilot

Will guide you to the Mare Mortuum,
Where you shall sink to fathoms bottomless.

(V.iii.111–20)

In his role as a dramatist, Alsemero scrupulously delivers stage directions that signify the hiatus dividing him from the traumatic 'scene of lust', and thus bear witness to his desire for visual mastery over it: 'Enter my closet' (V.iii.86); 'Take your prey to you, get you in to her' (V.iii.113); 'Rehearse again' (V.iii.114); 'Come forth, you twins of mischief' (V.iii.142). In fact, he implicitly redefines the marginality *vis-à-vis* the 'scene of lust' he eagerly produces as *self-inflicted* marginality. By doing so, he tries to turn 'his impotence and helplessness' into a 'form of potency: the power of superior discernment'.[105] This is a self-inflicted marginality that actively marginalizes, in that it is strictly co-simultaneous with his endeavour to re-create the boundaries of his body and identity through the abjection and expulsion of those 'deformed' creatures he confines to the private space of his closet.[106] Yet one needs only to take a second look at the way in which Alsemero sets up and visualizes the 'scene of lust' to realize that he not only invites Beatrice and De Flores to 'rehearse again' that 'scene of lust' he does not fail to represent *to* himself. He also continuously, if fantasmatically, crosses the threshold of the closet to re-present *himself* in the scene by means of an identificatory bond with a figure such as De Flores who acts as his double. In other words, the 'scene of lust' is also a 'phantasy scene' whose subject is a 'subject' that 'never avoids yielding to an identification and always confuses itself in some way with another (an alter ego – but one that is neither other nor self)'.[107] This identification manifests itself, more or less explicitly, in Alsemero's allocation of roles, which tends to play down De Flores's contribution to transgression as compared to Beatrice's. Indeed, De Flores is cast as Beatrice's 'prey', whilst she is fantasized as taking on the active role of a 'pilot' who 'will guide [him] to the Mare Mortuum'. This is not an unbiased reflection of the positions they respectively occupy when they first 'rehearse' the 'scene of lust' at the end of III.iv.[108] It is a partial reinterpretation that owes much to the fact that Alsemero, just as he enjoins De Flores to 'enjoy' in his place, invites him to *mime* the position he has come to identify as peculiar to *his own* relation with Beatrice. Given this 'imaginary' reversibility of positions, it makes perfect sense for Alsemero to refer to Beatrice as *De Flores*'s 'adult'ress'.

Alsemero's placing of himself in a position of *intimate* exteriority with respect to the re-enactment of the traumatic 'scene of lust' indicates some kind of blurring of clear-cut distinctions between outside and inside, self and other. It is thus hardly reconcilable with his simultaneous effort to re-view and re-present this scene to himself from the supposedly safe distance his role as a dramatist bestows on him.[109] More specifically, this is a position that complicates one of the most essential aspects of the movement towards visual mastery he devises: the re-creation of himself through the re-establishing of definite demarcations along class and gender lines. Alsemero's position of intimate exteriority suggests that the re-fashioning of his self does not so much correspond to an exclusion and abjection of both 'twins of mischief' (V.iii.142) as to an *including* exclusion, a 'cryptic incorporation' of De Flores that further abjects Beatrice.

As with the process of 'cryptic incorporation' described by Derrida, Alsemero's is 'an inclusion intended as a compromise' that turns out to be plagued by 'a certain ceaselessly threatening instability'.[110] By making De Flores into a man who *equally* falls 'prey' to Beatrice's 'change', and thus presenting himself as the rule rather than the exception, Alsemero somewhat defends himself against the anxiety about the possession of Beatrice; and, more generally, against the anxiety about the effeminizing effect of heterosexual desire.[111] However, he does not fail to reproduce these anxieties elsewhere and in a different form. His furtive bond with De Flores – his 'cryptic incorporation' of one of the 'twins of mischief' (V.iii.142) – registers, in a necessarily oblique way, 'the primacy and tenacity of the homosocial bond even among antagonists'.[112] Yet, at the same time, it does nothing but secretly compromise the politics of class exclusiveness the play's finale predominantly displays. This is even more so if one considers that the fantasmatic interchangeability between Alsemero and De Flores, occurring in the representation of the 'scene of lust' as imagined by the former, provides an uncanny mirror image of the substitution of De Flores for Alsemero as the active agent of 'class cleansing'. This is a substitution that guarantees Alsemero's impermeability from the shedding of blood in the play's finale. Yet, by the same token, it displaces him from the central position he claims for himself within the process of redefinition of class and gender boundaries he initiates. It is worth adding that what is from the dominant perspective of the play's finale a decontamination of abject matter is to De Flores the repetition of an absolute assimilation of Beatrice's blood, which he ecstatically recalls as follows:

De F. Her honour's prize
Was my reward; I thank life for nothing
But that pleasure: it was so sweet to me
That I have drunk up all, left nothing behind
For any man to pledge me.

(V.iii.167–71)

Interestingly, De Flores defines this heterosexual performance in relation not only to Beatrice but also to those male counterparts, including Alsemero, to whom he has 'left nothing behind ... to pledge [him]'. This shows, once again, how significant the male antagonist is within the articulation of male heterosexuality, even as, and at the very moment when, this antagonist is categorically excluded by the 'act'.[113]

The substitution of De Flores for Alsemero and Alsemero's cryptic bond of incorporation with De Flores superimpose upon each other to suggest that the play's finale is unable to present a proper and satisfactory closure or offer unproblematic instances of containment and ejection. This is a finale that operates by uneasily and unceasingly exchanging one form of anxiety for another in an effort to make class, gender and erotic boundaries cohere. The play thus ends *in* and *as* a compromise, but one, to have a final recourse to Derrida, that 'can only maintain in a state of repetition the mortal conflict it is impotent to resolve'.[114]

3 'A meer chaos'

Moles, abject bodies and the economy of reproductive discourses

Je suis mon fils, mon père, ma mère,
et moi;
niveleur du périple imbécile où s'enferre l'engendrement,
le périple papa-maman
et l'enfant,
suie du cul de la grand-maman,
beaucoup plus que du père-mère.

(Antonin Artaud)

The clouds conceive not rain, or do not pour
In the due birth time, down the balmy shower.
Th' air doth not motherly sit on the earth,
To hatch her season, and give all things birth.
Spring-times were common cradles, but are tombs;
And false conceptions fill the general wombs.

(John Donne)

Matter and detours

At the end of *The Changeling*, Beatrice-Joanna re-presents herself as the abject part of blood standing between Vermandero and his 'better health' (V.iii.151), between a father and further honourable male versions of himself. Significantly, the evacuation of this contaminated and contaminating female 'matter' paves the way for the final mirroring of the father in the newly acquired 'son' (V.iii.216). It ensures – although, as shown earlier, not unproblematically – that the 'name' (V.iii.180) of the father, unlike Beatrice's, be not 'blotted out' (V.iii.182) but passed on to a male heir. Also, it guarantees that the 'illegitimate' female child – one of the changelings of the play – be replaced by a 'legitimate' male child.[1] In *Cymbeline*, after Iachimo produces a 'corporal sign' (II.iv.119) as indubitable evidence of Imogen's supposed betrayal, Posthumus indulges in the fantasy of dismemberment typical of early modern scenarios of male sexual jealousy: 'O that I had her here to tear her limb-meal' (II.iv.147).[2] He then asks himself: 'Is there no way for men to be, but women / Must be half-workers? We are all bastards'(II.v.1–2).[3] To Posthumus, woman's contribution to the genesis of men cannot but threaten to adulterate what might have been a perfect and 'legitimate' doubling of the father in the son. Hence, his strenuous attempt to locate that 'woman's part in [him]' (II.v.20) he conceives as the inevitable, if deleterious, result of this contribution.[4] In *Hamlet*, as Patricia Parker observes, the melancholic prince notably juxtaposes 'woman' ('O most pernicious woman' [I.v.105]) to 'baser matter' (I.v.104). This is the 'matter' of previous inscriptions he endeavours to 'wipe away' (I.i.98), so that his father's 'commandment all alone shall live within the book and volume of [his] brain' (I.v.102–3).[5] For Parker, this female 'matter', which can be etymologically related to *mater* or *matrix*, 'undermines and adulterates the perfect copying or reproduction of parthenogenesis ..., the generative reproduction of a paternal original in a son who might be a faithful copy or representative, perfect instrument of a father's will.'[6]

To a large extent, the threat posed to the reproduction of the male self-same by the aberrant detour through the 'matter' of a body marked female agitates not only early modern plays but also coeval anatomical and gynaecological discourses on the reproductive body. In the course of this chapter, I focus on the way in which these discourses portray bodies that fail to come into being, or are brought to light but fail to qualify as adequately 'human': so-called false conceptions and/or moles, monstrous products of the womb attributed to female self-insemination or to a conception in which a defective male seed is overwhelmed by the over-abundance of female seed and/or menstrual blood. These 'unprofitable' and formless 'aequivocations of the womb',[7] emblematically characterized by an early modern anatomist such as Helkiah Crooke as 'illegitimate', signify the disruption of a male-centred and teleologically oriented economy of reproduction.[8] They induce specific anxieties about the 'work' respectively carried out by male and female reproductive fluids in the generation of offspring. At a later stage in the chapter, I argue that these abject bodies are metonymically contiguous with other 'dis-figured' bodily figures that interfere with the hierarchical construction of bodies and reproductive fluids; a construction whereby, according to Thomas Laqueur, bodies *and* reproductive fluids are 'arrayed according to their degree of metaphysical perfection, their vital heat, along an axis whose telos [is] male'.[9]

An 'unformed & rude masse'

One of the most extensive early modern discussions of false conceptions and/or moles is to be found in *Child-Birth, or The Happy Deliverie of Women*, a midwifery treatise by the French surgeon Jacques Guillemeau, Ambroise Paré's pupil and son-in-law, translated into English in 1612.[10] After stating that 'a false conception ... is as it were the beginning of Mola', Guillemeau continues as follows:

> False conception is a lump of flesh gathered together commonly like to the gizard of a fowle, which is bigger or lesser according to the continuance of it,

> which nature commonly expelleth in the second, third, or fourth month. But the Mola is farre bigger, and continues a yeare or two, yea ten or twelve, and sometime as long as the woman lives. Of this Mola there be two kinds, the one may be called a true, the other a false one. The true Mola is fleshy, being nothing else but an unprofitable masse, without shape or forme, hard and firme, bred within the Matrice, and cleaving to the sides thereof. The false Mola is of three sorts, the one windy, being a collection of grosse winds: the second watrish, or a heaping together of waters: the third humorall, or a meeting of many humours.[11]

Some anatomical and gynaecological treatises add a 'membranous' and even a 'pendent' mole – what probably corresponds to a *prolapsus uteri* – to Guillemeau's inventory of false moles.[12] Others disregard the distinction between true and false moles. For instance, Ambroise Paré chooses to speak of 'a tumor called Mola', and defines it as a 'false conception of deformed flesh, rude and imperfect, not distinguished into members'.[13] Similarly, Helkiah Crooke's *Microcosmographia* (1615) only refers to what Guillemeau's *Child-Birth* would call a 'true mola', describing it as 'an idle flesh without forme and hard, engendred onely in the wombe of a woman'.[14] For my purposes here, the impulse towards a detailed categorization, or lack thereof, is less remarkable than the range of interpretations of the genesis of the mole, and, in particular, of the 'true mole' in those treatises where it is differentiated from the 'false mole'. It is through these interpretations that one can begin to assess the extent to which discussions of the disruption of the 'legitimate' economy of reproduction serve as a way of upholding *a contrario* the hierarchical ordering of reproductive fluids, as well as of the bodies emitting these fluids.

After surveying ancient and coeval medical literature on the causes of the *mola*, which he also calls, like Jacques Guillemeau, the 'Mooncalfe', Helkiah Crooke concludes: 'This is the very truth: when a great aboundance of blood cloyet[h] a little ill disposed seede there cannot bee a lawfull conception, yet the belly swelleth as if the woman were with child.'[15] Thus, according to Crooke, this 'ill disposed' seed 'undertak[es] the Conformation' of a new being.[16] Yet, because of the great quantity of blood, it 'cannot atteine his own end'.[17] Instead of a creature, it 'generateth a lumpe of flesh', an 'unformed & rude masse having indeed the principles of life, but those so weake that they are presently suffocated and extinguished'.[18] For a 'lawfull' conception to take place, Crooke explains, the blood should not 'bear greater sway then the seed'.[19] The seed retained in the womb should be 'pure and fruitfull', not 'sickly or diseased, neither yet mingled with blood'.[20] In fact, blood (that is, menstrual blood) should play a part in the process of reproduction only at a later stage, providing nourishment for the embryo after its consolidation in the womb. It should intervene, that is, only after 'the action of the spermaticall parts' has been properly carried out.[21]

Crooke's account is far from being untypical. This can be shown by juxtaposing his interpretation to Guillemeau's and Paré's. In *Child-Birth*, Guillemeau invokes the authority of Galen and argues as follows:

> [The fleshy Mole] is bred when the mans seed is weake, barren, imperfect, or in little quantitie; and for the most part choked through the abundance of the menstruous bloud, which is grosse and thicke, unfit for the framing of a child, so that in stead thereof is bred a lumpe of flesh.[22]

Paraphrasing Fernelius (Jean Fernel), Paré maintains that 'the immoderate fluxes of the courses' lead to 'the generation of the mola'.[23] This outpouring of menstrual blood, 'overwhelming the mans seed, being now unfruitfull and weak, doth constraine it to desist from its enterprise of conformation already begun'.[24]

According to other anatomical and gynaecological works, menstrual blood is not the only female reproductive fluid contributing to the 'vanquishing' and 'overcoming' of the male seed and its 'enterprise'.[25] *The Expert Midwife*, a 1637 translation of *De Conceptu et generatione hominis*, a gynaecological treatise by the Swiss surgeon Jakob Rueff, authoritatively states that 'they which doe more narrowly pry and search into the Natures of things, doe attribute [the mole] to the more copious and abundant seed of the woman'. Predictably, this immoderate ejaculation of seed occurs 'especially in those women which are somewhat more lascivious than others are'. Rueff describes these women as follows:

> [Lascivious women], conceiving little seed from their husbands, dry by nature, by the desire of the Matrix, doe stirre up copious seed of their owne, which augmented with the flowers, by heat of the Matrix, is congealed together, and by the defect and want of mans seed, the proper worke-man and contriver of it, doth grow together into such a lump.[26]

Rueff underlines that the profusion of female semen is a crucial factor in the engendering of the mole – more crucial, in fact, than the copiousness of 'the flowers' (menstrual blood). He thus differentiates himself from Crooke, Guillemeau, or Paré. Like them, however, he accepts that 'nothing' – not even 'such a lump' of flesh – can be 'ingendred without the seed of man'.[27] In other words, he acknowledges, and even emphasizes, the role the male seed plays, at the very moment when he illustrates its failure to fulfil its 'proper' role as an active and 'in-forming' agent.

To conclude this brief examination of representative early modern medical interpretations of the genesis of the *mola*, it is worth referring to two Italian physicians: Scipione Mercurio (also known as Mercurialis) and Giovanni Marinelli (or Marinello). In *La Commare o riccoglitrice* (1601), Mercurio spurns Aristotle's opinions on the *mola uteri* to embrace the superior wisdom of the medieval Arabic physician Avicenna (ibn-Sina).[28] To Mercurio, the production of the *mola* is *not* to be related to the lack of sufficient heat in the womb, but, rather, to the 'overcooking' of menstrual blood in a womb that is already too hot because of the excessive inflow of this blood; an 'overcooking' that is in turn attributed to copulation.[29] The emission of seed, either by a man or a woman or both, is uninfluential.[30] Giovanni Marinelli would agree with Mercurio that the intemperate heat of the womb is of paramount importance to false conceptions. Yet, he comes to rather different conclusions as regards the interplay of elements involved in such a process. In *Le medicine partenenti alle infermità delle donne* (1563), he claims that 'the cause … [of the *mola*] is heat'. But he continues as follows: 'Whenever the matrix is hot and dry, it draws its own sperm to itself and retains it. This sperm being only the woman's, it cannot generate a living creature'.[31] Moreover, coition is not as indispensable for the production of the *mola* as in Mercurio. Whilst asleep, women (especially virgins, widows and those women whose 'natural purgations' have stopped for at least two or three months) may inseminate themselves. Moved by the 'imagination' of sexual intercourse with a man, they may involuntarily cast forth their seed and mix it with menstrual blood, thus conceiving what will eventually become a misshapen piece of flesh as hard as a rock.[32] It is worth adding that Marinelli does not categorically dismiss all the other theories on the genesis of the *mola* he considers. (He entertains alternative notions such as: the *mola* may be produced when male and female seed do not properly commingle; when the male seed flows out of the womb too soon; when the mixture of male and female seed is potentially fertile but the woman's menstrual blood is unfit to receive an adequate 'impression'; when older people copulate with younger people, and so forth.) However, unlike the anatomists and gynaecologists mentioned so far, he is undoubtedly prepared to give more credence to the opinion that the *mola* owes its origin to the combination of female semen and menstrual blood, and that the intervention of the male seed is unnecessary.

Moles, reproductive anxieties and the 'body of knowledge'

In *Making Sex. Body and Gender from the Greeks to Freud*, Thomas Laqueur argues:

> It is empirically true, and known to be so by almost all cultures, that the male is necessary for conception. It does not of course follow that the male contribution is thereby the more powerful one, and an immense amount of effort and anxiety had to go into 'proving' that this was the case.[33]

As Laqueur points out, medical discussions of the *mola* need to be seen within the context of this more general rhetorical attempt to demonstrate the powerfulness of man's seed compared to woman's. They are meant to prove that woman's reproductive fluids cannot by themselves 'ensoul matter'.[34] They are supposed to show *a contrario* that 'the seede of the male being cast and received into the wombe, is … the principall and efficient cause, but the seede of the female is … the subjacent matter, or the matter whereon it worketh'.[35] Laqueur is also right in underlining that there is a great amount of anxiety involved in this 'will to truth'. Indeed, he suggests in passing that the confident assertion of the 'truth' of the hierarchy of bodies and reproductive fluids – what he identifies as 'an exercise in preserving the Father'[36] – is nothing but a defence mechanism; it anxiously compensates for the 'fact' that 'the work of generation available to the senses is wholly the work of the female'.[37]

However, Laqueur seems to shy away from the implications of this insight. If the hierarchization of bodies and reproductive fluids inhering in the one-sex model is an anxious response to 'the *pressing* … question of whether there needs to be a male [contribution to conception]';[38] if it is haunted, that is, by this 'intolerable truth', then one needs to reconsider its coherence, stability or predominance. In other words, if one chooses *not* to exorcize the ghost Laqueur himself raises, one must agree with Patricia Parker on the necessity 'to interrogate the sheer repetition of the [one-sex model] … as symptomatic and ideological rather than as a descriptive discourse, to focus … on the rhetoric of insistence'.[39] In this sense, discussions of the *mola* turn out to be not so much an illustration by antithesis of the 'truth' of the hierarchy of bodies and reproductive fluids as a discursive area onto which anxieties about this hierarchy are displaced only to be re-marked.

Anxiety also informs the reassertion of the 'proper' ranking of reproductive fluids that often precedes or follows the narration of the process of 'illegitimate' conception. In fact, it helps to explain why there is this reassertion in the first instance; why, that is, early modern anatomical and gynaecological treatises find it necessary to supplement a narration that should already be in itself a clear demonstration of the 'truth' of 'the hierarchical ordering of the one sex'.[40] To refer to Rueff's *The Expert Midwife* again, the description of a conception in which a defective male seed is defeated by female elements, as well as the abjection of its outcome, do not seem to suffice. A few basic truths need to be restated:

> For nothing can be ingendred without the seed of man; as neither any can be ingendred of the seed of women onely: for the seede of woman doth only inclose the seede of man conceived in the wombe …. For as of the white and yolke of it selfe, nothing can be ingendred, unlesse the seede of the Cocke be infused into it, although the copiousnesse of them is much greater in comparison of the seed: so also of woman's seed alone, nothing can be ingendred, unlesse mans seed be added to it.[41]

One can read this passage in terms of what it explicitly states, as an unproblematic reiteration of the disparity between male and female reproductive fluids Rueff has already advanced in other contexts. Or, alternatively, one can read it 'against the grain', by focusing on how the repeated disavowals of woman's ability to be the formal and/or efficient cause of generation anxiously defer, and defend against, the question of whether man's seed can engender anything alone; or, in fact, whether it contributes anything at all to conception.[42] Yet, even if one interprets this passage as an uncomplicated reiteration, one cannot fail to observe that, as he moves on to the example of 'the white and yolke' to re-emphasize his point, Rueff redefines the male seed as that which is 'infused' into a female 'matter' that is still as threateningly marked by 'copiousnesse' as in the process of false conception. He describes it, moreover, as that which is 'added' to a seed by which it has just been said to be 'inclose[d]'. In this latter case, the reiteration of the 'truth' brings about a rearrangement of the 'proper' timing of male and female contributions, so that the male seed begins to play a belated and supplementary role that is uncannily similar to the one Rueff ascribes to the female seed in his first account of reproduction at the beginning of his treatise. In the section 'Of the mixture of the seede', he maintains that it is only *after* the womb has 'conceived' the seed of man that woman 'admix[es] and mingle[s] her seed also to it'.[43]

The foregoing observations are not meant to dispute what is most thought-provoking about Laqueur's general line of analysis, namely that the body, its fluids or the supposedly natural facts of sex are cultural constructs, discursively produced in the service of social and political interests. It is easy to see, for instance, that debates about who contributes what, and to what extent, to the genesis of this 'unprofitable masse' have little to do with neutral truth-claims about the body or its fluids.[44] The labelling of women who 'ejaculate' in excess as 'lascivious' in Rueff, or the definition itself of the mole as 'illegitimate' conception in Crooke, suggest as much.

The concluding part of Paré's chapter on the generation of the *mola* can also be read along these lines. It shows once again that there is no 'demonstration' that is unmarked by cultural assumptions about gender and sexuality: 'If all men were not perswaded that the conflux of mans seed must of necessity concurre to the generation of the mola, it would bee no small cloake or cover to women to avoide the shame and reproach of their light behaviour.'[45]

In this passage, Paré delineates the deleterious effects men's belief in female self-insemination might have on the patriarchal system. More specifically, he suggests that this belief might make men compliant with women's attempt to shun the 'proper' reprisal for their sexually transgressive behaviour; and, more obliquely, that this compliance would be nothing but a repetition at a different level of that threatening 'subjection' to female 'matter' he has just described.[46] Conversely, men's collective rejection of female self-insemination might somehow make up for the inability on the part of some men to enact the masculinity that is supposed to be an intrinsic feature of their bodies and bodily fluids. Thus, Paré's concluding remarks not only shed light on the (gendered) principles governing his discussion of the *mola*. They are also an attempt to negotiate some of the anxieties about the precarious performance of masculinity emerging from this discussion, not least because of the fact that they put in the foreground a 'masculine' body of knowledge and truth about the *mola* as the site of a potential, if vicarious, re-creation of the powerfulness and stability of the male body. To pursue the implications of Paré's concluding remarks a little further, one can add that this fantasmatic re-creation goes hand in hand with an aggressive 'removal' of the 'cloake or cover' mistakenly bestowed on women. It is tantamount to a 'dis-covery' or a 're-dis-covery', a bringing *back* to light that is also, at one and the same time, an indictment of what women would rather keep concealed or secret.[47]

Masculinity and bodily extensions: the emblematic case of Ambroise Paré

The reordering of bodies and identities along the lines of dichotomized gender does not end here. It is given a new impetus by Paré's repeated appeals to the surgeon's 'mechanical art', one of which takes place at the end of the chapter on the signs that distinguish the *mola* from a true conception: 'To conclude, whatsoever resembles being with child, if it not be excluded at the due and lawfull time of child birth by its own accord or by strength of nature, then must be expelled by art.'[48] This is an 'art' that – literally – brings forth to view what is hidden. As such, it is no less than the 'material correlative', as well as the point of reactivation, of the desire to lay open to scrutiny, know and control the female body. In the course of this chapter, Paré gives an example of his 'art' at work, in the form of an anatomical dissection of the body of the deceased wife of one Guillaume Roger, a pewterer. Cutting open her womb, he relates, in the presence of other fellow surgeons, he 'found a lumpe of flesh as bigge as both [his] fists … cleaving to the sides of the wombe but in certain places, of a very thicke, unequall and cloddish substance, with many bodies as are found in wennes and gristles'.[49] This 'lumpe of flesh' turns out not to be what he expected – it was originally a *mola*, Paré assures us, but in time it 'degenerated into a schirrous body'.[50] After all, the woman is alleged to have carried it for seventeen years. Yet, this metamorphosis is less significant than the fact that the surgeon invests his anatomical performance – the opening and display of the womb – with the power to tell and disclose the ultimate truth about the *mola*, which is a *de facto* marginalization of other, more traditional sources of authority about this 'lumpe of flesh'. Arguably, this performance also functions as a form of displaced punishment. It brings to a climax the 'un-covery' of woman's 'light behaviour'.[51]

In the following section of his *Workes*, specifically dedicated to the cure of the *mola*, Paré reiterates the indispensability of a surgical supplement counteracting Nature's insufficient strength. He does so as he considers the case of a *mola* that is carried loose in the womb – an occurrence, incidentally, that contradicts what he has previously argued, namely that a *mola* that does not 'cleave fast' to the sides of the womb inexorably 'falleth away within three or four months'.[52] To Paré, this kind of *mola* can only be extracted with the help of 'Gryphons Talons', a surgical instrument so called because of its three acuminate endings:

> [The *mola*] cannot be taken hold on otherwise, by reason of the roundness thereof, for it hath no place whereon it may be taken hold of: therefore, when one taketh hold on it with his hand, it cannot be holden fast by reason of the slipperinesse thereof, but will run and slip backe into the hollownesse of the wombe, like unto a bowle or a great ball.[53]

This strenuous exercise of power/knowledge bears witness to the fact that early modern anatomical and gynaecological works attempt to provide alternative solutions to anxieties about the truth of the proper organization of bodies and bodily fluids; anxieties, as I have argued, that are displaced on to discussions of the *mola* only to be re-marked. They do so through strategies of evasion, by changing the terms of the issue. Paré's treatise is emblematic in this respect, in that it offers not only a 'masculine' body of knowledge, but also fetishized surgical instruments as identificatory props for those vacillating male bodies whose fluids are said to be 'vanquished or wholly overcome'.[54] These are 'tools', therefore, that 'supply the defects of nature' – one of the aims of surgery, according to Paré – in more senses than one.[55]

In the course of the early modern period, one witnesses a strengthening of the hold over the female body that is made possible by, and is part of, an emerging 'culture of dissection' centred upon the ocular;[56] a culture that aggressively proceeds by viewing, anatomizing and dichotomizing along gender lines, and thus *de facto* displaces the logic of the 'one-sex'.[57] This strengthening is also linked to male practitioners' encroachment upon a domain of knowledge such as midwifery that was traditionally associated with women. The history of this encroachment has often been told.[58] Here I only want to underline, with Elizabeth D. Harvey, that surgical instruments – instruments such as a Sadler's '*Pes griphius*',[59] Paré's 'Gryphons Talons', and various kinds of crochets employed in the 'delivery' of the *mola* – 'metonymically express the control man-midwives and surgeons came to wield'.[60] These were instruments midwives were not allowed to utilize – at least not officially.[61] However, as the emblematic case of Paré illustrates, the adoption of prosthetic extensions to penetrate and display the hidden recesses of the female body is not wholly unproblematic. In Paré's treatise, this adoption disavows a lack on the masculine side – specifically, a lack of heat – but also brings into relief the performative character of masculinity. To borrow from a theoretically related argument by Judith Butler, it exposes masculinity's status as a 'heterosexualized gender' that 'is always in the process of imitating and approximating its own phantasmatic idealization of itself'.[62] To take hold of a slippery *mola* – with one's hands or even with technological extensions of the body such as the 'Gryphons Talons' – in order to fashion or re-fashion one's masculinity is still *not* to take hold of the phallus.[63] In other words, the surgical extraction covers up but does not annul the gap between desire and its realization. As Lacan succinctly puts it, in a way that can suggestively be juxtaposed to the passage in question, 'the phallus … always slips through [one's] fingers'.[64] To sum up, the excerpt from Paré articulates wide-ranging tensions about masculinity. On the one hand, the French surgeon presents himself as fully in control of his performance, getting a firm grip on the monstrous product of the inversion of the 'natural' properties of bodies and reproductive fluids. On the other, he obsessively lingers on the deferral of the 'hold' he ostensibly affirms. Put differently, Paré's is a mastery that is found only to be lost; a mastery that is lost only to be found: a *desire for*, or even a *différance* of, mastery. This compulsive seesawing is part of the dubious, morbid pleasure of the surgical exercise. It is also a sign, however, of the latter's precariousness and instability. In fact, it re-inscribes anxiety at its very centre.[65]

Pleasure, abjection and the construction of the womb

In early modern discourses on the reproductive body it is not only the mole that is defined as 'slippery'. 'Slipperiness' or one of its cognate lexemes is also frequently used to connote that by which the *mola* is contained – the womb. Or, to be more precise, the womb's 'in-capacity', its inability, from a male point of view, 'to containe ..., cherish, preserve and nourish' the mixture of the seeds,[66] and thus unproblematically guarantee the reproduction of the father in the son – the engendering of a baby girl remaining, to a large extent, an anomaly, a kind of 'illegitimate' and 'false' conception.[67] A few pages after his narration of the removal of the slippery mole, Paré emphasizes that women cannot conceive if 'the womb be overslippery, or more loose, or slack, or overwide'.[68] In *A Directory for Midwives* (1651) Nicholas Culpeper invites women 'to preserve the womb in due decorum', admonishing them to 'use not the Act of Copulation too often'.[69] This is an 'act', he points out, that 'makes the womb slippery' and 'more willing to open than shut'.[70] Nicholas Fontanus's *The Womans Doctour* (1652) extols 'the temperate Matrix ..., namely that which obtaines a mediocrity, approaching to no excesse',[71] but deprecates 'those [women] that are luxuriant, and the whorish crew'. The former are infertile 'because by frequent coition their bodies become empty of seed'. As to 'the latter sort',

> [they] conceive not partly by reason that many, and various seeds are mingled together, and partly also by reason of their frequent cohabitation with men, whereby the neck of the Matrix is made so slippery, that it cannot retaine the mans seed.[72]

Helkiah Crooke observes that 'in women that are full of lust', the *collum uteri* (i.e. the part of the female reproductive system that should 'receive the yard fitly like a sheath') stretches excessively, so as to become 'smooth and slippery'. [73]

Thus, the ultimate result of the immoderate 'use of venery'[74] is some kind of deformation of the womb that makes it unable to be the proper 'receptacle of human seed'[75] – one might be tempted to say, quite simply, unable to *be*.[76] In other words, in the logic of early modern discourses on reproduction, the womb becomes uncannily similar to that deformed and 'inarticulate peece of flesh'[77] which is often seen as the effect of untimely coition (i.e. coition during menstruation). Interestingly, in their narration of the reproductive impasse represented by the *mola*, the anonymous authors of *The Compleat Midwife's Practice Enlarged* juxtapose untimely and immoderate sexual intercourse. By doing so, they implicitly reinforce the metonymic association between the 'dis-figured' content of the womb – the *mola*, they stress, is 'without any figure or order'[78] – and the womb itself as an amorphous container, a 'vessel' that does not contain. In a way that should be familiar by now, they argue that '[t]he cause of the fleshy mole doth not alwayes proceed from the mother, for the man doth often contribute to the encrease of it, when the seed of the man is weak, imperfect, and barren, or though it be good ... is choked by the menstrual blood.'[79] But they also point out that the *mola* can be engendered by 'superfetation'.[80] This happens 'when the woman lies with a great desire and lust with her husband, *after* she hath conceived'.[81] Presumably, the woman's intemperate desire causes the womb to alter.[82] To use Culpeper's lexicon again, it 'makes the womb slippery' and 'more willing to open than shut'.[83] This eventually leads to the production of a 'false conception' and its parasitical fastening to a 'true conception' that often ends with the destruction of the latter. The mole can also be 'a cruell beast'.[84]

This is not to suggest that early modern discourses on the reproductive body deplore sexual pleasure as such, especially the woman's.[85] Nicholas Fontanus, for instance, explains that 'the use of Venery is exceeding wholsome, if the woman will confine herself to the lawes of moderation'. When undertaken within the legitimate bounds of marriage for the purpose of procreation, these 'pleasant conflicts' have therapeutic qualities.[86] To Fontanus, 'wives are more healthfull than Widowes, or Virgins, because they are refreshed with the mans seed, and ejaculate their own'.[87] The retention of the seed and *menstruum* by marriageable maids and 'lusty widows that are prone and apt to venery' is likely to cause a variety of dreadful diseases,[88] such as the 'Suffocation of the Mother'; a disease so called, John Sadler explains in *The Sick Womans Private Looking-Glasse* (1636), 'not because the wombe is strangled, but for that it causeth the woman to bee choked'.[89] Edward Jorden, who writes a whole treatise on this subject, describes its symptoms as follows:

> The matrix is drawne upwards or sidewards, according as the repletion is, whereupon followeth a compression of the neighbour parts, as of the midrif which causeth shortnes of breath, by straightning the instruments of respiration of their due scope.[90]

Therefore, for a woman *not* 'to play in the courts of Venus' at all is just as harmful as the immoderate 'use of venery'.[91] Not only does it have damaging repercussions on her sexual make-up, it also 'affect[s] … the principal parts of the bodie by consent'.[92] For my purposes here, I only want to emphasize that in medical discussions of *passio hysterica* the uterus is interpreted once again as that which differs from itself, as an organ whose identity is to a great extent an abject and deformed non-identity. In Jorden's treatise, it re-presents itself as 'drawne upwards or sidewards'.[93] Sadler speaks of the 'retraction of the wombe'.[94] Like most early modern physicians, Fontanus rejects Plato's idea of the womb as 'some straggling creature, wandering to and fro thorough several parts'.[95] However, he concedes that in women suffering from 'that disease which we commonly call the mother', the womb 'doth remove, and slip from its proper place'.[96] Indeed, he adds, it is 'loosened and exceedingly stretched'.[97]

But just how stable is the internal physiology of a woman who 'confine[s] herself to the lawes of moderation'?[98] Does the matrix ever 'obtaine … a mediocrity, approaching to no excesse'?[99] If one moves from the margins to the centre, from narratives recounting the disruptive effects of inappropriate, excessive or non-existent copulation to accounts of successful reproductive intercourse, one finds that the womb is still construed as a 'non-entity' exceeding its 'proper' limits and situated at the boundaries of the human. As recent interpretations of reproductive biology in early modern culture have pointed out, especially Laqueur's, most anatomical and gynaecological texts insist on the causal relation between female sexual pleasure and successful conception.[100] Arguably, it is this causal relation that facilitates the re-emergence at the very centre of these texts of a 'dis-figured' figure they ostensibly marginalize – that of the roaming womb. Helkiah Crooke, for instance, in the context of his discussion of the fact that it is not 'so uncouth in Nature, that those parts which in some creatures are prominent and apparent, should in others be veyled and covered', defines the female genitalia as 'captives', by which he means 'not those which are not at all, but which are in restraint or in bonds'.[101] However, as he proceeds to consider the process of 'legitimate' reproduction, he implicitly shows that it is exceedingly difficult to keep these 'captives' in check. Men and women, according to Crooke,

> in their mutual imbracements doe either of them yeeld seede the mans leaping with greater violence. The woman at the same instant doth not onely eiaculate seede into her self, but also her womb *snatcheth* as it were and *catcheth* the seed of the man, and *hideth* it in the bottom and bosome thereof.[102]

Later in the text, he specifies that the simultaneous emission of seed is not really necessary for a successful conception to take place. This does not prevent him from calling attention to the advantages of this simultaneity: 'If at the same time both sexes yeelde their seede, then is the conception sooner … because the wombe at that time being as it were *enraged*, doth *more greedily draw* and *more narrowly embrace* the seede which is cast unto it.'[103] For Paré, the womb '*allures or draws* the masculine seed into itself by the mouth thereof and it receives the womans seed by the hornes from the spermatick vessel'.[104] Jacques Duval poetically describes the encounter between sexual organs:

> This mouth [of the womb] [*cervix uteri*] opens easily, freely and voluptuously when it has a chance to receive the male sperm, which it loves and enjoys most marvellously. This is the reason why, during coitus, the man feels it fluttering like a butterfly or moving like a tench, coming at intervals to kiss or suck the extremity of the balanus, eager to gain its natural balm.[105]

In *The Sick Womans Private Looking-Glasse*, John Sadler states that in the act of conception 'there must be an Agent and a Patient'.[106] Man, of course, is 'the Agent, [woman] the Patient or weaker vessell, that she should be subject unto the office of the Man'.[107] The least that can be said about the passages from Crooke, Paré and Duval is that they show, instead, that this 'weaker vessell' *actively* pursues its 'passive' aims, which is nothing but a blurring of the distinction between 'Agent' and 'Patient'. In other words, once woman's capacity for (hetero)sexual desire and pleasure is inserted in accounts of successful procreation, the part that metonymizes this capacity re-emerges as a hybrid, less-than-human or super-human 'entity' that remains nonetheless the condition of possibility for the (re)production of the human. This part can thus hardly be said unproblematically to fall within the boundaries of the constraining production of the female body as a colder, inverted version of the male.[108] In fact, to paraphrase one of Judith Butler's crucial arguments in *Bodies That Matter*, the womb qua double of the penis is re-marked as a site of ambivalence, as the 'dis-figured outside' of the phallomorphic logic of the one sex/flesh, providing 'the necessary support' for this logic but also continuously posing a threat to its coherence.[109] In short, it is a largely unthematizable and yet *constitutive* matrix/outside. In psychoanalytic terms, one can hypothesize that the excerpts from Crooke, Paré and Duval also indicate the extent to which the womb embodies the 'imaginary' threat of castration.[110] In Crooke, for instance, the womb is represented as that which 'snatcheth … and catcheth the seed of the man', as that which 'greedily draw[s] and more narrowly embrace[s] the seede'.[111] But one needs to clarify that the 'lack' the womb represents – a 'lack' that exceeds, in any case, the conceptualization of the womb as 'passive' matter seeking 'active' form – is itself the result of a process of disavowal that does not fail to draw attention to that which is disavowed: men's precarious possession of the phallus; or, to use a Lacanian terminology, their unstable parading of that which they do *not* have.[112] Arguably, it is because of this precariousness and instability that Jacques Duval recommends that men emit sperm into the womb without delay, explaining that 'too long a friction of the genital parts provokes such a dissipation of the [vital] spirits that the virile member waxes soft';[113] or that Paré, using almost the same terms, but displacing the fear of male inadequacy onto the seed, takes the trouble of giving the following advice:

> for generation it is fit the man cast forth his seed into the womb with a certain impetuosity, his yard being stiffe and distended …, lest that through delay the seed waxe cold, and so become unfruitfull by reason that the spirits are dissipated and consumed.[114]

Coda

I conclude by citing at length from the opening of Michel de Montaigne's essay 'Of Idlenesse':

> As we see some idle-fallow grounds, if they be fat and fertile, to bring foorth store and sundry roots of wilde and unprofitable weeds, and that to keep them in ure we must subject and imploy them with certain seeds for our use and service; and as we see some women, though single and alone, often to bring foorth lumps of shapelesse flesh, whereas to produce a perfect and naturall generation, they must be manured with another kinde of seed; so is it of mindes, which except they be busied about some subject, that may bridle and keep them under, they will here and there wildely scatter themselves through the vast field of imaginations.[115]

I shall not attempt to offer an analysis of this brief but crucial essay, or fully explore the extended analogy grounds/wombs/minds and its implications for the general discursive economy of the *Essayes*.[116] I shall only note, first of all, that the metaphorical construction of the womb as a fertile 'ground' is not peculiar to Montaigne.

Crooke, for instance, speaks of the womb as a 'fruitful field or garden of nature'.[117] For Duval, 'it is not without reason that [the womb] is called *physis*, because if it is properly cultivated, attended to, and supplied with semen, it always produces something of its own'.[118] In *The Midwives Book* (1671), Jane Sharp points out that 'man in the act of procreation is the agent and tiller and sower of the ground, woman is the patient or ground to be tilled'.[119] However, the passage from Montaigne's 'Of Idlenesse' also suggests that there is a disorderly and yet *natural* fruitfulness of the womb that *precedes* the intervention of a masculine inseminating agent; that there is some kind of *natural* fecundity whose 'monstrous' sign is the womb's bringing forth of 'lumps of shapelesse flesh'. Moreover, the passage indicates that this productivity needs to be curbed for the womb to be inserted into a teleological narrative leading to the (re)production of the Same – what the passage calls 'a perfect and naturall generation' but is in fact a departure from a 'natural' disorderliness, a deviation from an 'original' deviation that is arguably constitutive. In this sense, the differential and hierarchical construction of the male as 'sower of the ground' and the female as 'ground to be tilled' in Sharpe, or the definition of the womb as *physis* producing 'something of its own' only if 'properly cultivated' in Duval, are themselves forms of a process of 'constraining production'.[120] They are signs and symptoms of the contraction of a wider field of interpretive possibilities. Put differently, these are constructions and definitions that are gendered more than once, with the figure of the womb qua 'patient' and 'ground to be tilled' coming to mark the simultaneous inclusion and exclusion of female pleasure and (re)productive power.[121]

But just how stable is this constraining economy of reproduction? How successful is this veritable structural doubling of the *assujettissement* to masculine principles signified by the proper tilling of the *matrix*? If one follows the logic of the argument developed in 'Of Idlenesse', one cannot but conclude that the notion of 'proper cultivation' as a form of restricted and restrictive economy of (re)production is emphasized only to be problematized and put under erasure. Montaigne keeps on bringing (back) to the fore, with a mixture of pleasure and shame, his 'extravagant Chimeraes, and fantasticall monsters, so orderlesse, and without any reason, one hudling upon another'.[122] These 'extravagant Chimeraes, and fantasticall monsters' seem to proceed from some kind of self-impregnation, and are identifiable with nothing less than the *Essayes* themselves.[123]

Following a different route, I have argued in this chapter that the construction of female bodies and bodily fluids as colder, less perfect and inverted versions of those of the male is to a large extent an anxious reiteration, and thus in no simple sense original, natural or dominant. Indeed, 'construction' may not be the most appropriate term to describe the complex dynamics whereby, to cite from Judith Butler's Irigarayan argument, 'what *has to be excluded* for [these] economies to function as self-sustaining systems' and 'posture as internally coherent' – the 'un-constructed' but constitutive 'outside' – ceaselessly poses the threat of a terrifying return.[124] I have analysed some constructions of the womb as paradigmatic of these paradoxical and threatening dynamics, and noted how in these constructions the 'container' bears an uncanny similarity to its monstrous and deformed content.[125] I have also emphasized that discourses on the *mola* do not simply function as a way of confirming *a contrario* the 'legitimate' economy of reproduction. They are, instead, one of the discursive areas onto which male anxieties about reproduction are displaced but not fully assuaged. These anxieties are mainly about the adequacy and efficacy of the performance of male bodies and bodily fluids *vis-à-vis* the 'matter' of a body marked female. They are arguably enhanced by the causal, but perhaps not entirely desirable, correlation between female pleasure and conception. I have pointed out that male anxieties induce a number of 'imaginary' solutions. With the emergence of the 'culture of dissection', one such solution, and perhaps the most conspicuous, is the recourse to surgical instruments. These technological extensions and supplements of the male body attempt to circumvent a sense of powerlessness. They endeavour to give form, mostly *ex post facto*, to what is perceived as inchoate 'feminine' matter, with ambiguous results.

ΜΙΚΡΟΚΟΣΜΟΓΡΑΦΙΑ:

A

DESCRIPTION

of the Body of Man.

TOGETHER

VVITH THE CONTROVERSIES

THERETO BELONGING.

Collected and Translated out of all the Best Authors of Anatomy, Especially out of Gasper Bauhinus *and* Andreas Laurentius. By HELKIAH CROOKE Doctor of *Physicke, Physitian to His Maiestie, and his Highnesse* PROFESSOR *in Anatomy and Chyrurgerie.*

Published by the Kings Maiesties especiall Direction and Warrant according to the first integrity, as it was originally written by the AVTHOR.

——*Etiam Parnassia Laurus*
Parua, sub ingenti matris se subiicit vmbra.

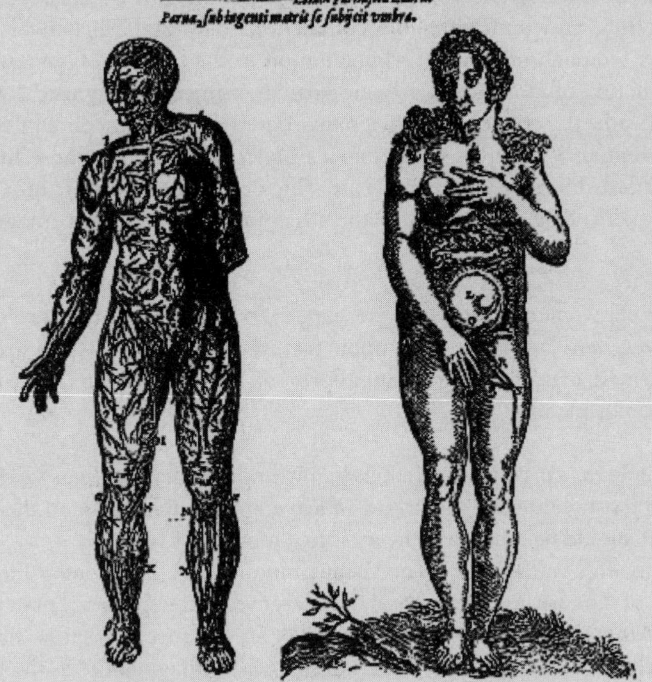

Printed by William Iaggard dwelling in Barbican, and are there to be sold, 1615.

Figure 2 Helkiah Crooke, *Microcosmographia. A Description of the Body of Man* (1615)

4 'Strange flesh' and 'unshap't bodies'

Monstrosity, hyperbolic masculinity and 'racial' difference

The female monster

Rosi Braidotti argues that 'the peculiarity of the organic monster is that s/he is both Same and Other. The monster is neither a total stranger nor completely familiar; s/he exists in an in-between zone.'[1] S/he is the 'foreign' at the heart of the 'domestic', a paradoxical entity – or non-entity – the rhetoric of the 'human' represses but does not fully suppress. In short, s/he is the uncanny.

In order to develop her point, Braidotti focuses on early modern discourses on reproduction, and underlines the connection they establish between the role played by women and women's imagination in the process of 'generation' and the production of monsters. Early modern anatomical and gynaecological treatises are, indeed, replete with advice to women on how to conduct themselves during pregnancy. Jacques Guillemeau's *Childe-Birth* (1612), whose first book is aptly entitled 'The government and ordering of a woman the nine monethes that she goes with childe', enunciates the disciplining of women's imagination as follows:

> Discreet women … will not give eare unto lamentable and fearefull tales or storyes, nor cast their eyes upon pictures or persons which are uglie or deformed, least the imagination imprint on the child the similitude of the said person or picture.[2]

To Guillemeau, a pregnant woman is highly impressionable, a passive recipient of *fictio* who has nonetheless the power to leave an indelible mark on the child and turn what should be a happy delivery into a monstrous birth.

Guillemeau's warning is by no means unique. The burgeoning literature on monsters of the early modern period routinely evokes the spectre of maternal imagination. Ambroise Paré's *Des Monstres* (1573), for instance, a treatise that contributed much to the 'naturalization' of monsters, lists 'imagination' as the fifth of the thirteen causes of monsters.[3] The French physician quotes the opinion of those who believe that 'the infant once formed in the wombe … is in no danger of the mothers imagination', but concludes that it is 'best to keep the woman, all the time she goeth with child, from the sight of [deformed] shapes and figures'.[4]

It has often been claimed, in relation to the early modern sex-gender system, that women do not simply *have* a body. They *are* the body. As Phyllis Rackin points out, there is an inextricable linkage between femininity and that negatively connoted and reviled entity that is the body/flesh. 'The body itself', she sums up, 'was gendered feminine' and subordinated to a 'masculine' soul/spirit.[5] The title page of Helkiah Crooke's *Microcosmographia* (see Fig. 2) emblematizes this distinction between 'masculine' spirit and 'feminine' flesh.[6] It presents two bodies standing next to each other. The male body has had its skin removed and exhibits its arteries, veins and muscles. It disquietingly looks like a hypermasculine armour. It is almost a cyborg *avant la lettre*. It stays in mid-air, as if to signify some kind of virtual transcendence of the flesh. This is compounded by the fact that it is sexually undifferentiated.[7] It bears no sexual organs. To recall Judith Butler's work once again, this is a body that matters precisely because it is a figure of 'dis-embodiment'.[8] Moreover, although it is fully exposed, it haughtily averts the eyes of the observer. The female figure, instead, meets the eyes of the – potentially male – observer. She is an object on display, and conscious of being so. Unlike the male figure, she is sexed. In fact, to an extent, she is the only body there is. She 'em-bodies' the realm of the flesh, which belongs to the earth and lacks transcendence. She bashfully hides her breasts and genitals and yet, by doing so, she draws attention to them. Moreover, this gesture of covering herself seems to be simultaneous with her folding back of the layer of skin standing underneath her breasts, which reveals her insides and reproductive organs. Arguably, this is a body that matters only insofar as it is inserted in an ocular economy, an economy that displays to the eye and – sadistically – partitions the body. As it unfolds, Crooke's treatise shows, first of all, that the womb synecdochically stands for the female body; secondly, that they are both signs of a radical 'dis-figuration', formlessness and deformity.[9] In this sense, even before considering the extent of the involvement of female 'imagination' in the making of monsters, one needs to underline that the female body always-already bears the mark of monstrosity.[10]

Moving from anatomical discourses to early modern tragedy, this chapter explores some of the most significant ways in which masculinity figures itself in relation to this 'uncanny monster'. It focuses on three Shakespearean tragedies – *Antony and Cleopatra*, *Coriolanus* and *Othello* – and a lesser-known play, Thomas Goffe's *The Courageous Turke*. It argues that they dramatize *and* problematize the dividing line between bodies that matter and bodies that do not matter. They articulate masculinity as that which is exceedingly powerful *and* intimately threatened. In short, the construction of masculinity in these plays is part of an unstable 'deconstructive dynamic', and this is especially the case when this construction finds itself implicated in questions of 'racial' and cultural difference.

'Strange flesh' in Shakespeare's Roman plays

Judith Butler's work has had some impact on recent studies of early modern masculinity. Mark Breitenberg refers to Butler to corroborate his hypothesis that masculinity is nothing but the inherently anxious performance of its outward signs and expressions; and that these external signs can hardly be opposed to a stable and invulnerable kernel of masculine identity.[11] Laura Levine sets Butler's understanding of performativity against much new historicism's blindness to the theatricalization of gender. She also argues, in an attempt to historicize Butler's work, that in the early modern texts she examines, it is only masculinity (rather than gender as such, as is the case with Butler's approach)[12] that needs to be performed in order to exist. Femininity, instead, is 'the default position, the otherness one [i.e. man] is always in danger of slipping into'.[13] Moreover, Levine sees the early modern performance of masculinity as emerging from a diffuse sense of powerlessness and fear: the fear, in fact, that there might be 'no real masculinity, no masculine self' at all.[14] She opposes this historically specific masculine 'panic' to Butler's sense of the 'liberating possibilities implicit in regarding gender as an act'.[15]

Yet Butler would probably object to Levine's portrayal of her work on gender. *Bodies That Matter* explicitly dismisses interpretations of her argument in *Gender Trouble* that read like Levine's.[16] She would in fact agree with Levine that gender is a series of 'highly codified, culturally rigid, externally defined' performances.[17] She would probably add that reiterated performances of gender, taking place within a field of cultural constraints, eventually coagulate into bodies that matter/mean; and that this process of materialization of bodies is simultaneous with the crafting of a domain of abjected and formless bodies.[18] Following Butler's approach to the process of materialization and de-materialization of bodies, I am therefore in partial disagreement with Levine's (or Rackin's) association of the 'feminine' with the body *tout court*. The 'feminine' is not simply the unperformable 'default body' man is always in danger of falling back into. It emblematizes a terrifying formlessness that fails to materialize as a body (that is, as a body that matters) but often refuses to stay put. It stands for a monstrous indistinction haunting those bodies that pose – and matter – as legitimate and normative.

In the light of these remarks, one can re-read some of the examples from *Antony and Cleopatra* Laura Levine uses in *Men in Women's Clothing* to pursue her argument on early modern masculinity. That Antony's body fails to hold its 'visible shape' (IV.xiv.14), a visibility that is a function of masculine ratification, does not simply suggest emasculation and/or effeminization. Rather, it points to the uncanny and monstrous dissolution of the boundaries of gender themselves.[19] Antony's body has become as 'indistinct as water is in water' (IV.xiv.10–11). Yet the distinct 'shape' of masculinity the Roman soldier cannot cling to is itself a construct that already belongs to the realm of unsubstantial 'signs'. It is part of 'black vesper pageants' (IV.xiv.7–8). Moreover, the remedy to such a loss of – artificial – embodiment, which is typically figured as the reassertion of the bleeding body of the warrior ('For with a wound I must be cured') (IV.xiv.78), is itself a 'dis-figuring' of the body. Thus, paradoxically, the re-inscription of a masculine body that matters is nothing but the evacuation of the body and its transformation into something undifferentiated and porous, disquietingly analogous to the 'indistinct' formless femininity Antony attempts to escape from.[20] This is even more so if one considers that the – literal – extinguishing of Antony's body in the play is an emulation of an emulation (in other words, an emulation of Cleopatra's fake suicide as well as Eros's), and a botched one to boot: 'How? Not dead? Not dead?' (IV.xiv.103), which inexorably undercuts any attempt on Antony's part to be a masculine 'conqueror of [himself]' (IV.xiv. 62).[21]

The 'masculine origin' Antony departs from is but a sign. The cure is but a poison. In spite of, or because of this, the play continuously looks back to the point in time when Antony was fully himself. However, an extended analysis of the play would reveal the extent to which this nostalgically evoked masculine presence is implicated in the 'deconstructive dynamics' I have begun to develop. One of the most striking instances of this nostalgia is, of course, Caesar's recollection of Antony's military and dietary exploits. In Caesar's lines, the body is a hypermasculine body that renegotiates the boundaries of the human, and so much so that it turns out to be a scarcely habitable construct: 'Thou didst drinke / The stale of horses, and the gilded puddle / Which beasts would cough at …; Thou didst eat strange flesh, / Which some did die to look on' (I.iv.61–3; 67–8). It is simultaneously a 'dis-figured' figure of abjection *and* a figure that matters as long as it undergoes a process of 'dis-embodiment': 'And all this … / Was borne so like a Soldier, that thy cheek / So much as lank'd not' (I.iv.68; 70–1).[22]

The wounded body of the warrior takes centre stage again and again in early modern tragedy. (In *Antony and Cleopatra* we even have a minor character called Scarus.) As in *Antony and Cleopatra*, it presents itself as the epitome of masculinity as well as the symptom of its ambiguity. *Coriolanus* is a case in point.[23] Coriolanus' wounded body matters, in its masculine form, only in so far as it transcends the flesh. The 'blood' the hero may happen to 'drop' is not synonymous with the vanishing of the body. It is 'rather physical than dangerous' (I.v.18–19) to him. It does reinvigorate the body but only by becoming the sign of its sublation. As Cynthia Marshall argues in her perceptive reading of the play, the question of masculinity revolves around Martius' highly fetishized wounds. Yet, the *vulnera* of this quasi-android being do not merely emblematize heroism and valour. As the play progresses, they increasingly tend to reinscribe themselves as signs of vulnerability. On the one hand, his haughty refusal to display them in the market place is a rejection of a version of himself as feminized spectacle, as the object of the gaze of the populace. On the other, just as he 'embraces masculinity as a construct', he does not fail to mark 'his lack of self-guaranteed identity'.[24] This can be interpreted, in Lacanian terms, as the lack of the phallus. In other words, even before the 'gang rape' of the 'boy' Coriolanus (V.vi.104) taking place at the end of the play, the 'dis-embodied' body of the warrior displays, in spite of itself, its uncanny proximity to formless penetrable 'femininity'.

A monster 'too hideous to be shown': *Othello* and alterity

In *Shakespeare and Masculinity* Bruce R. Smith cogently describes four categories in relation to which early modern masculinity defines itself: women, foreigners, persons of lower social rank, and sodomites.[25] His approach is a useful corrective of interpretations such as Breitenberg's that emphasize that masculinity is constantly dependent upon its own construction of 'woman as an Other who either confirms or disrupts masculine identity'.[26] Shakespeare's *Othello* bears out the complexity of the construction of early modern masculinity Smith underlines. The Moor *does* anxiously define himself in relation to what he and other male characters construe as a 'feminine Other'. Yet, because of his labile status as 'honorary white',[27] as a body that matters but not quite, he is also forced to present himself as a martial, royal and 'anti-physical' hero, and set this construction against the version of himself as a black, lascivious, 'extravagant, and wheeling stranger of here and everywhere' (I.i.136–7) that powerfully circulates within the play.[28]

To Othello, Desdemona unmistakably stands for a body that matters. It matters especially because it consolidates, or is supposed to consolidate, his transformation – what the play ambiguously calls 'redemption' (I.iii.138) – from the monstrous black and Islamic 'other' to the valiant noble white Moor of Venice. She is 'the fountain, from the which [his] current runs' (IV.ii.60), as well as a shield from 'chaos', as Othello states in the poignant lines: 'I do love thee, and when I love thee not / Chaos is come again' (III.iii.92–3). Crucial to this transformation is the acquisition of the body of white masculinity, which is constructed, in early modern discourses, in opposition to lust – a desire to desire, a bestial appetite that is tantamount to a monstrous undermining of manhood. The early modern name for this delusion is effeminacy, and the 'racial other' is seen as particularly susceptible to it.[29] As a result, soon after pleading with the senators to let Desdemona go to Cyprus with him, Othello feels the need to justify himself, not only as a man but also as an outsider: 'I … beg it not / To please the palate of my appetite, / Nor to comply with heat' (I.iii.261–3). In fact, he promises that 'light-wing'd toys, and feather'd Cupid' (I.iii.268–9) will not 'corrupt and taint [his] business' (I.iii.271): the 'business' of war against 'the general enemy Ottoman' (I.iii.49).

From Othello's point of view, therefore, to gain access to the body of an aristocratic Venetian maiden is yet another step towards the attainment of the 'normative' body of white masculinity. This has a price: Othello cannot but 'put into circumscription and confine' (I.ii.27) his treasured 'unhoused free condition' (I.ii.26), which speaks obliquely of the boundlessness of desire.[30] From Iago's point of view, instead, Othello's access to the body of Desdemona is yet another episode in the Moor's 'travel's history' (I.iii.139). It shows the extent to which he pursues his career as an 'erring' (I.iii.356) Barbarian pirate in Venice. Talking to Cassio about Othello's marriage, Iago half-jokingly observes: 'He to-night hath boarded a land carrack: / If it prove lawful prize, he's made for ever' (I.ii. 50–1). In other words, to Iago, as well as to other characters who operate through strategies of demonization of 'racial' alterity, Othello remains 'an extravagant and wheeling stranger, / Of here and everywhere' (I.i.136–7), an oxymoronic fluctuating monstrous 'non-identity' that confounds ethnic, religious, cultural and sexual affiliations.

Daniel J. Viktus persuasively argues that there is a spectre haunting early modern English and European imagination: the spectre of 'turning Turk', a conversion to Islam that, given the damning of this religion as licentious, is regularly construed in sexual terms. Indeed, for Viktus, as a result of the greater frequency of Anglo–Islamic contacts in the Mediterranean during the late sixteenth and early seventeenth centuries, we witness a spate of demonizing representations of the Islamic 'other', 'not from the perspective of cultural domination but from the fear of being conquered, captured and converted'.[31] Viktus adds that this fear of conversion does not fail to leave its imprint on *Othello*. The play continuously raises the spectre of 'turning Turk'. Yet, its reverse form (that is, conversion from Islam to Christianity) does not cause less panic. To the proto-racist *imaginaire* of the play, the Moor's 'redemption' (I.iii.138) simply means that the one who 'turns', even the one who 'turns Christian', is bound to turn again or turn back. 'Turning Christian' is, as far as the Moor is concerned, nothing but the symmetrical uncanny equivalent of 'turning Turk'. It speaks the same lascivious story. In this sense, one does not have to wait for Othello to metamorphose into a 'turban'd Turk' (V.ii.354) at the end of the play. He has been one all along. In short, a renegade is a renegade is a renegade. To borrow from a later text, a sermon preached by Henry Byam in 1627, Othello can be seen as one of those who are 'Musselmans in Turkie and Christians at home; doffing their religion, as they doe their clothes, and keeping a conscience for every Harbor wheere [sic] they shall put in'.[32]

Representations of the 'Christian-Turned-Turk' proliferate in travel writings and religious literature of the early modern period. The English translation of the lavishly illustrated *Navigations, Peregrinations and Voyages, Made into Turkie* (1585), for instance, describes the French traveller Nicholas de Nicholay's encounter with the multitude of renegades living in Algiers. They are typically portrayed as the 'dis-located' and 'dis-locating' antithesis of an incipient sense of European normativity and civilization:

> The most part of the Turkes of Algers … are Christian renied, or Mahumetised, of al Nations, but most of them Spaniards, Italians, and of Provence, of the Ilands and Coastes of the Sea Mediterane, given all to whoredome, sodometrie, theft, and all other most detestable vices, lyving onely of rovings, spoyles, & pilling at the Seas.[33]

If these depreciatory constructions of the renegade are brought to bear on Shakespeare's play, one is in a better position to gauge Othello's reaction to the 'barbarous brawl' (II.iii.163) breaking out in Cyprus in the second act of the play: 'Are we turned Turks?' (II.iii.161) This question, of course, is part of a speech in which Othello appeals to Christian values in order to mark his distance from the Ottoman 'other' just vanquished by a providential storm: 'For Christian shame, put by this barbarous brawl' (II.iii.163). Yet this is also a speech that furtively announces the eruption of the Islamic enemy within, the monstrous adversary who is none other than Othello himself.[34]

Early modern discourses on Islam situate themselves within a long-standing Western tradition that routinely interpreted it as nothing but idolatry, in fact, as no religion at all. For these discourses, Islam is indistinguishable from devilish witchcraft. Mohammed, in turn, is often branded as 'a Iuggler, a Mount-bank, a bestiall people-pleaser'.[35] The attraction of Islam has to do with the fact that it is a religion of sensuality, a cover for monstrous sexual practices. For Edward Aston, the success of this 'pestilent religion' is due to Mohammed's 'giving to his people free liberty and power to pursue their lustes and all other pleasures'.[36] Its followers keep on converting, and converts are Islam's most zealous 'sexual' adherents. In his account of his voyages to Turkey, Nicholas de Nicholay speaks of a sect of Islam called 'the men of the religion of love'. These are men, according to the French traveller, who

> secretly and under pretext of religion do of a fervent love draw unto them, the hearts of many faire women, & likewise of the fairest yonglings, of which they are no lesse amorous than they are of the woman kind, so much are they given unto the abhominable sinne of luxurie against nature.[37]

He adds that 'if there were such an order and profession amongst us …, the most part of our youth would sooner give themselves to the avowing and profession of such a religion, than to that of chastity and observance'.[38] Whether this is said tongue-in-cheek or not, Nicholas de Nicholay's conclusion suggests that the pull of a 'sexualized' Islam is irresistible.

It is this kind of enticing 'sexual proselytism' that obsessively informs Brabantio's speeches and dreams: 'Thou hast enchanted her' (I.ii.63); 'Thou has practis'd on her with foul charms' (I.ii.73). To Desdemona's father, Othello is an impostor, 'an abuser of the world, a practiser / Of arts inhibited, and out of warrant' (I.ii.78–9). Of course, Brabantio would not concede that his daughter is 'half the wooer' (I.iii.176). As he learns of her active role in the affair – what Desdemona herself calls a 'downright violence' (I.iii.249) – he contents himself with instilling into the Moor the suspicion that it may be impossible to put an end to the trespassing of the boundaries of gender: 'Look to her, Moor, have a quick eye to see: / She has deceiv'd her father, may do thee' (I.iii.292–3).[39] The changeability of the 'wheeling convert' Othello thus begins to intersect with the unpredictability of the 'converted' Desdemona. The fickleness of the monstrous female convert will be most famously enunciated as follows: 'She can turn, and turn, and yet go on / And turn again' (IV.i.249–50).[40] The tragedy of the play mostly lies in the fact that it is precisely by speaking and acting from the orthodox and rigid position that damns them both that Othello will terminate all kind of 'turning'.[41]

It has often been observed that Othello's insecurity in relation to the 'object' Desdemona is dependent upon his position as an outsider. As Iago intimates, he does not 'know our country disposition well' (III.iii.205). He is unaware of Venetian women's 'pranks' (III.iii.206), blind to their promiscuity. Yet, as the play develops, Iago's 'pestilence' (II.iii.347) is more and more effective also because Othello is unable to occupy, or fall back into, any discursive position in relation to such an 'object' that is free from anxiety. In other words, the 'other' in relation to which Othello's masculinity defines itself becomes, or has always been in a surreptitious way, a changeable and abject other, whether she is construed as a Christian Venetian woman or a Muslim woman from Barbary (North Africa). In the eighth book of Leo Africanus's *A Geographical Historie of Africa*, often referred to as one of the sources of Shakespeare's play and translated into English by John

Pory in 1600, one finds that the women in Cairo are 'costly attired', ambitious and proud:

> They vouchsafe great libertie unto their wives: for the good man being gone to the taverne or victualling-house, his wife tricking up her selfe in costly apparell, and being perfumed with sweet and pretious odours, walketh about the citie to solace herself, and parley with her kinsfolks and friends .... It falleth out oftentimes that the wife will complaine of her husband unto the iudge, that he doth not his dutie nor contenteth her sufficiently in the night season, whereupon (as it is permitted by the Mahumetan law) the women are divorced and married unto other husbands.[42]

Juxtaposed to the construction of the abjected body of Othello qua 'Islamic other' is the casting of the Moor as a stereotypically rampant black male. Given the recent surge of criticism focusing on the volatile context of the Mediterranean to re-situate a number of early modern texts such as *Othello*, it is easy to play down the vocabulary of colour.[43] Yet, one cannot simply replace the black pagan with the Islamic 'other' as the embodiment of the external and internal threat to the dominant. In short, Othello is not only figured as a monstrous 'Barbary horse' covering Brabantio's daughter; he is also imagined as 'an old black ram ... tupping [a] white ewe' (I.i.88–9).

For Leo Africanus, a Moor born in Granada who converted, or was forced to convert, to Christianity after being captured by Italian pirates, Barbaria 'is the most noble and worthie region of all Africa, the inhabitants whereof are of a browne or tawnie colour, being a civill people, and prescribe wholsome lawes and constitutions unto themselves'.[44] Yet, Leo's panegyric of the people of Barbaria seems to be a function of the utter abjection of one of the remaining four principal 'nations' of Africa,[45] which he calls 'the land of the Negroes': 'The negroes ... lead a beastly kinde of life, being utterly destitute of the use of reason, of dexteritie of wit, and of all artes .... They have great swarmes of harlots among them'.[46] Later on, he adds that they live 'a brutish and savage life, without any king, governour, common wealth, or knowledge of husbandrie'. He continues:

> Clad they [are] in skins of beasts, neither [have] they any peculiar wives ...: when night [comes] they [resort] ten or twelve both men and women into one cottage together, using hairie skins in stead of beds, and each man choosing his leman which he [has] most fancy unto.[47]

Yet, the distinction between Barbaria and sub-Saharan Africa is often inconsequential in most early modern texts.[48] One form of demonization feeds upon the other. Lasciviousness provides the code that allows writers to move with nonchalance from blacks to Muslims and back. Iago, for instance, effortlessly switches from the 'old black ram ... tupping [a] white ewe' (I.i.88–9) to the 'Barbary horse' covering Brabantio's daughter to 'the beast with two backs' (I.i.116). To Iago, all these 'dis-figured' figures emblematize a monstrous sodomitical conjunction.[49]

However, monstrosity does not merely lie in sodomitical acts. Iago also evokes the spectre of the production and reproduction of a new breed of Venetians: 'You'll have your nephews neigh to you; you'll have coursers for cousins, and gennets for germans' (I.i.112–13). I now want to associate Iago's fantasy of a 'monstrous progeny' with a passage from Paré's *Des Monstres*. In this passage the French physician discusses the monstrous offspring of bestial copulation, which is the result of the sodomitical 'mixture or mingling of seed':

> There are monsters that are born with a form that is half-animal and the other human, or retaining everything about them from animals, which are produced by sodomists and atheists who 'join together' and break out of their bounds – unnaturally – with animals, and from this are born *several hideous monsters that bring great shame to those who look at them or speak of them.*[50]

Martin Orkin argues that Shakespeare's play 'reverses the associations attached to the colors white and black that are the consequences of racist stereotyping. It is Iago, the white man, who is portrayed as amoral and anti-Christian'.[51] It is Iago who takes on the traits of the stereotypical Moor or the 'cruel Turk'. He embodies deceit, duplicity, cruelty and lasciviousness. He can thus be identified as the 'civil monster' (IV.i.64) he mentions in the first scene of the fourth act. He can also be associated with almost everything else he claims the 'other' to be. Bearing this in mind, I want to return to the passage from Paré I have just cited, to the 'hideous monsters that bring great shame to those who look at them or speak of them'. Of course, given the problems Paré had with censorship, this is literally a kind of justification, an anticipatory self-defence.[52] Yet, I want to interpret Paré's words allegorically, as words that speak otherwise. They can be read as summarizing the highly charged cultural dynamic of monstrosity within and without the play. Paré's words suggest that there is 'great shame' and monstrosity at the centre of the process of conjuring monsters into being, at the heart of the dominant production of monsters as abject and deformed 'others'. It is this, perhaps, this monstrosity at the centre, the monster 'too hideous to be shown' (III.iii.112).

'Unshap't' bodies: Thomas Goffe's *The Courageous Turke*

Othello shows that the deconstructive – and violent – relation between bodies that matter and bodies that do not matter does not merely correspond to the binary masculinity versus femininity. It also clarifies that that in relation to which man defines himself – in fact, that which masculinity forcefully *produces* as its other – is far from occupying a position of absolute exteriority. Put differently, the Other (Desdemona qua Venetian courtesan; Othello qua 'turban'd Turk' [V.ii.354]) never seems to be *at a safe distance* from the bodies that embody and re-enact the dominant discourses by which they are invested and through which they are constituted (Desdemona qua Venetian Lady; Othello qua Christian Venetian general).

Never at a safe distance: this works both ways but obviously in an asymmetric way. The excluded/abjected induces anxiety, which is symptomatic of the destabilizing effect it has on the fabrication of legitimate bodies. Anxiety, in turn, often activates or reactivates violence. Therefore, those bodies failing to count as bodies can become sites of further exclusions or abjections. To paraphrase Jonathan Dollimore, there is never safety in exclusion or abjection.[53]

I want to conclude with a brief analysis of Thomas Goffe's *The Courageous Turke or Amurath the First* (1632), a play first performed in 1619, which has been read by Samuel Chew as part of the Irene-saga and, in more recent years, by Daniel Viktus in conjunction with, and as informed by, *Othello*.[54] The play presents, from its very beginning, and in a much-stylized way, the opposition between masculine military valour and effeminizing lust. Lala-Schahin, tutor to Amurath, enters at one door, with warlike music and soldiers and Amurath 'in State' at the other, with Eumorphe, his Greek concubine and other ladies.[55] Amurath immediately tells his tutor to stop the belligerent music that is being played: 'Be dumb those now harsh notes, our softer eares / Shall never be acquainted with such sounds, / Peace' (I.i.1–3). He proudly speaks the language of war to articulate his transformation into a doting lover: 'In loving Combats now I valiant prove, / Let others warre, great Amurath shall love' (I.i. 55–6). Yet, as early modern texts repeatedly stress, in 'loving combats', there is only one loser: the man. As Amurath himself admits, 'I conquered Greece, one Grecian conquered me' (I.i.32). In early modern terms, that Amurath willingly subjects himself to lust, and keenly admits to it, is bad enough. What is worse is that the object of his desire is geographically, ethnically and religiously 'other': the Greek concubine Eumorphe, called Irene in 'The Argument', the female captive who has captivated and conquered the conqueror.[56]

I now want to focus on Schahin's interpretation of Amurath's predicament, because it is through the tutor's speeches that one can begin to consider the extent to which the performance of masculinity, or lack thereof, is associated with specific figurations of the male body. According to Schahin, Amurath has relinquished 'those Acts, / Which 'ene the Furies would have trembled at: / Treading downe Armies, as if by them he meant / Of dead mens backes to build up staires to Heaven' (I.ii.16–19). In other words, he has given up the only masculinity that seems to matter, a masculinity that exceeds itself, since it is equivalent to transcending the flesh – transcending one's flesh, but also, one might surmise, 'transcending' the flesh of others. Amurath is now identified with an effeminized body that threatens to leak and overflow its boundaries.[57] He 'lyeth lurking in a womans armes / Drencht in the Lethe of ignoble lust' (I.ii.20–1). Having been appointed as 'the wanton Enginere / To keepe [Amurath's] so loose thoughts in smoothing tune' (I.ii.22–3), Schahin makes the best of a bad job. Being both a soldier *and* a scholar, and having probably read parts of *Hamlet* and Thomas Heywood's *Apology for Actors*, he devises two masques as an antidote to the dangerous porosity afflicting the body of his master, and even takes the trouble to impersonate the ghost of his master's father. In one of these masques, Alexander the Great shows Amurath the true meaning of masculinity.[58] He turns down 'exquisite form'd Ladies' (I.v.24) and 'a Troope of such shapt Ganimedes / That Iove not equals' (I.v.26–7), setting these 'effeminate presents' (I.v.41) against the hyperbolic masculinity of 'a man, a Souldier, strong with his wounds, / 'Mongst fate and ruine, *upright and unshap't,* / His minde being all his guard, his wall, and armour' (I.v.47–9).[59] This truly masculine man is oblivious to, and even welcomes 'all the darts / Stucke in his sides, making him all one wound' (I.v.51–2). The all too obvious message Schahin conveys through Alexander the Great is not wasted upon Amurath. After meeting the ghost of his father, he decides to 'rend … / That putrid Wenne which cleaves unto [his] flesh' (II.iv.39). He strikes off Eumorphe's head before his counsellors, after having invited them into the bedchamber to witness her beauty. The bond between men, which is essential to early modern structurations of masculinity, is thus reconstituted over and against the body of the woman, in a way that does not fail to involve desire, even if only in its repudiated form:

Amurath There, kisse now (Captaines) doe! and clap her cheeke;
This is the face that did so captive me:
These were the lookes that so bewitcht mine eyes;
Here be the lips, that I but for to touch,
Gave over Fortune, Victory, Fame, and all;
These were two lying mirrors where I lookt
And thought I saw a world of happinesse.

(II.v.73–9)

The – literal – 'de-formation' of the beautiful shape of 'Eu-morphe' counteracts the temporary loss of proper masculinity. It reinstates the 'upright and unshap't' (I.v.48) masculine body of the warrior, a fully erect body that refuses to be determined from without (in other words, 'unshap't'). This reinstatement is followed by the renewal of the war against Christendom: 'Now Tutor, shall our swords be exercised, / In ripping up the breasts of Christians. Say Generals! Whether is first?' (II.v.80–2). Yet the images that are meant to complement the hyperbolic masculinity of the warrior seem, in fact, to supplement it: a 'Trunke' with 'darts / Stucke in [its] sides'; a body that is nothing but one gigantic 'wound' (I.v.51–2).[60] Like in the Roman plays earlier referred to, the re-creation of a masculine body that matters goes hand in hand with the metamorphosis of the body into an amorphous mass that is disquietingly similar to the 'drenched' femininity one repeatedly and apotropaically endeavours to keep at bay. Put differently, the masculine body remains to a large extent blatantly 'unshap't' (that is, shapeless), and violence against one of masculinity's others turns out to be an upshot of the half-perceived uncanny similarity between bodies that are in fact proximate to one another.[61]

5 'Un-pleasurable' detours

Figurations of desire and the body erotic

Levidulcia Our creation has no reference
To man but in his body, being made
Only for generation .... If reason were
Our counsellor, we would neglect the work
Of generation for the prodigal
Expense it draws us to of that which is
The wealth of life. Wise Nature, therefore, hath
Reserv'd for an inducement to our sense
Our greatest pleasure in that greatest work.

(Cyril Tourneur, *The Atheist's Tragedy*)

The woman was ordayned to receive and conceive the seed of the man, to beare and nourish the infant, to governe and moderate the house at home, to delight and refresh her husband ... and therefore her body is soft, smooth and delicate, made especially for pleasure, for that whosoever useth them for other doth almost abuse them.

(Helkiah Crooke, *Microcosmographia*)

Along history, forever
some woman dancing
making shapes on the air;
forever a man
riding a good horse,
sitting the dark horse well,
his penis erect with
fantasy.

(Muriel Rukeyser, 'Along History')

'A strange and violent kinde of delight'

Taking as his starting point Galen's *De usu partium*, the seventeenth-century English anatomist Helkiah Crooke argues:

> Nature hath given to all creatures both the instruments of conception, and hath also infused into them a strange and violent kinde of delight, that none of the kindes of the creatures should perish but remayne ever after a sort immortall.[1]

Crooke adds that this irresistible 'delight' compels the body – a body that is paradigmatically male – to overcome some kind of deep-seated reluctance towards the 'act of generation:'

> And truely it was very necessary that there should be a kind of pleasant force or violence in the Nature of Mankind to transport him out of himselfe or behind himselfe as it were, in the act of generation: to which otherwise being maister of himself he would hardly have been drawne.[2]

Of course, as Crooke clarifies in another section of his treatise, this 'instinct of lust or desire' induces a loss of mastery that is only temporary, 'for a time'.[3] It is 'incredible' – a veritable 'sting or rage of pleasure' – but is inextricably bound up with the propagation of the species.[4] It unbinds the self providentially to secure some kind of immortality, although this is not equally true for 'all creatures'.[5] Echoing an idea that can already be found in Plato's *Laws,* and moving once again with nonchalance from generic to gendered constructs, Crooke surmises:

> The individuum extending it selfe as it were in the procreation of another like unto itself, groweth young againe and becommeth after a sort eternall. The father liveth in the sonne, and dyeth not as long as his expresse and living image stands up on the earth.[6]

In a way that is not untypical of early modern medical treatises, these passages delineate a male-centred and teleologically oriented restricted economy of the erotic and reproductive body whereby one loses only to gain; one 'dies' – the 'instinct of lust' eventually leading to a metaphorical death[7] – only to 'grow ... young againe', to postpone death.[8] In this sense, man's difference from himself – his being 'transposed' out of himself or behind himself[9] – is consistent with the compulsory but strategic heterosexual detour of male homosocial desire. This is a detour through the body of the female 'other' that is subordinated to, and culminates in, homosocial satisfaction. It eventually leads to the 'extension' of the (masculine) self, the narcissistic re-creation of images of this self.[10] By imprinting bodies with 'a strange and violent kinde of delight' Nature herself seems to subscribe to the structure of male homosocial desire.[11]

Irreversible detours: the paradoxical 'content' of desire in Jacobean tragedy

The 'instinct of lust or desire' medical treatises such as Crooke's refer to is unequivocally 'natural'. It is not 'inordinate such as by sinne is super-induced in man'.[12] In early seventeenth-century English tragedy, instead, male desire is most often represented as that which is irredeemably 'inordinate' and 'super-induced', exceeding the regulation of bodies and identities effected by the 'deployment of alliance'. This is a *dispositif* Foucault defines as 'a system of marriage, of fixation and development of kinship ties, of transmission of names and possessions', structured around 'a system of rules defining the permitted and the forbidden, the licit and the illicit', and 'firmly tied to ... the transmission or circulation of wealth'.[13] In other words, the detour of desire that inscribes itself in Jacobean tragedy is irreversible. As such, it fails to guarantee relations between men, or between a man and further versions of himself.

Duke Brachiano's adulterous passion for Vittoria in Webster's *The White Devil* is at odds with, and disrupts, the 'alliance' with Monticelso and Francisco he has secured through his marriage to Isabella. This is a disruption with ominous consequences. Brachiano's desire takes the form of an unconditional attachment to a unique 'object', and so much so that he envisages some kind of utopian rearrangement of erotic and political priorities that is comparable to Edward II's repeated attempts to subordinate his political responsibilities as a king to his amorous bond with Gaveston:[14]

Brach. [G]overnment [shall not]
Divide me from you longer than a care
To keep you great: you shall to me at once
Be dukedom, health, wife, children, friends and all.
(I.ii.254–7)[15]

'[D]ukedom, health, wife, children, friends and all': this is also an appropriate description of what Marcelia is to Sforza in Philip Massinger's *The Duke of Milan*. Sforza's desire does not involve an adulterous object. It is entirely confined within the bounds of marriage. Nonetheless, in early modern terms, his immoderate passion for his wife breaches the 'unwritten law' that regulates the economy of male heterosexual desire in the period; a law, to borrow from Jonathan Dollimore, establishing that 'desire for [women] precludes identification [with them]'.[16] Put differently, Sforza exhibits those characteristics that are associated, within the play and in the culture at large, with effeminacy.[17] The Duke's following speech is a paradigmatic example of this effeminizing marital excess:

Sforza Such as are cloy'd with those they have embrac'd
May think their wooing done. No night to me
But is a bridal one, where Hymen lights
His torches fresh, and new; and those delights,
Which are not to be cloth'd in airy sounds,
Enjoyed, beget desires as full of heat,
And jovial fervour, as when first I tasted her virgin fruit.
(I.iii.41–8)[18]

If Brachiano's pledge erases his previous detour through Isabella, suspending public bonds of friendship with powerful men, and symbolically disowning his legitimate child Giovanni,[19] Sforza's detour through Marcelia is an endless repetition of a detour, *not* a means to an end but an end in itself: enjoyment only ever 'beget[s] desires'. The inappropriateness of Sforza's passionate attachment is enhanced by the fact that it is enunciated at the most critical of moments, as his dukedom is threatened by military invasion.[20] The celebrations for Marcelia's birthday – a birthday 'solemniz'd with all pomp, and ceremony' (I.i.100) – go ahead in spite of this military threat. This lays the duke open to charges of dotage and effeminacy. These charges are unfailingly levelled at him by his mother, sister and some of the courtiers. This is a birthday, Lord Tiberio observes, 'in which the duke is not his own, but her's' (I.i.101). He goes on to specify that 'every day, indeed, he is her creature, for never man so doted' (I.i.102–3).

However, the signs of the war between the French (the Duke's allies) and the Spanish do not fail to infiltrate these birthday celebrations, in the form of letters delivered at regular intervals. On receipt of one of them, Sforza throws the letter away, dismissing the post and embracing Marcelia:

Sforza Out of my sight!
And all thoughts that may strangle mirth forsake me ....
Though the foundation of the earth should shrink ...,
Supported thus, I'll stand upon the ruins,
And seek for new life here.

(I.iii.123–4; 125; 127–8)[21]

In a sense, the Duke wants to be an actor in a different kind of play. He longs for a transformation of his bond with Marcelia. He is seeking a 'new life' in her embrace, a new arrangement of bodies and identities. He is looking for a *dispositif* from within which his desire will no longer be seen as an effeminizing substitute for the more appropriate enactment of masculinity in the battlefield. Nonetheless, once the 'state affairs', 'deferr'd' for so long (I.iii.121), impose themselves upon him, the only transformation one witnesses is the metamorphosis of the trajectory desire–enjoyment–desire he has previously delineated – a trajectory that is seemingly devoid of anxiety – into an intense anxiety about the possession of the object of desire. This is an anxiety that Francisco, an Iago-like 'new man', is only too willing to exploit.[22] In the end, the integrity of the dukedom and the erotic bond with Marcelia turn out to be utterly incompatible. Sforza regains the former through a newly forged alliance with the victorious Spanish king, but loses the latter, and loses himself in the process.

In Middleton's *Women Beware Women*, the Duke, not unlike Brachiano, violates the law he is supposed to found and embody as a ruler. He falls in love – at first sight, as is invariably the case in Jacobean tragedies[23] – with the wife of one of his subjects: 'a creature', in the words of one of the courtiers, who is 'able to draw a state from serious business' (II.ii.17–18).[24] Significantly, and paradoxically, it is within the context of a ritual display of power (the Duke's procession through the streets of Florence *in state*) that this effeminizing and destructive desire surfaces, as the Duke, almost unperceived, catches a glimpse of Bianca, who is leaning from a window to admire 'such a solemn and most worthy custom' (I.iii.105).

Bianca suspects the Duke has looked up: 'Me-thought he saw us' (I.iii.106). Her mother-in-law reacts as follows:

> *Mother* That's everyone's conceit that sees a duke:
> If he look steadfastly, he looks straight at them –
> When he perhaps, good careful gentleman,
> Never minds any, but the look he casts
> Is at his own intentions, and his object
> Only the public good.
>
> (I.iii.107–12)

As Slavoj Žižek points out, to look at a thing straight on – in the play's own terms, to 'look steadfastly' at one's 'own intentions' – is to keep desire at bay. Conversely, to deflect one's gaze, however slightly, is to call into being the 'fatal' object of desire.[25] In the play the deflection of the gaze corresponds to the Duke's defection. To be more precise, the movement of desire this deflection triggers coincides with the Duke's turning away from 'the public good', as well from the idealized image of himself the gaze of his subjects and beholders mirrors back to him.

Therefore, the Duke's is *not* a 'love' that is 'like a good king, that keeps all in peace' (I.iii.48). Nor is it a 'love which is respective of increase' (I.iii.47). His desire is beyond the 'pleasure principle'.[26] It also inexorably marks its difference, to refer to a related argument by Catherine Belsey, from the 'conspicuous excess which puts ... courtly magnificence on display'.[27] In this latter sense, the masque (or anti-masque) that concludes the play, by confounding the lines of sight as well as the possibility of making sense of the events, brings to a climax the lethal discrepancy between desire's excess and the *meaningful*, if equally excessive, display of power the third scene of the first act initially dramatizes.[28]

In the early modern period, as Catherine Belsey points out, desire was in the process of being 'thoroughly contained and confined within the institution of marriage, and thus brought under the control of the Law (and the law)'. She continues: 'The project was to ground desire in true love, its moralized, domesticated version, based on partnership, companionship, the fitness of mind and disposition.'[29] The drama of the period plays a part in this attempt 'to differentiate increasingly systematically, increasingly solemnly, between love and lust, propriety and licence, natural and unnatural passion'; to implement, that is, a system of binary and hierarchical differences in which 'the privileged term becomes incorporated into the meaning of marriage'.[30] Yet, according to Belsey, in play after play desire regularly resurfaces to mark the precariousness and instability of any such attempt. Middleton's *Women Beware Women* can be read along these lines, as a play that exhibits the project to bring desire 'within the bounds of propriety and orthodoxy', but is unable to sustain it beyond the first act.[31] In effect, the Duke's excessive desire, which is indicative of an irreversible detour and loss of mastery, is not only destructive to his public role as a ruler – the only self he has – but also to the marital bond between Leantio and Bianca; a bond that is inflected by the emerging ideology of companionate marriages.[32] But, in an important sense, his desire successfully impinges upon this bond also because of the tensions that agitate the latter from its very inception.

Significantly, in Middleton's play the endeavour to confine and domesticate desire mostly comes from below, from the lower end of the social hierarchy, in the person of Leantio, a 'factor'.[33] The opening of the play shows Leantio, just returned from Venice with his 'most unvalued'st purchase' (that is, Bianca) (I.i.12), drawing the boundaries between love and lust, love and adultery, the fulfilment of desire and a desire that does not 'content' or has no 'content', and firmly situating himself on the side he sees as more conducive to the maintenance and strengthening of the marital bond:

Leantio Beauty able to content a conqueror,
Whom earth could scarce content, keeps me in compass;
I find no wish in me bent sinfully
To this man's sister, or to that man's wife:
In love's name let 'em keep their honesties,
And cleave to their own husbands, 'tis their duties.
Now when I go to church, I can pray handsomely;
Nor come like gallants only to see faces,
As if lust went to market still on Sundays.

(I.i.26–34)

This newly acquired bond marginalizes 'lust' but does not indiscriminately proscribe pleasure and desire, as shown by the following intimate and playful exchanges between Bianca and Leantio:

Bianca You have not bid me welcome since I came.
Leantio That I did, questionless.
Bianca No sure, how was't?
I have quite forgot it.
Leantio Thus. [*kisses her*]
Bianca Oh sir, 'tis true,
Now I remember well: I have done thee wrong,
Pray take't again, sir. [*kisses him*]
Leantio How many of these wrongs
Could I put up in an hour? and turn up the glass
For twice as many more.

(I.i.143–8)

Thus, pleasure and desire are not erased.[34] They are made 'proper' and consigned to the private space in which the new conjugal couple operates. This is a space that is apparently impermeable to anxieties of any kind. It is in this space that 'quiet innocent loves' find their 'shelter' (I.i.52) and come to fruition. The body through which the couple's sedate affection manifests itself is imagined as eminently prolific. It is clearly distinguishable from the unreproductive body of the privileged classes. This is how Leantio comments on the difference between these bodies:

Leantio Honest love ... knows no wants but, mocking poverty,
Brings forth more children, to make rich men wonder
At divine Providence, that feeds mouths of infants,
And sends them none to feed, but stuffs their rooms
With fruitful bags, their beds with barren wombs.

(I.i.95–100)[35]

The antithesis Leantio sets up may be a retrospective, anxious justification of his 'theft' (I.i.43) of Bianca.[36] It is almost as if Bianca *had* to be saved from a potentially 'barren' upper-class bed in order to become reproductive elsewhere – in a private place where she can 'enjoy all her desires' (I.i.126). In any case, this 'honest' and fruitful love inescapably bears the imprint of the disruption of the relations of alliance between men secured through a 'dynastic' marriage, a marriage Bianca was clearly destined for. In this sense, the retreat into domesticity as the proper locus of articulation of the erotic is simultaneously a choice, informed by self-restraint, *and* a *de facto* protection against this disruption:

Leantio From Venice her consent and I have brought her,
From parents great in wealth, more now in rage;
But let storms spend their furies. Now we have got
A shelter o'er our quite innocent loves,
We are contented.

(I.i.49–53)

'We are contented.' Nonetheless, the emergence of the companionate bond between Leantio and Bianca goes hand in hand with the appearance of Leantio's anxiety about the possession of what cannot but be called the *object* of his desire, variously defined as a 'purchase' (I.i.12), a 'treasure' (I.i.14), a 'piece of theft' (I.i.43), a 'jewel' (I.i.170), and so forth. Arguably, this anxiety far exceeds any external threat or *ex post facto* socially induced guilt about the 'theft' (I.i.43) of Bianca. It is intrinsic to the dynamics of a desire that presents itself as that which is present *to* itself – a desire knowing 'no wants' (I.i.96) – but is in fact structured from within by the anticipation of 'absence' (I.i.173). In the following speech Leantio evokes the spectre of 'absence', an absence that is necessitated by the attempt to fill the lack of a domestic unit that is 'full of wants' (I.i.120). He also depicts, in a way that is quite unusual for the drama of the period, recognizably modern forms of distribution of work and pleasure:

Leantio This day and night I'll know no other business
But her and her dear welcome. 'Tis a bitterness
To think upon tomorrow, that I must leave her
Still to the sweet hopes of the week's end.

That pleasure should be so restrained and curbed
After the course of a rich workmaster,
That never pays till Saturday night!

(I.i.153–9)

The precise and regular cadence of a restricted economy dictates its rhythms to the 'sweet hopes' of the conjugal couple. But, as Leantio's speech progresses, his regret about pleasure being 'so restrained and curbed' gives way to anxiety about Bianca's 'restraint':

Leantio The jewel is cased up from all men's eyes:
Who could imagine now a gem were kept,
Of that great value, under this plain roof?
But how in times of absence – what assurance
Of this restraint then?

(I.i.170–4)

'Absence' irremediably infiltrates presence and possession, and so much so that the relegation of pleasure and desire to a private realm begins actively to produce the anxiety it is designed to occlude. Evidently, Leantio's own 'assurance' to his mother that Bianca is 'contented / With all conditions that [his] fortunes bring her to' (I.i.88–9), and that she intends 'to keep close as a wife that loves her husband' (I.i.90), does nothing to reassure him. Likewise, Bianca's obliteration of her former self ('I have forsook friends, fortunes and my country; /And hourly I rejoice in't' [I.i.131–2]) and modest self-(re)fashioning do not seem to assuage Leantio's anxiety, even if they are unmistakably carried out in the name of a love that is unassailable and firmly based on 'content':[37]

Bianca Heaven send a quiet peace with this man's love,
And I am as rich as virtue can be poor –
Which were enough, after the rate of mind,
To erect temples for content placed here.

(I.i.127–30)

Foucault observes that the 'deployment of alliance' is 'attuned to a homeostasis of the social body, which it has the function of maintaining'.[38] Jacobean tragedy mostly dramatizes a 'lust' that, by undermining the marital tie or exceeding it from within, is 'like an insurrection in the people' (I.iii.44–5). This 'insurrection' often emanates from the centre of the body politic that should 'keep… all in peace' (I.iii.48). Indeed, as Franco Moretti argues, the very fact that even authoritative male figures irremediably succumb to the compulsive nature of desire makes the latter 'an agent of destruction in a social hierarchy based on the diametrically opposed principle of *inequality*'.[39] As mentioned earlier, in *Women Beware Women* the Duke's desire not only signifies the negation of the relations of alliance secured though marriage; it also violently marks the invasion of an emerging conjugal bond that is uneasily involved in the creation of an alternative *dispositif* of regulatory production of bodies and identities.

The Duke's 'invasion' takes the form of a rape, which brings about 'the most sudden'st, strangest alteration' (III.i.63) in the victim. According to the logic of the play, this is an invasion that erases Bianca's obliteration of her former identity. By the same token, it instigates the re-emergence of that unsatisfied desire which is ostensibly banned from the private realm of the conjugal couple: 'I laid open all defects to her; / She was contented still. But … nothing contents her now' (III.i.72–3).

Bianca's 'content' is by now elsewhere: 'I have had the best content Florence can afford' (III.i.121–2), she says, implicitly referring to the Duke.[40] In effect, from the point of view of the project of domestication of pleasure and desire, she becomes, at least momentarily, the 'stranger within'.[41] She starts thwarting Leantio's hopeful development of a 'love' that 'is respective of increase' (I.iii.47) and deferring *ad infinitum* his return to 'a happiness / That earth exceeds not' (III.i.82–3); a 'happiness' comfortably 'locked up in woman's love' (III.i.86) and symbolized by a series of concealed private spaces. Yet however demonized Bianca's 'alteration' may be in the first scene of the third act, her being 'in-between' – neither quite outside nor inside the private realm of the conjugal couple – enables her to lay bare some of the faultlines of the ideology of companionate marriage.[42] Especially significant is her reaction to Leantio's scheme to confine her to the most secret and inaccessible place of the house, which he contrives after the Duke sends for her. He intends to lock his 'life's best treasure up' (III.i.247) in the secluded place that was his father's 'sanctuary' (III.i.246) when sought for manslaughter. She retorts as follows:

Bianca Would you keep me closer yet?
Have you the conscience? Y'are best ev'n choke me up, sir!
You make me fearful of your health and wits,
You cleave to such wild courses.

(III.i.248–51)

In her rejoinder, Bianca exposes the final transformation of an idealized 'honest love … which knows no wants' (I.i.95–6) for what it is: a murderous fantasy of cancellation of the object as the most 'proper' way of securing absolute mastery over it, and assuaging that anxiety about possession repeatedly raised by less drastic forms of confinement.[43] One might go so far as to argue that the project of domestication of a desire that is 'beyond the pleasure principle' is uncannily subjected – maybe from its very outset – to the 'wild courses' of a desire that is itself 'beyond the pleasure principle'.

Bodily supplements: the clitoris as uncanny double

In the preceding section, I have analysed some of the vicissitudes of male heterosexual desire in Jacobean tragedy as examples of an immoderate and irreversible detour that exceeds from within the regulation of bodies and identities intrinsic to the 'deployment of alliance'. I have also considered this tragedy's emerging investment in the private world of the conjugal couple, with its sedate pleasures and desires, which also marks a departure from the 'deployment of alliance', but in the opposite direction to the one taken by the powerful aristocratic male figures of Jacobean tragedy.[44] I now want to return to the medical treatises with which I began, and suggest that even in these treatises the male detour through the body of the female is *not* an unproblematic and insignificant diversion, and not only when the 'instinct of lust or desire' instigating it is 'inordinate' and 'super-induced'. In Chapter 3, I have shown some examples of how this detour falls short of guaranteeing procreation and the re-creation of man's mirror images of himself; of how, moreover, it fails to secure the perpetuation of the 'constraining production' of the female body as a colder, less perfect and inverted version of that of the male, even when it (the detour) is part of a narrative of successful reproductive intercourse. In this section I want to focus on another type of diversion that equally conjures up the spectre of the impossibility of an unproblematic reproduction of the male self-same: the male detour through a body that is endowed with the clitoris anatomical science claims to have just discovered or rediscovered.[45]

One of the primary purposes of the construction of the female body as having a set of genitals analogous to those of its male counterpart is that of ensuring that man's difference *from* himself – his being 'transposed' or 'transport[ed]' out of himself or behind himself – by a detour *through* another 'himself' that eventually leads to the reproduction of the male self-same.[46] The passage through a body equipped with the newly discovered clitoris problematizes this re-articulation of the 'old dream of symmetry'.[47] This is mostly because the clitoris turns out to be a double too many, a less-than-reassuring uncanny double of the male penis that also stands side by side the penis duplicate woman is already alleged to bear within. In this section, therefore, I want to investigate the tenuous borders of anatomical and gynaecological discourse where masculine specul(ariz)ation is at its strongest *and* at its weakest, exceedingly powerful and intimately threatened. These are borders where the male body's radical exclusion of the other of *its* other fails to shun the possibility of the disruptive return of that which it excludes.

The first recorded use of the word 'clitoris' in English is to be found in Helkiah Crooke's *Microcosmographia*. 'Clitoris', the English anatomist writes, 'commeth of an obscoene worde signifying contrectation but properly it is called the womans yard'. He goes on to describe this part of female anatomy in great detail:

> It is a small production in the upper, forward and middle fatty part of the share [i.e. pubic bone], in the top of the greater cleft where the Nymphes [i.e. labia] doe meet, and is answerable to the member of man, from which it differs in length, the common passage and the want of a pair of muscles; but agrees in situation, substance and composition. For it consisteth of two nervous bodies … round without, hard and thick; but within spongy and porous, that when the spirits come into it, it may bee distended and grow loose when they are dissipated [;] these bodies, as those of the mans yarde, are full of blacke, thicke and sprighfull blood …. The head is properly called Tentigo by Juvenall, which is covered with a fine skin made of the conjunction of the Nymphae as it

> were with a fore-skinne. It hath an entrance but no through passage; there are vessells also running along the back of it as in a man's yarde.[48]

This passage dwells on both the similarities and dissimilarities between the clitoris and the penis. The former, however, is irresistibly drawn into the orbit of the latter. It is, after all, a 'yard'. In this sense, the passage seems to corroborate Laqueur's argument that Crooke, despite his repeated questioning of the Galenic model of introverted homology, speaks the only language he knows: the language of the one-sex body.[49] More specifically, his demonstration of 'how little likeness there is betwixt the neck of the womb [i.e. vagina] and the yard [i.e. penis], the bottom of it [i.e. the womb proper] and the cod [i.e. scrotum]', does not go so far as to affirm a radical incommensurability between male and female sexual organs.[50] Rather, Crooke implicitly seems to replace one organ with another as the closest analogue of the male penis.[51]

I shall return to Laqueur's interpretation. For the moment, I want to stress that in those texts that more explicitly abide by the Galenic model, the assertion of an essential isomorphism between the clitoris and the penis is juxtaposed to the description of the vagina as an inverted penis. In Jane Sharp's *The Midwives Book*, the vagina is not only 'the passage for the yard', but also that which 'resembleth it turned inward'. They are so much alike that they only 'differ like a pipe, and the case for it'.[52] Like in Crooke, the clitoris 'differs from the yard in length, the common pipe and the want of one pair of muscles … but is the same in place and substance'.[53] It is also susceptible to erection and detumescence in much the same way as the penis. It 'will stand and fall as the yard doth'.[54] If the clitoris is an erectile organ just like the penis, so is the vagina. According to *The Compleat Midwife's Practice Enlarged*, 'the action of the clitoris is like that of the yard, which is erection'. But it is also true that 'the action of the neck of the womb [i.e. vagina] is the same with that of the yard; that is to say, erection'.[55] Even in Crooke, who is sceptical of the Galenic homology, the *collum uteri* is described as 'more or less turgid, more open or more contracted & direct', depending on woman's sexual excitement.[56] Indeed, 'in women that are full of lust, or in the time of any womans appetite, it strutteth … and the Cavitie *growes very straight*'.[57] In a sense, Luce Irigaray's observations apropos the construction of femininity in psychoanalytic thought may be equally applied to these 'theories' of sexual difference:

> [W]oman's erogenous zones never amount to anything but a clitoris-sex that is not comparable to the noble phallic organ, or a hole-envelope that serves to sheathe and massage the penis in intercourse: a non-sex, or *a masculine organ turned back upon itself, self-embracing*.[58]

After Realdo Colombo's highly disputed 'discovery' of the clitoris, which he calls 'the love or sweetness of Venus',[59] anatomical and gynaecological texts increasingly invest in this 'miniature penis' as one of the most significant loci – or even *the* locus – of female sexual pleasure. This is simultaneously a proliferation of discourses on the body erotic of the female *and* a radical synecdochical reduction of its erotic power to a masculinized bodily part that comes to signify it *in toto*, and so much so that it becomes almost synonymous with this power.[60] Anatomical and gynaecological texts systematically reiterate Colombo's definition of this 'production' or 'protuberance' (*processus*)[61] as 'the principal seat of women's pleasure, when they engage in sexual intercourse [*venerem*]'.[62] For Crooke, the clitoris is 'the especiall seate of delight in [women's] veneral imbracements'.[63] *The Compleat Midwife's Practice Enlarged* describes it as 'the seat of venereal pleasure'.[64] Nicholas Venette calls it 'the fury and rage of love'. He continues: 'there Nature has placed the seat of pleasure and lust …; there it has placed those excessive ticklings, and there is lechery and lasciviousness established.'[65] Nicholas Culpeper stresses that the clitoris is 'that which causeth lust in women, and gives delight in copulation, for without this a woman neither desires copulation or hath pleasure in it, or conceives by it'.[66]

As this last passage from Culpeper suggests, another aspect of the 'contraction' of the body erotic, which is the reverse side of the discursive amplification surrounding the clitoris as an 'erogenous zone', is the attempt to reassert, through this bodily part, the customary contiguity of desire, pleasure and conception, and, with it, the dominant ideology of reproduction.[67] This is already in Colombo, who underlines that the rubbing of this excrescence – with one's penis or even with one's little finger[68] – gives rise to an overwhelming pleasure, and that this pleasure, in turn, 'causes their seed [that is, women's seed] to flow forth in all directions, swifter than the wind, even if they don't want it to'.[69] Helkiah Crooke describes with greater precision the reproductive function of the clitoris, showing how it governs that pleasurable emission of female seed that is essential to successful 'generation':

> The use of this part is the same with the bridle of the yard: because the testicles of the woman are far distant from the yard of the man, the imagination is carried to the spermatic vessels by the motion and attrition of this clitoris, together with the lower ligatures of the wombe whose originall toucheth, cleaveth and is tyed to the leading vessels of the seed, and so the profusion of their seed is stirred up for generation …: wherefore although by this passage their seed is not eiaculated, yet by the attrition of it their imagination is wrought to call that out that lyeth deeply hidden in the body.[70]

For the clitoris to 'stir up' the 'profusion' of female seed, Crooke specifies in the brief passage I omitted, 'it was not necessary it should be large'.[71] Arguably, Crooke's elucidation is related to the fact that, in late sixteenth- and seventeenth-century anatomical and gynaecological treatises, including his own, the *enlarged* clitoris is construed as a bodily supplement that tends to exceed reproductive and heterosexual framing.[72] As Valerie Traub points out, 'clitoral hypertrophy' increasingly comes to 'metonymize … women's supposedly inordinate capacity for pleasure', and especially the tribade's 'nonreproductive misuse of pleasure'.[73] For Crooke, the 'head' of the clitoris is 'but a small production hidden under the Nimphes and hard to be felt but with curiosity'. Yet, he continues,

> sometimes it groweth to such a length that it hangeth without the cleft like a man's member, especially when it is fretted with the touch of cloaths, and so

> strutteth and groweth to a rigidity as doth the yarde of a man. And this part it is which those wicked women doe abuse called Tribades (often mentioned by many authors, and in some states worthily punished) to their mutuall and unnaturall lustes.[74]

Thomas Bartholin expands on women's use and abuse of this part as follows:

> In some women [the clitoris] grows as big as the yard of a man: so that some women abuse the same, and make use thereof in place of a Mans Yard, exercising carnal copulation one with another, and they are termed Confricatrices [and] Rubsters.[75]

The late seventeenth-century English midwife Jane Sharp rephrases Crooke's passage, adding some observations on the national 'otherness' of these 'unnaturall' erotic practices (or making explicit what is only implicit in Crooke):[76]

> The head of this counterfeit yard … is but a small sprout, lying close hid under the wings, and not easily felt, yet sometimes it grows so long that it hangs forth at the slit like a yard, and will swell and stand stiff if it be provoked, and some lewd women have endeavoured to use it as men do theirs. In the Indies and Egypt they are frequent, but I never heard but of one in this country: if there be any, they will do what they can for shame to keep it close.[77]

Thomas Laqueur argues that 'the elaboration in medical literature … of a "new" female penis and specifically clitoral eroticism … was a re-presentation of the older homology of the vagina and the penis, not its antithesis'.[78] Relatedly, he observes that 'tribadism, women 'rubbing' one another …, [was] merely another variation of an old theme'.[79] In fact, doesn't medical literature present a female homoerotic scenario in which 'rubbing' is a 'rubbing' of penises? Moreover, isn't this 'rubbing' homologous to the 'friction of two like parts' that takes place in heterosexual intercourse, 'whether these be the male penis with the vagina or the clitoris'?[80] I shall argue, first of all, that if there is a 're-presentation of the older homology', it is prevalently in the sense of a reiteration that displaces and dislocates; secondly, that seventeenth-century writers do *not* remain 'undisturbed', as Laqueur maintains, 'by the clitoris's supposed dual function – licit pleasure in heterosexual intercourse and illicit pleasure in "tribadism"'.[81] On the one hand, as one moves from Realdo Colombo to Jane Sharp, woman's 'counterfeit yard' is still that which 'makes women lustful and take delight in copulation', causing 'the vessels to cast out that seed that lieth deep in the body'. It remains that body part that 'will stand and fall as the yard doth'.[82] On the other hand, this 'yard' seems to be increasingly unable to 'suffer erection' without extending beyond its 'proper' bounds and prompting women to desire to copulate with other women.[83] This is not merely a futile effort to imitate the 'real thing', to mimic, that is, the 'heterosexual thing'.[84] It is, rather, to borrow from a related argument by Jonathan Dollimore, a simultaneous appropriation, inversion and replacement of the privileged signifier of masculinity.[85] In other words, the clitoris, once enlarged, is so much *like* the male penis that it inexorably and threateningly turns into its uncanny double. It begins to proliferate outside heterosexual and reproductive scenarios, becoming part of a process of supplementarity that problematizes definite distinctions between the 'original' and the 'copy' and puts under erasure any proper return to the 'real heterosexual thing'. In this respect, my interpretation parallels Valerie Traub's. She evokes the 'Derridean instrument' of the supplement to suggest that 'early modern women's prosthetic supplementation of their bodies is … both additive and substitutive'. It is 'a material addition to the woman's body and … a replacement of the man's body *by* the woman's' that not only 'displaces male prerogatives, but exposes "man" as a simulacrum and gender as a construction built on the faulty ground of exclusive, binary difference'.[86]

I want to re-emphasize some of these points by looking more closely at Bartholin's discussion of the 'woman's yard or prick'.[87] I shall start by comparing it to Colombo's. For the latter, the swelling of this organ exclusively takes place within the boundaries of a 'heterosexual' scenario – or, at least, of a scenario in which the clitoris is a reassuring double of the penis:

> If you touch that part of the uterus while women are eager for sex and very excited as if in a frenzy and aroused to lust [and] they are eager for a man, you will find it a little harder and oblong to such a degree that it shows itself a sort of male member.[88]

Furthermore, as shown earlier, the friction of the clitoris during heterosexual intercourse is eminently pleasurable and reproductive, and so much so that it causes women to release their seed even if they are not willing to do so. Bartholin, instead, even as he cites Colombo's definition of the clitoris, confines the ejaculation of female seed to *specific* circumstances. He thus cuts down to size, as it were, the reproductive role of the clitoris: '[The clitoris is] the chief Seat of Delight in carnal copulation: which if it be gently touched *in such as have long abstained from carnal embracements, and are desirous thereof*, seed easily comes away.'[89] Moreover, he obsessively returns to the potentially excessive endowment of women's bodies, which allows or encourages them to engage in nonreproductive erotic practices.[90] After the passage already cited, in which he highlights the 'abuse' of the clitoris and the replacement of the original by the copy,[91] he continues as follows:

> Its Size is commonly small; it lies hid for the most part under the Nymphs in its beginning, and afterward it sticks out a little. For in Lasses that begin to be amorous, the Clitoris does first discover itself. It is in several persons greater or lesser: in some it hangs out like a mans Yard, namely when young Wenches do frequently and continually handle and rub the same, as Examples testifie. But that it should grow as big as a Gooses neck, as Platerus relates of one, is altogether praeternatural and monstruos. Tulpius hath a like Story of one that had it so long as half a mans finger, and as thick as a boys Prick, which made her willing to do with Women in a carnal way. But the more this part encreases,

> the more does it hinder a man in his business. For in the time of copulation it swells like a mans Yard, and being erected, provokes to Lust.[92]

There are several elements in this excerpt that are worth underlining. First, the enlarged clitoris, as distinct from its 'heterosexualized' counterpart, is simultaneously effect and cause of nonreproductive erotic practices, ranging from masturbation to tribadism. Second, its difference from the clitoris that 'lies hid' or 'sticks out a little' is not simply one of size. Its size is the objective anatomical correlative of a desire that is *actively* pursued. By contrast, its heterosexualized counterpart 'lies hid' to then 'discover itself'. This is a coming into visibility that occurs almost automatically, quite independently from the 'subject' of desire (the 'Lasses that begin to be amorous'). Third, and most importantly for my argument here, the enlarged clitoris comes back to haunt the heterosexual scenario it marks its difference from, reappearing as that 'part' that menacingly stands in between man's desire and its realization: 'But the more this part encreases, the more does it hinder a man in his business'. As such, it infuses this scenario with the fear that the 'sex' that sets itself up as the 'original' – 'sex' both in the sense of masculine organ and sexual practice – may be nothing but a rather inadequate copy of its copy.[93] In this sense, Bartholin's addendum, which intriguingly takes the form of an explanation ('For in the time of copulation [the clitoris] swells like a mans Yard, and being erected, provokes to Lust'), is *less* a reaffirmation of the original, or a recasting of the enlarged clitoris as the proper counterpart of the penis within a heterosexual context, *than* an anxious attempt to evade the threat posed to heterosexual 'sex' by the repeated appearance of the clitoris qua *uncanny* double of the penis. Indeed, the 'swelling' of the clitoris, as numerous treatises including Bartholin's illustrate, does *not* unproblematically 'provoke ... to [heterosexual] Lust'. It does not guarantee a desire for a 'proper' heterosexual object. This anxiety may also help to explain why Bartholin proceeds with his description of the clitoris by making a distinction between its 'outmost end or Head', which is 'sticking out like the nut of a mans yard', and 'the rest', which is 'lying hid'.[94] One may suggest that the fact that part of the clitoris erects but 'the rest' does *not* offers some kind of fetishistic solution to the anxiety raised by the implicit *and* explicit acknowledgement that there is an inextricable link between the swelling of the clitoris and nonreproductive erotic practices.[95]

Thus, the prominence early modern medical literature gives to the clitoris is highly ambiguous. Indeed, much of this ambiguity has to do with the clitoris's 'prominence', with the ever-present possibility of it growing beyond its heterosexual and reproductive limits and turning into, or returning as, an uncanny double of the 'sex which is one'. As suggested earlier, the investment in the clitoris is not simply a celebration of female sexual pleasure and desire. It is coterminous with, or even predicated upon, a number of assumptions and restrictions: the clitoris, as an erogenous *part*, is an adequate stand-in for the whole; it is the woman's *yard*; it is a *reproductive* organ. During the course of the seventeenth century, whilst these assumptions and restrictions remain, the clitoris also becomes one of the sites of a further, intense problematization of the meanings of the 'body erotic'. In Valerie Traub's words, it is increasingly subjected to the 'growing cultural pressure to differentiate between legitimate and illegitimate desire'. This is a 'pressure', she adds, that is 'in part a function of an intensifying investment in the [legitimate] desire of the conjugal couple'.[96] In the light of these remarks, it comes as no surprise that a text such as Nicholas Venette's *Tableau de l'amour conjugal*, which was written in a period intensely marked by this investment, describes 'the pleasures of the wedlock' as 'something divine, when not passing the bounds of right reason'.[97] This is a text that also construes the bodily part standing for 'illegitimate' pleasures as extending well beyond these 'bounds' – exceeding, in effect, that which other medical texts see as excess:

> This part lascivious women abuse. The *lesbian Sappho* would never have acquired such indifferent reputation, if this part of her's had been less. I have seen a girl eight years of age, that had already the *clitoris* as long as one's little finger; and if this part grows with age, as it is probable it may, I am persuaded it is now as long as that of the woman mentioned by Platerus, who had one as big as the neck of a goose.[98]

Therefore, one witnesses the emergence of a process of 'regulatory production' of the clitoris, as well as of the pleasures and desires it embodies, which re-marks an already problematic investment. As shown in relation to the emblematic case of *Bartholinus Anatomy*, this process is continually haunted by the spectre of the return of that which it marginalizes, and so much so that it articulates, in spite of itself, the untenability of the distinctions it draws, *even as* it draws them. It is worth adding that if this spectre induces anxiety, this anxiety easily turns into an active, if displaced, will to punish and correct. Hence, the appearance of an exoticized fantasy, or even of practical advice, regarding the excision of that part which symptomatizes a body erotic increasing beyond its 'proper' bounds: sometimes of the enlarged clitoris, sometimes of the extended 'nymphae' or 'wings', sometimes of both.[99] Helkiah Crooke states that the 'nymphae', like the upper part of the clitoris, can 'grow to such a length on one side, more rarely on both; and not so ordinarly in maidens as in women'. The cause is either 'the affluence of humours' or 'attrectaction'. He continues:

> [F]or the trouble and shame ... they neede the Chirurgions to cut them off (although they bleed much and are hardly cicatrised) especially among the Egyptians, amongst whom this accident (as Galen saith) is very familiar. Wherefore in Maidens before they grow too long they cut them off, and before they marry.[100]

Jane Sharpe specifies that it is 'not only the clitoris that lieth behind the wings [i.e. labia], but the wings also' that sometimes 'hang forth at [women's] privities'.[101] She then sets up a fantasmatic scenario of excision that follows Crooke's very closely. Venette classifies the enlarged clitoris and labia amongst the 'many infirmities incident to a woman's privy parts, that hinder the consummation of marriage, and consequently generation', without explicitly 'othering' these 'infirmities'.[102] If the clitoris, he argues, 'in some … swells to such a bigness, as to prevent the entrance of the yard', the labia are at times 'so long and flouting, that there is a necessity of cutting them in maids before they marry'.[103] In the section dedicated to the clitoris, the authors of *The Compleat Midwife's Practice Enlarged* assert that this organ can 'grow out of the body the breadth of four fingers'.[104] They use the word 'tentigo'[105] to describe the 'disease of the neck of the womb' that occurs when 'the clitoris increases to an over-great measure', recommending as a remedy a 'diet' or 'taking away the excrescence'.[106]

A 'jouissance en plus'

'La jouissance, c'est ce qui ne sert à rien'.[107] Citing in passing this concise statement by the French psychoanalyst Jacques Lacan, Thomas Laqueur argues that depictions of *jouissance* such as Lacan's are 'a distinctly modern possibility'.[108] They only make sense, that is, within 'our' horizontal model of incommensurability and biological divergence between the sexes. This is a model that has replaced the age-old hierarchical and teleological arrangement of bodies Laqueur chooses to call the 'one-sex/flesh body', and, with it, the close link it established between female sexual pleasure and 'generation'. My analysis suggests, instead, that Lacan's point about the 'uselessness' of *jouissance* is relevant to an understanding of early modern medical treatises' articulations of female sexual pleasure and desire, and especially of their fraught investment in the clitoris as the 'seat' of this pleasure and desire. These treatises, to rephrase part of my analysis in Lacanian terms, are informed by the tension between a *jouissance* that is profitable, useful and governed by the necessity of inscription (that is, a *jouissance* Lacan defines as 'phallic') and a *jouissance en plus*, a *jouissance* in excess that, from the point of view of the Law and its restricted economy, is unprofitable and meaningless.[109] They also obliquely show how easy it is for one to tip over into the other. As suggested earlier, the reiteration of the homology between the penis and the clitoris, as well as of the reproductive pleasures they afford, is in fact a re-marking that 'dis-places'. It inadvertently but irresistibly brings into being something more, something *en plus*, both literally and metaphorically – in Lacanian terms, a *supplementary jouissance* that is neither beyond the phallus nor entirely centred around it.[110] I have added that, from the point of view of the male *imaginaire* informing these treatises, this re-marking coincides with a 'dis-figuring' of the reflection of like to like, which complicates the heterosexual detour of male homosocial desire and raises the spectre of the impossibility of any proper return to the (male) self-same.

Jacobean tragedy, too, as I have shown, continually raises this spectre. The plays I have referred to dramatize detours through the female body that are 'beyond the pleasure principle'. They irremediably defer homosocial satisfaction, and undermine the ordering of bodies and identities inhering in the *dispositif* of alliance. Marking a non-reproductive surplus, these detours exceed the attempts at closure that are regularly enunciated at the end of the plays; attempts that are the prerogative of discursive positions whose authority is directly proportional to the absence or renunciation of desire (for example, the Cardinal in *Women Beware Women*, Duke Brachiano's young son in *The White Devil*, the Marquis of Pescara in *The Duke of Milan*). These irreversible diversions are also countered, and equally ineffectively, by an emerging project of domestication of pleasure and desire insisting on a 'love' that is 'respective of increase', prolific and confined to private spaces. In this sense, Jacobean tragedy is a cultural form that predominantly revolves around the gap between lack and excess, but is also infiltrated, however marginally, by a project aimed at reaching a formation of compromise between the two. This is a project, however, that does not cease *not* fully inscribing itself.

Notes

Introduction

1 Keir Elam, '"In What Chapter of His Bosom?": Reading Shakespeare's Bodies', in Terence Hawkes (ed.), *Alternative Shakespeares: Vol. 2* (London and New York: Routledge, 1996), pp. 140–63 (p. 143). For an earlier account of the renewed interest in the early modern body, see Dympna Callaghan, '"And All Is Semblative a Woman's Part": Body Politics and *Twelfth Night*', *Textual Practice*, 7, 3 (1993), 428–52. For an analysis of the explosion of body criticism in various academic disciplines and contemporary popular culture, which also provides a useful historicization of the concept of the body, see Caroline Bynum, 'Why All the Fuss about the Body? A Medievalist's Perspective', *Critical Inquiry*, 22 (1995), 1–33. Domna C. Stanton calls this explosion 'bodyology'. See her 'Introduction: The Subject of Sexuality', in Domna C. Stanton (ed.), *Discourses of Sexuality: From Aristotle to Aids* (Ann Arbor: The University of Michigan Press, 1992), pp. 1–46.

2 References are, respectively, to Francis Barker, *The Tremulous Private Body: Essays on Subjection* (London and New York: Methuen, 1984); Thomas Laqueur, 'Orgasm, Generation, and the Politics of Reproductive Biology', *Representations*, 14 (1986), 1–41, Thomas Laqueur, *Making Sex: Body and Gender From the Greeks To Freud* (Cambridge MA, and London: Harvard University Press, 1990) and Stephen Greenblatt, 'Fiction and Friction', in *Shakespearean Negotiations: The Circulation of Social Energy in Renaissance England* (Oxford: Clarendon Press, 1988), pp. 66–93; Peter Stallybrass, 'Patriarchal Territories: The Body Enclosed', in Margaret W. Ferguson, Maureen Quilligan and Nancy J. Vickers (eds), *Rewriting the Renaissance: The Discourses of Sexual Difference in Early Modern Europe* (Chicago and London: Chicago University Press, 1986), pp. 123–42; Frank Whigham, 'Reading Social Conflict in the Alimentary Tract: More on the Body in Renaissance Drama', *English Literary History*, 55, 2 (1988), 333–50; Peter Stallybrass, 'Reading the Body: *The Revenger's Tragedy* and the Jacobean Theater of Consumption', *Renaissance Drama*, 18 (1987), 121–48; Peter Stallybrass and Allon White, *The Politics and Poetics of Transgression* (London: Methuen, 1986); Laura Levine, *Men in Women's Clothing: Anti-theatricality and Effeminization 1579–1642* (Cambridge: Cambridge University Press, 1994); Gail Kern Paster, *The Body Embarrassed: Drama and the Disciplines of Shame in Early Modern England* (Ithaca and New York: Cornell University Press, 1993); Jonathan Goldberg, *Sodometries: Renaissance Texts, Modern Sexualities* (Stanford CA: Stanford University Press, 1992); Jonathan Sawday, *The Body Emblazoned: Dissection and the Human Body in Renaissance Culture* (London and New York: Routledge, 1995); Keir Elam, 'The Fertile Eunuch: *Twelfth Night*, Early Modern Intercourse and the Fruits of Castration', *Shakespeare Quarterly*, 47, 1 (1996), 1–36; David Hillman and Carla Mazzio (eds), *The Body in Parts: Fantasies of Corporeality in Early Modern Europe* (New York and London: Routledge, 1997). I add to the list this last text, published after Elam's article.

3 Elam, '"In What Chapter of His Bosom?"', p. 14.

4 Barker, *The Tremulous Private Body*, p. 13.
5 Ibid., p. 12.
6 Friedrich Nietzsche, *On the Genealogy of Morals and Ecce Homo*, trans. by Walter Kaufmann (New York: Vintage Books, 1989), p. 80.
7 Ibid., pp. 77–8.
8 Judith Butler, *Gender Trouble: Feminism and the Subversion of Identity* (London and New York: Routledge, 1990), p. 7.
9 Laqueur, *Making Sex*, pp. 5–6.
10 Ibid., p. 8. Ann Rosalind Jones and Peter Stallybrass also argue that 'in the Renaissance there was no privileged discourse (as biology was to become in the nineteenth century) that could even *claim* to establish a definitive method by which one distinguished male from female' ('Fetishizing Gender: Constructing the Hermaphrodite in Renaissance Europe', in Julia Epstein and Kristina Straub [eds], *Body Guards: The Cultural Politics of Gender Ambiguity* [London and New York: Routledge, 1991], p. 80). According to this study, the ensuing Renaissance paradox is that 'one of the main grounds for the distribution of political and legal power … could not itself be grounded' (Ibid., p. 104); and that hermaphroditism was, in a sense, the 'bodily norm'. In other words, gender dichotomy had to be *produced* by a variety of complex, often contradictory, discourses. Yet Jones and Stallybrass also put forward the more general hypothesis that gender is always a production. The 'phantasized biology of the "real"' of post-Renaissance reproductive biology is nothing but a disavowal of this fact (Ibid., p. 106). Phyllis Rackin also pursues the line of investigation opened up by Laqueur by arguing that 'the reason we cannot locate gender difference in Renaissance accounts of the body is that the body itself – male as well as female – was gendered feminine' and subordinated to a 'masculine' soul/spirit; and that 'the reason we cannot find [gender difference] in medical texts is that the distinctions that separated men and women, like those that separated aristocrats from commoners, were grounded not in the relatively marginal discourse of the new biological science but in the older and traditionally privileged discourses of theology and history' ('Historical Difference/Sexual Difference', in Jean R. Brink [ed.], *Privileging Gender in Early Modern England: Sixteenth Century Essays & Studies Vol. XXIII* [Ann Arbor: Michigan University Press, 1993], p. 39.)
11 See also Laqueur, *Making Sex*, pp. 61–2.
12 Ibid., p. 11.
13 Ibid., p. 15.
14 Ibid., p. 12.
15 *Hamlet* is quoted from The Arden Edition, ed. Harold Jenkins (London: Methuen, 1982).
16 Laqueur, *Making Sex*, p. 23.
17 For a critique of Laqueur's approach, see Katharine Park and Robert A. Nye, 'Destiny Is Anatomy', *The New Republic*, 18 February 1991, pp. 53–7. They argue that Laqueur's one-sex model is 'a hybrid of individual and sometimes mutually contradictory features assembled from the two dominant and fundamentally incompatible traditions of early writing on the subject, the Aristotelian and the Hippocratic/Galenic' (p. 54). See also Paster, *The Body Embarrassed*, especially pp. 78–84, where she challenges Laqueur's argument on the interchangeability of male and female bodily fluids; and pp. 166–84, where she questions his optimistic reading of early modern attitudes towards the female body's role in reproduction. Valerie Traub disputes Laqueur's 'reliance on texts that inscribe the dominant ideology, which leads to his own (re)inscription of a hegemonic medical model', especially in relation to early modern constructions of the clitoris and same-gender female eroticism. See Valerie Traub, 'The Psychomorphology of the Clitoris', *GLQ: A Journal of Lesbian and Gay Studies* (Special issue: *Pink Freud*, ed. Diana Fuss), 2, 1–2 (1995), 81–113 (p. 84).
18 I use 'supplementary' in a Derridean sense. See Jacques Derrida, *Of Grammatology*, trans. by Gayatri Chakravorty Spivak (Baltimore and London: The Johns Hopkins University Press, 1976), pp. 141–64. The 'sex which is one' is an allusion to Luce

Irigaray, *This Sex Which Is Not One*, trans. by Catherine Porter (Ithaca and New York: Cornell University Press, 1985), esp. pp. 23–33.

19 The reference is to Raymond Williams, *Marxism and Literature* (Oxford: Oxford University Press, 1977), pp. 121–7. Laqueur does not deny that there are heterogeneous and/or incompatible representations of the body in pre-Enlightenment texts. Yet, to Laqueur, the body can 'register and absorb any number of shifts in the axes and valuations of difference' because it is 'construed as illustrative rather than determinant' (*Making Sex*, p. 62). On the one hand, therefore, the body is marked by a certain unfixity and malleability. It has not yet been reduced to one of its parts – 'sex' – to posture as the indubitable and biological foundation for a rigidly dichotomized regime of gender. On the other, it is nothing but a function of 'cultural truths purer and more fundamental than biological fact' (Ibid., p. 55). It endlessly represents and upholds the more stable, extra-textual and 'extracorporeal reality' (Ibid., p. 35) of patriarchal culture and institutions; a 'reality' that makes it redundant and supplementary. In other words, the reverse side of the unfixity and malleability of the body is a monologic, incontrovertible and largely de-historicized socio-political 'truth' of patriarchy that remains unchanged from Hippocrates to Rousseau.

20 Patricia Parker, 'Gender Ideology, Gender Change: The Case of Marie Germain', *Critical Inquiry*, 19 (1993), 337–64 (p. 340). Patricia Parker's essay focuses on early modern narratives of gender transformations. She objects to Laqueur's indiscriminate repetition of some medical authorities' claim that these transformations are only ever unidirectional, from the less perfect female to the more perfect male. See Laqueur, 'Orgasm, Generation, and the Politics of Reproductive Biology', p. 13; and Laqueur, *Making Sex*, p. 127.

21 Laqueur, *Making Sex*, p. 12; p. 14.

22 See Judith Butler, *Bodies That Matter: On the Discursive Limits of 'Sex'* (London and New York: Routledge, 1993), pp. 10–11.

23 Ibid., p. 8.

24 Nineteenth-century discourses on homosexuality, as described by Michel Foucault, exemplify this process. For Foucault, these discourses 'made possible a strong advance of social control into this area of "perversity".' Yet, they also 'made possible the formation of a "reverse" discourse: homosexuality began to speak in its own behalf, to demand that its legitimacy or "naturality" be acknowledged, often in the same vocabulary, using the same categories by which it was medically disqualified.' (*The History of Sexuality: An Introduction*, trans. by Robert Hurley [Harmondsworth: Penguin Books, 1981], p.101.) More generally, it can be argued that, for Foucault, 'points of resistance' are neither fully outside nor totally inside the power network. They are 'the *odd* term … inscribed *in* [relations of power] as an irreducible *opposite*' (Ibid., p. 96) (emphasis mine). It is only within the logic of the Law and juridical power that one can speak of an inside and an outside that are clearly demarcated from one another. What Foucault calls 'the strictly relational character of power relationships' is a displacement of this logic (Ibid., p. 95).

25 Butler, *Bodies That Matter*, p. 34.

26 Ibid., p. 9.

27 Ibid., p. 35. Of course, this domain remains 'dematerialized' from the point of view of the bodies that matter and their enforceable forms and norms.

28 Ibid., p. 16.

29 Ibid.

30 In 'Sexual Inversions' Judith Butler offers an extraordinarily perceptive re-reading of Foucault's *The History of Sexuality: An Introduction*. Without denying that sexuality is a historical construct, she casts doubts upon the historical shift from juridical power (that is, the repressive law saying no to 'sex') to productive power (that is, the power producing the object it disciplines). She persuasively argues that there is no prohibition that is not, at one and the same time, a production; and, conversely, no production that is not, simultaneously, a prohibition. As she puts it, there is only 'a production that is *at the same time* constraint', a 'constraining production' ('Sexual Inversions', in Domna C. Stanton

[ed.], *Discourses of Sexuality: From Aristotle to Aids* [Ann Arbor: The University of Michigan Press, 1992], pp. 344–61 [p. 350].) Regulation and production are thus internal to the functioning of power. They are not opposing features of two historically distinct regimes. In a sense, Foucault seems to be saying as much. It is the advent of the 'identitarian' category of sex that brings about a fundamental reversal in the relationship of power to sexuality. ('Sex' is here conceived as the 'imaginary point' that operates by making the biological, the anatomical, the sexual and the psychic into mutually reinforcing entities. Qua 'fictitious unity', it postures as 'a causal principle, an omnipresent meaning' one has to submit to in order to gain access to one's intelligibility, body and identity. See Foucault, *The History of Sexuality: An Introduction*, pp. 154–5.) It is the emergence of 'sex' that causes sexuality to be reduced to an 'irreducible urgency which power tries as best it can to dominate' (Ibid., 155). It is 'sex', moreover, that 'makes it possible to evade what gives "power" its power; *it enables one to conceive power solely as law and taboo*' (Ibid.) (emphasis mine). Law and taboo are thus produced *within* and *by* the *dispositif* of sexuality as the latter's imaginary outside, as modalities of juridical power that, by saying no to 'sex', conceal the proliferation of power/sexuality. And yet, at the same time, law and taboo, as well as the cognate problematics of the permitted, the forbidden and transgression, are seen by Foucault as historically distinct from, and in a position of exteriority in relation to, the *dispositif* of sexuality, in that they are pivotal to the organization and regulation of relations of 'sex' in what he calls the deployment of alliance (Ibid., pp. 106–7; 147–8). The relation of mutual exclusion *and* mutual implication between juridical and productive power – and the corresponding historico-sexual regimes – undoubtedly raises a number of more general questions concerning the axiomatic of history in Foucault's *The History of Sexuality*. I would group these questions under the heading of 'haunting', a 'dis-figured' spectral figure Jacques Derrida has recently evoked, in the context of a discussion of the position of Freud and psychoanalysis in Foucault's *Madness and Civilization*, to underline what 'threatens the logic that distinguishes between one thing and the other, the very logic of exclusion or foreclosure, as well as the history that is founded upon this logic and its alternatives' ('"To Do Justice to Freud": The History of Madness in the Age of Psychoanalysis', trans. by Pascale-Anne Brault and Michael Naas, *Critical Inquiry*, 20 [1994], 227–66 [p. 242]). To Derrida, the figure of haunting calls for another logic of history, beyond the reassuring notions of *episteme*, age, epoch and paradigm. The following pages are haunted by the question of haunting. Yet, they do not constitute a decisive break with the logic of 'epistemic breaks'. Nonetheless, in the sections of the book in which I develop arguments concerning the body erotic, I problematize the historical narrative Foucault presents in *The History of Sexuality: An Introduction*. I suggest, especially in the first and fifth chapters, that the 'symbolics of blood' and the 'deployment of alliance' do not fully inform early modern texts; that these texts at times dramatize the emergence of something *like* the sedate heterosexualized pleasures of the conjugal couple, as well as of an 'anatomical essentialism' through which some pleasures are legitimated and others abjected. For a more 'deconstructive' reading of Foucault's *History of Sexuality*, which mostly deals with early modern material, see Jonathan Goldberg's (dis)seminal *Sodometries*. Goldberg's study oscillates 'between the recognition that the Renaissance does not distinguish two forms of sexuality as if they were totally distinct' and a sense of 'the precariousness of the present aegises which declare that impermeable boundary now to be in effect' (Ibid., p. 22). It shows alertness to the difficulty in using, in relation to the early modern period, 'categorical terms' such as male and female, masculinity and femininity, heterosexuality and homosexuality. Indeed, these categories are not 'ontologically pregiven' but, rather, 'in the process of a deconstitutive construction' (Ibid., p. 129). 'Deconstitutive construction' is an expression that accentuates the divisibility of the partition between different sexual regimes and marks the remainder at the centre of dominant constructions then and now. However, to Goldberg, the historically problematic status of these 'categorical terms' does not preclude but *calls for* an investigation of 'how relations between men (or between women or between men and women) in the [early modern] period provide the sites upon which later sexual orders and later sexual identities could batten' (Ibid., p. 22).

31 Elam, '"In What Chapter of His Bosom?"', p. 143. This is not to imply that the critical works mentioned by Elam, unlike mine, can be categorized in this way.

32 Ibid.

33 The 'ex-timate object' is neither interior nor exterior. As Mladen Dolar points out, it is 'located there where the most intimate interiority coincides with the exterior and becomes threatening, provoking horror and anxiety'. It is simultaneously 'the intimate kernel and the foreign body' ('"I Shall Be with You on Your Wedding Night": Lacan and the Uncanny', *October*, 58 [1991], 5–23 [p. 6]). Lacan relates this *extimité*, this 'intimate exteriority', to the – Maternal – Thing. In *The Ethics of Psychoanalysis* he argues: '*das Ding* is at the center only in the sense that it is excluded. That is to say, in reality *das Ding* has to be posited as exterior …, in the form of something *entfremdet*, something strange to me, although it is at the heart of me.' (Jacques Lacan, *The Seminar of Jacques Lacan. Book VII: The Ethics of Psychoanalysis 1959–60*, trans. by Dennis Porter [New York and London: W.W. Norton, 1992], p. 71.) For a suggestive reinterpretation of the Lacanian Real/Thing, see Slavoj Žižek, *The Sublime Object of Ideology* (London and New York: Verso, 1989). Žižek also provides an interesting account of the shifts in Lacan's thinking on these matters. See esp. pp. 169–99 and pp. 131–6.

34 Jacques Derrida, *The Post Card: From Socrates to Freud and Beyond*, trans. by Alan Bass (Chicago: The University of Chicago Press, 1987), p. 263.

35 For the notion of cryptic incorporation, see Jacques Derrida, 'Fors', trans. by Barbara Johnson, *The Georgia Review*, 31, 1 (1977), 64–116.

36 As he discusses Desdemona's subject positions in *Othello*, Jonathan Dollimore argues: 'Because the subordinate is so often the subject of displacement there is never safety in obedience' (*Sexual Dissidence: Augustine to Wilde, Freud to Foucault* [Oxford: Clarendon Press, 1991], p. 161.)

37 To Laqueur, there is a strict correlation between the 'nature' of the body and the 'nature' of society. Culture is essentially a second nature, which produces circular arguments such as: 'In a public world that was overwhelmingly male, the one-sex model displayed what was already massively evident in culture more generally: *man* is the measure of all things' (*Making Sex*, p. 62).

38 Leonard Tennenhouse, *Power On Display. The Politics of Shakespeare's Genres* (London and New York: Methuen, 1986), p. 118. See also his 'Violence Done to Women on the Renaissance Stage', in Nancy Armstrong and Leonard Tennenhouse (eds), *The Violence of Representation: Literature and the History of Violence* (London and New York: Routledge, 1989), pp. 77–97.

39 Following Foucault's idea that in the old regime 'power spoke *through* blood' (*The History of Sexuality: An Introduction*, p. 147), Tennenhouse argues that blood is symbolically and historically more important than gender and sexuality in marking and determining difference within the social body. Within this perspective, the aristocratic female's gender and sexual transgressions inevitably 'represent … [the] loss of political boundaries', the blurring of the distinction between 'what belongs to the body politic … [and] what must be kept outside' (Tennenhouse, *Power On Display*, p. 120). In fact, they only ever *represent*. They stand for, and are subsumed into, something else. According to Ania Loomba, Tennenhouse's interpretation amounts to an erasure of the *specific* threat posed by female sexuality to the mechanisms governing the unequal apportionment of power in the early modern period. She observes that in Jacobean drama 'active female sexuality … directly threatens the power base of patriarchy which is dependent upon its regulation and control'. She adds that this sexuality is 'disruptive of patriarchal control not just because it is an emblem for, or analogous to, other sorts of rebellion' (*Gender, Race, Renaissance Drama* [Manchester and New York: Manchester University Press, 1989], p. 56). One must clarify that Loomba does not argue that female (hetero)sexuality in Jacobean drama can be read in isolation from other categories. She only points out that the intricate interweaving of axes of domination

such as class, gender, race and sexuality can be reduced neither to a homology nor to a univocal and *unidirectional* articulation of one through the other.

40 See Barbara Maria Stafford, *Body Criticism: Imagining the Unseen in Enlightenment Art and Medicine* (Cambridge MA: MIT Press, 1991).

41 That internal divisions split the dominant even before pollution takes place is never seriously considered by Tennenhouse. His picture of Jacobean society is oddly harmonic, as is also made clear by his uncritical appropriation of Mary Douglas's argument that 'pollution is a type of danger which is not likely to occur except where the lines of structure, cosmic or social, are clearly defined' (*Purity and Danger: An Analysis of the Concepts of Pollution and Taboo* [London and New York: Routledge, 1991], p. 113, cited in Tennenhouse, *Power On Display*, p. 117).

42 For the recent critical interest in these discourses, see especially Daniel J. Viktus, 'Turning Turk in *Othello*: The Conversion and Damnation of the Moor', *Shakespeare Quarterly*, 48, 2 (1997), 145–76; Nabil Matar, *Turks, Moors, and Englishmen in the Age of Discovery* (New York: Columbia University Press, 1999); Lisa Jardine and Jerry Brotton, *Global Interests: Renaissance Art Between East and West* (London: Reaktion Books, 2000); Jerry Brotton, *The Renaissance Bazaar: From the Silk Road to Michelangelo* (Oxford: Oxford University Press, 2003); Gerald MacLean, *Rise of Oriental Travel. English Visitors to the Ottoman Empire, 1580–1720* (Houndsmill and New York: Palgrave, 2004).

43 I am using the expression *pater familias* in connection with the king because, to Tennenhouse, the 'parallel between the husband–wife relationship and that of the sovereign and subject' is the *explanandum* of *all* the gender relations dramatized in Jacobean tragedies (Ibid., p. 121). See also Loomba, *Gender, Race, Renaissance Drama*, p. 56.

44 For Barker, 'that the body we see [in Jacobean tragedy] is so frequently presented in fragments, or in the process of its effective dismemberment ..., indicates that contradiction is already growing up within this system of presence, and ... the deadly subjectivity of the modern is already beginning to emerge and to round vindictively on the most prevalent emblem of the discursive order it supersedes' (*The Tremulous Private Body*, pp. 24–5). However, Barker often speaks of the elimination of *the* body, not only of a 'macro-system' of regulatory production such as the one emblematized by the visible body of the sovereign. In this sense, he is closer to a certain Foucault, who refers to the Nietzschean concept of genealogy to argue that the latter's task is 'to expose a body totally imprinted by history and the process of history's destruction of the body' ('Nietzsche, Genealogy, History', in Donald F. Bouchard [ed.], *Language, Counter-Memory, Practice. Selected Essays and Interviews* [Ithaca and New York: Cornell University Press, 1977], pp. 139–64 [p. 148]). This is a Foucault, one might argue, who accepts the 'repressive hypothesis' he was later to contest. In *The History of Sexuality: An Introduction*, for instance, Foucault explicitly questions the idea that 'the bourgeoisie signifies the elision of the body and the repression of sexuality' (p. 125). As Barker's argument develops, it becomes clearer that it is not the disappearance of *the* body that is mainly at stake in his argument, but, rather, the emergence of a 'supplementary body [that] is both more present and more absent than the old body' (*The Tremulous Private Body*, p. 64).

45 Franco Moretti, 'The Great Eclipse: Tragic Form as the Deconsecration of Sovereignty', in *Signs Taken for Wonders: Essays in the Sociology of Literature*, trans. by Susan Fischer, David Forgacs and David Miller (London and New York: Verso, 1988), pp. 42–82 (p. 42).

46 Ibid., p. 72.

47 Ibid., p. 74.

48 Ibid., p. 75.

49 Ibid., p. 74. However, by suggesting that 'it is preferable to define lust as "passion" rather than "desire", for it is clearly something that one passively undergoes', something 'external and objective, a burden that overwhelms its bearer'; by adding that pleasure itself, 'lacking entirely the essential dimension of freedom, becomes a repetition compulsion' (Ibid., p. 75), Moretti sets up a problematic dichotomy between a 'passive'

and a potentially 'active' subject of desire. In other words, he construes desire as a function of a *telos*, an ideal spatial and temporal point where the lack of the sovereign is eventually filled up with presence: a point, that is, where the sovereign re-presents himself in the guise of an active – sovereign – 'subject' in full possession of his desire.

50 Foucault, *The History of Sexuality: An Introduction*, pp. 105–6.
51 Eve Kosofsky Sedgwick, 'A Poem Is Being Written', in *Tendencies* (London: Routledge, 1994), p. 204.
52 Moretti, 'The Great Eclipse', p. 74. My emphasis.
53 I stress 'potentially' because, as I argue in the case of the relationship between the Duchess and Antonio in *The Duchess of Malfi*, Beatrice and De Flores in *The Changeling*, and, to a certain extent, Leantio and Bianca in *Women Beware Women*, differential markers of power never entirely disappear, or are immediately re-emphasized.
54 In these formulations, I have been much helped by Francis Barker's analysis of the project of sovereignty's nomination of the forces other than itself, an analysis which is pursued in relation to Shakespeare's high tragedies. See Francis Barker, *The Culture of Violence: Essays on Tragedy and History* (Manchester: Manchester University Press, 1993), esp. pp. 17–19 and pp. 62–7; and more generally, his reflections on pp. 70–92.
55 My analysis of the drama of masculinity in the fourth chapter also bears this out.
56 Catherine Belsey, 'Desire's Excess and the English Renaissance Theatre: *Edward II, Troilus and Cressida, Othello*', in Susan Zimmerman (ed.), *Erotic Politics: Desire on the Renaissance Stage* (New York and London: Routledge, 1992), pp. 84–102 (p. 95).
57 *The Duchess of Malfi* is quoted from the Revels edition, ed. John Russell Brown (Manchester: Manchester University Press, 1976). References are included parenthetically in the text.
58 In so far as my argument is concerned with the gender politics of the period, I agree with Ania Loomba's rejection of the polarization of the debate on the political valence of Jacobean drama as *either* contestatory *or* complicit with patriarchal ideology. Discussing seemingly contradictory evidence in the work of feminist historians and literary critics, she points out that 'the literary representations of women [in Jacobean drama] emerge as both constructed by and radically disruptive of an authority which was historically simultaneously being consolidated and in crisis' (*Gender, Race, Renaissance Drama*, pp. 67–8). She surmises that 'repression is likely to intensify precisely when authority is challenged' (Ibid., p. 70).
59 The allusion, of course, is to Stephen Greenblatt's 'Invisible Bullets', in *Shakespearean Negotiations*, pp. 21–65. This re-fashioning has little to do with any form of reinvestment in the sovereign qua centre.
60 Dollimore, *Sexual Dissidence*, p. 86. Here Jonathan Dollimore is discussing and problematizing the terms of what has come to be known as the 'subversion–containment debate'.
61 Ibid., p. 90.

1 'That body of hers'

1 This can be compared to the 'tragic lodging' of Othello's bed (V.ii.364), a 'lodging' that, like the Duchess's body, 'poisons sight' (V.ii.365) and must therefore 'be hid' (V.ii.366). All references to *Othello* are from the New Arden Edition, ed. M.R. Ridley (London and New York: Methuen, 1965), and are included parenthetically in the text.
2 For a study of the contradictory figurations of the female body in early modern drama that is relevant to my argument here, see Peter Stallybrass, 'Reading the Body: *The Revenger's Tragedy* and the Jacobean Theater of Consumption', *Renaissance Drama*, 18 (1987), 121–48. Stallybrass underlines the 'desire to *fix* the body as a spectacle of transparency', and the simultaneous figuration of the body, especially the female body, 'as exceeding all categories, as the vanishing point of legibility itself' (p. 122).

3 Jacques Lacan, *Le Séminaire, livre XX: Encore 1969–70* (Paris: Editions du Seuil, 1975), esp. pp. 67–82. Two sessions of Lacan's 1969–70 seminar are translated into English in Juliet Mitchell and Jacqueline Rose, *Feminine Sexuality: Jacques Lacan and the Ecole Freudienne* (London: Macmillan, 1982), pp. 137–61. See also Jaqueline Rose's 'Introduction–II' to this book for comments on the construct '*The* woman' or 'Woman', a translation of Lacan's *La femme*, esp. pp. 44–57.

4 According to Antonio, 'You never fix'd your eye on three fair medals, / Cast in one figure, of so different temper' (I.i.188–9).

5 Bosola is implicitly and explicitly associated with the 'dissolute and infamous persons' (I.i.8–9) a sensible king should be willing to relinquish: 'I observe his railing / Is not for simple love of piety; / Indeed he rails at those things which he wants, / Would be as lecherous, covetous, or proud, / Bloody, or envious, as any man, / If he had means to be so' (I.i.22–8).

6 In the case of Cardinal, there is more than an analogy: 'the spring in his face' (I.i.158), unlike the 'common fountain' of the idealized French court pouring forth 'silver drops', is, to Antonio, 'nothing but the engendering of toads' (I.i.158–9). Here is Antonio's full description: 'Some such flashes superficially hang on him, for form; but observe his inward character: – he is a melancholy churchman; the spring in his face is nothing but the engendering of toads' (I.i.156–9). Later on, Ferdinand is characterized as follows: 'A most perverse, and turbulent nature: / What appears in him mirth, is merely outside .... He speaks with others' tongues, and hears men's suits / With others' ears; will seem to sleep o' th' bench / Only to entrap offenders in their answers; / Dooms men to death by information, rewards by hearsay' (I.i.169–70; 173–7).

7 Franco Moretti, 'The Great Eclipse: Tragic Form as the Deconsecration of Sovereignty', in *Signs Taken for Wonders: Essays in the Sociology of Literature*, trans. by Susan Fischer, David Forgacs and David Miller (London and New York: Verso, 1988 [1987]), pp. 42–82 (p. 72). This is a centre in which 'the loss of meaning ... is concentrated' (Ibid.).

8 In other words, Antonio's initial speech emphasizes, in spite of itself, the process of reconstituting 'a condition of dependent membership in which place and articulation are defined ... by incorporation in the body politic which is the king's body in its social form' (Francis Barker, *The Tremulous Private Body: Essays on Subjection* [London and New York: Methuen, 1984], p. 31). In the course of this process, the 'other' of the 'fix'd order' of sovereignty, even as it is ostracized, is dangerously brought into visibility and made available for resignification. Yet, at the same time, the bringing into visibility of sovereignty's 'other' is precisely just this: a bringing into visibility of *sovereignty's* 'other', which occludes other alternatives (that insubordination may come from different quarters and in a different form, that the king may be the 'poison ... near the head', and so on). For reflections on this, see Francis Barker, *The Culture of Violence: Essays on Tragedy and History* (Manchester: Manchester University Press, 1993), pp. 3–92*:*

9 See Jacques Lacan, *The Seminar of Jacques Lacan. Book VII: The Ethics of Psychoanalysis 1959–60*, trans. by Dennis Porter (New York and London: W.W. Norton, 1992), esp. pp. 139–60. Slavoj Žižek provides an interesting account of this less emphasized aspect of the Lacanian Lady of courtly love in *The Metastases of Enjoyment. Six Essays on Woman and Causality* (London and New York: Verso, 1994), pp. 89–112.

10 Emphasis mine.

11 As Karin S. Coddon points out, this is equivalent to a 'visual penetration of a private, female space' ('*The Duchess of Malfi*: Tyranny and Spectacle in Jacobean Drama', in James Redmond (ed.), *Madness in Drama* [Cambridge: Cambridge University Press, 1993], p. 6).

12 Patricia Parker, '*Othello* and *Hamlet*: Dilation, Spying, and the "Secret Place" of Woman', *Representations*, 44 (1993), 60–95. There has been a recent revival of interest in the subject of spies and secret informers in the early modern period. See, amongst other works, Alan Haynes, *Invisible Power: The Elizabethan Secret Services 1570–1603* (Stroud:

Alan Sutton, 1992) and J.M. Archer, *Sovereignty and Intelligence: Spying and Court Culture in the English Renaissance* (Stanford: Stanford University Press, 1993).

13 *The White Devil* is cited from The New Mermaids edition, ed. Elizabeth M. Brennan (London: Ernest Benn, 1966). *The White Devil* and *The Duchess of Malfi*, like countless other Jacobean plays, are pervaded by the quasi-paranoid atmosphere of spying and being spied upon. In *The Duchess of Malfi* the Cardinal is said to 'strew … in his way flatterers, panders, intelligencers, atheists, and a thousand such political monsters' (I.i.161–3). As for Ferdinand, he 'dooms men to death by information, rewards by hearsay' (I.i.176–7).

14 Parker, 'Dilation, Spying, and the "Secret Place" of Woman', esp. pp. 64–7.

15 Jacques Guillemeau, *Child-Birth or, The Happy Deliverie of Women* (London, 1612) (repr. Amsterdam: Theatrum Orbis Terrarum, 1972), p. 1. In the section dedicated to 'the signes to know whether a woman be with childe, or no', after listing the most common signs of pregnancy which are also reported by Bosola, Guillemeau refers to Hippocrates: 'if thou canst not finde by any [other] meanes, her very eyes will tell thee: for their eyes be more hollow, and sunke inward; and the white is turned bluish' (Ibid., p. 2, p. 5).

16 Michel Foucault, *Discipline and Punish: The Birth of the Prison*, trans. by Alan Sheridan (New York: Pantheon, 1977), p. 27.

17 Ibid., p. 28.

18 See also Coddon, '*The Duchess of Malfi*: Tyranny and Spectacle in Jacobean drama', esp. pp. 8–11.

19 For the 'deployment of alliance', see Michel Foucault, *The History of Sexuality: An Introduction*, trans. by Robert Hurley (Harmondsworth: Penguin, 1981), pp. 105–6. See also my comments in the 'Introduction'.

20 On 'companionate marriages', see Lawrence Stone, *The Family, Sex and Marriage in England 1500–1800* (Harmondsworth: Penguin, 1979) (abr. ed.), pp. 100–5; 217–53. For a much earlier account of Reformation theories of marriage, see William and Malleville Haller, 'The Puritan Art of Love', *Huntington Library Quarterly*, 5 (1941–42), 235–72. Kathleen M. Davies provides a useful summary of the debate amongst historians about the impact of these new ideals of marriage on the early modern system of gender relations. She also argues that there is a fundamental continuity between Catholic and Puritan understanding of marriage and the position of women within it. See 'The Sacred Conditions of Equality – How Original Were Puritan Doctrines of Marriage?', *Social History*, 5 (1977), 563–81. In a recent reconsideration of this debate, Karen Newman, whilst mostly agreeing with Davies's argument, also suggests that there are 'important differences in *how* this marital advice is presented, and in the ways in which these texts represent and produce femininity' (*Fashioning Femininity and English Renaissance Drama* [Chicago and London: The University of Chicago Press, 1991], p. 20). To Newman, there is a shift in the organization of marital advice texts from 'the rhetorical principles and practices of *copia*', used by Catholic and early Reform writers, to 'the practice of classifying concepts by dichotomies', whose shorthand term is 'method', employed in the 1590s and early seventeenth century (Ibid., pp. 20–1). This shift is indicative of changes in the way in which femininity is fashioned in the early modern period. To Newman, if the rhetorics of *copia* is related to the managing of femininity by means of spectacles of public shaming in which the submission of the unruly female body combines with some kind of acknowledgement of its 'troubling power', 'method' is connected with the interpellation of women 'as subjects through an ideology of the family that represented "an imaginary relation of [women] to their real conditions of existence"' (Ibid., p. 26). (Newman is using 'interpellation' in an Althusserian sense, and quoting from Louis Althusser, 'Ideology and Ideological State Apparatuses', in *Lenin and Philosophy and Other Essays*, trans. by Ben Brewster [London: New Left Books, 1971], pp. 127–86 [p. 162].)

21 Catherine Belsey, *The Subject of Tragedy: Identity and Difference in Renaissance Drama* (London and New York: Methuen, 1985), p. 197; p. 206; p. 198. More generally, see esp. pp. 192–221 for an exploration of the emergence of the 'liberal' concept of

marriage as well as of the limits of this concept. Belsey's argument does not imply that the emergence of 'companionate marriages' is synonymous with a weakening of patriarchal authority: 'Once the family is outside politics, the power relations within the family are excluded from political analysis .... In consequence a new and more insidious form of patriarchy, a "chosen" patriarchy, comes to rule unchallenged' (Ibid., p. 193). Yet, to Belsey, for women 'to have a place in discourse, even a domestic one, to have a subject-position from which to speak, however inadequate, is to be able to protest' (Ibid.). Cf. Ania Loomba, *Gender, Race, Renaissance Drama* (Manchester and New York: Manchester University Press, 1989), pp. 71–3, and Alan Sinfield, *Faultlines: Cultural Materialism and the Politics of Dissident Reading* (Oxford: Clarendon Press, 1992), pp. 42–7.

22 As Theodora A. Jankowski argues, elaborating on Belsey's points, the 'fruit' she will bear are not 'the heirs or commodities in a dynastic marriage, but ... offspring who need a mother's care' ('Defining/Confining the Duchess: Negotiating the Female Body in John Webster's *The Duchess of Malfi*', *Studies in Philology*, 87 [1990], 221–45 [p. 240].) She refers to the Duchess's request to Cariola later in the play to support this argument: 'I pray thee, look thou giv'st my little boy / Some syrup for his cold, and let the girl / Say her prayers, ere she sleeps' (IV.ii.203–5.) As for Antonio, what counts is 'the bare name / Of being a father, or the weak delight / To see the little wanton ride a-cock-horse / upon a painted stick, or hear him chatter / Like a taught starling' (I.i.399–402), rather than the transmission of the name, status and property that is characteristic of the 'dynastic' version of marriage. See also Belsey, *The Subject of Tragedy*, pp. 198–9.

23 Emphasis mine.

24 Frank Whigham, 'Sexual and Social Mobility in *The Duchess of Malfi*', *PMLA*, 100 (1985), 167–86 (p. 176).

25 Emphasis mine.

26 For a rather different interpretation of the Duchess's speech, and the notion of 'progress' in particular, see Kathleen McLuskie, 'Drama and Sexual Politics: The Case of Webster's Duchess', in James Redmond (ed.), *Drama, Sex, and Politics* (Cambridge: Cambridge University Press, 1985), p. 79. In an excellent article on Webster's play, Andrea Henderson, making use of Jean-Christophe Agnew's *Worlds Apart: The Market and the Theatre in Anglo-American Thought, 1550-1750* (Cambridge: Cambridge University Press, 1986), points out that this speech by the Duchess 'could serve as a textbook example of the interrelations of the expanding market economy, theatricality, and the bourgeois notion of the self' ('Death on the Stage, Death of the Stage: The Antitheatricality of *The Duchess of Malfi*', *Educational Theatre Journal*, 48 [1987], 194–207 [p. 198]).

27 This is liable to be read as inconstancy. As Belsey observes, female characters seem to speak 'with equal convictions from incompatible subject-positions, displaying a discontinuity of being, an "inconstancy" which is seen as characteristically feminine' (*The Subject of Tragedy*, p. 149).

28 Emphasis mine.

29 See, for instance, Barbara J. Todd, 'The Remarrying Widow: A Stereotype Reconsidered', in Mary Prior (ed.), *Women in English Society 1500–1800* (London and New York: Methuen, 1985), pp. 54–92. See also Lisa Jardine, *Still Harping on Daughters: Women and Drama in the Age of Shakespeare* (Hemel Hempstead: Harvester, 1983), pp. 68–93. It is in relation to the issue of widows' independence that a text as sober as *The Law's Resolutions of Women's Rights* (1632) adopts an ironic stance: 'But, alas, when she hath lost her husband, her head is cut off, her intellectual part is gone, the very faculties of her soul are (I will not say) clean taken away, but they are benumbed, dimmed, and dazzled .... Time must play the physician, and I will help him a little. Why mourn you so, you that be widows? Consider how long you have been in subjection under the predominance of parents, of your husbands; now you be free in liberty, and free ... at your own law; you may see ... that maidens' and wives' vows ... were all disavowable

and infringable by their parents or husbands unless they ratified and allowed them .... But the vow of a widow or of a woman divorced, no man had power to disallow of, for her estate was free from controlment.' I cite from Joan Larsen Klein (ed.), *Daughters, Wives and Widows: Writings by Men abut Women and Marriage in England, 1500–1640* (Urbana and Chicago: University of Illinois Press, 1992), p. 50.

30 I cite from The New Mermaids edition of *Women Beware Women*, ed. Roma Gill (London: Ernest Benn, 1968).

31 On this point, see Jankowski, 'Defining/Confining the Duchess', p. 240.

32 Homi Bhabha, 'Of Mimicry and Man: The Ambivalence of Colonial Discourse', *October*, 28 (1984), 125–33. See also the use of Bhabha's argument by Loomba, *Gender, Race, Renaissance Drama*, esp. pp. 93–104.

33 Emphasis mine.

34 Valerie Traub notes that female characters in early modern drama have 'minimal room within which to manoeuvre; even a minimum of erotic "warmth" is quickly transmogrified into intemperate heat'. Referring to *Hamlet*, *Othello* and *The Winter's Tale*, she adds that 'what the drama enacts is the disappearance of any middle ground, with the rigidity of this bifurcation following a unidirectional narrative: from a projection of too much movement, warmth, openness, to an enclosing fantasy of no movement or heat at all' (*Desire and Anxiety: Circulations of Sexuality in Shakespearean Drama* [London and New York: Routledge, 1992], p. 28). In a kind of postscript to this chapter of her book, she confesses to having 'unwittingly adopted the viewpoint of Hamlet, Othello and Leontes' (Ibid., p. 49). *Mutatis mutandis*, one can argue that to read the erotic system dramatized in Webster's play exclusively in terms of rigid dichotomies such as mobility and stasis, heat and cold, open and close, would be to adopt Ferdinand's viewpoint. The Duchess is precisely in search of what Traub calls a 'middle ground'. Yet this turns out to be not a synthesis but a compromise that compromises the interiority of each of the terms of the dichotomy in relation to the other.

35 Emphasis mine.

36 See Jacques Derrida, *Dissemination*, trans. by Barbara Johnson (Chicago: Chicago University Press, 1981), esp. pp. 209–22.

37 For this aspect of the play, see Whigham, 'Sexual and Social Mobility in *The Duchess of Malfi*', pp. 171–2. However, Whigham sees the 'martial' and the 'erotic' as mutually exclusive. To Whigham, the Duchess constitutes a threat (the threat of social and gender mobility), but this threat is not articulated in sexual terms. In fact, he compares and contrasts Julia's erotic 'self-giving will' to the Duchess's 'project', a project that 'does not aim at self-subjecting relational identity but itself founds substantial identity in the normatively masculine sense'. According to this interpretation, Julia's erotic status qua adulteress and mistress to the Cardinal serves to 'deflect the judgmental charge of lasciviousness away from the duchess' (Ibid., p. 172). The Duchess's 'project' is therefore an appropriation of male prerogatives, predicated upon the suspension of the erotic, as the latter would endlessly reinscribe, as it does for Julia, her subjection to men.

38 There are only characters such as Ferdinand who long to 'fall to action indeed' (I.i.92), but whose military exploits consist in bawdy jokes on 'sexual' fighting, or are equivalent to the exercise of violence in private places of confinement; a violence, moreover, that is meted out mostly 'by a deputy' (I.i.100).

39 On *différance*, see Jacques Derrida, *Margins of Philosophy*, trans. by Alan Bass (Chicago: University of Chicago Press, 1982), pp. 1–28.

40 The Duchess counts on Cariola's 'known secrecy' (I.i.350). Cariola has pledged herself to 'conceal this secret from the world' (I.i.352). For comments on Cariola's concluding remarks, see Coddon, '*The Duchess of Malfi*: Tyranny and Spectacle in Jacobean drama', pp. 9–10.

41 Judith Butler, *Bodies That Matter: On the Discursive Limits of 'Sex'* (London and New York: Routledge, 1993), p. 16.

42 Ibid.

43 Parker, 'Dilation, Spying, and the "Secret Place" of Woman', p. 66. See also Jonathan Sawday's reflections on the figure of the Medusa's head in the discourses of anatomy, as 'emblematic of a fragmented and dispersed body-interior – a profoundly ambivalent region – whose power can be somehow harnessed for good or ill' (*The Body Emblazoned: Dissection and the Human Body in Renaissance Culture* [London and New York: Routledge, 1995] p. 9).

44 Helkiah Crooke, *Microcosmographia. A Description of the Body of Man* (London, 1615), p. 237; pp. 238–9. Subsequent page references will be included parenthetically in the text. For the controversies surrounding Crooke's work, see G.N. Clark, *A History of the Royal College of Physicians*, 3 vols (Oxford: Clarendon Press, 1964), I, 204–6. See also C.D. O'Malley, 'Helkiah Crooke, MD, FRCP (1576–1648)', *Bulletin of the History of Medicine*, 42 (1968), 1–18.

45 Luce Irigaray is behind these formulations. See Luce Irigaray, *This Sex Which Is Not One*, trans. by Catherine Porter (Ithaca and New York: Cornell University Press, 1985) esp. pp. 23–33.

46 For a fuller exploration of Crooke's position in relation to Galenic and Aristotelian models of sexual difference, see Chapter 3 and Chapter 5.

47 Parker, 'Dilation, Spying, and the "Secret Place" of Woman', p. 71.

48 This is also wonderfully explored by Michael Neill, 'Changing Places in *Othello*', *Shakespeare Survey*, 37 (1984), 115–31, and 'Unproper Beds: Race, Adultery, and the Hideous in *Othello*', *Shakespeare Quarterly*, 40 (1989), 383–412. For the relevance of this 'ob-scene' locus to a Derridean analysis of hospitality as the impossible, see Maurizio Calbi, 'Being a Guest But Not Quite … White: *Othello* and Hybrid Hospitality in the Mediterranean', *Anglistica-AION*: *Shakespeare and the Genres of Hospitality*, ed. Lidia Curti and Silvana Carotenuto, 6, 2 (2002)–7, 1 (2003), 27–42.

49 'Let not youth, high promotion, eloquence … sway your high blood' (I.i.95–7).

50 All the subject positions delineated here are intricately related to the opening of the 'examination scene', in which the Cardinal invites the Duchess to embody the split between a chaste and 'luxurious' widow, and thus become a self-regulating and divided identity visible not only to others but also to herself: 'We are to part from you: and your own discretion / Must now be your director. (I.i.292–3). That the 'examination' proceeds, in spite of the fact that these lines seem to make it redundant, is already in itself a sign that the 'interpellation' of the Duchess is not particularly successful. As the 'wooing scene' shows, she does not identify, at least not fully, with the place from which she is being observed by her two brothers.

51 The enunciation of the prohibition of transgression by the Duchess's brothers uncannily resembles a staging of her desire, and reads almost like an anticipation of her 'dangerous venture' (I.i.348). As Loomba notes, the two brothers' fears 'anticipate, and perhaps contribute to the formulation of, her plans' (*Gender, Race, Renaissance Drama*, p. 111).

52 Mikhail Bakhtin, *Rabelais and his World*, trans. by Hélène Iswolsky (Cambridge MA: MIT Press, 1968), as especially used and reinterpreted in Stallybrass, 'Reading the Body', *passim.*

53 In the Revels edition of the play John Russell Brown glosses 'whispering-rooms' as 'intimate, private closets' (p. 28n.). He also notes that this and Bosola's reference to Antonio in III.ii.257 are the only recorded examples of this expression in the *Oxford English Dictionary*.

54 Francis Barker, *The Tremulous Private Body: Essays on Subjection* (London and New York: Methuen, 1984), p. 28.

55 As far as medical texts are concerned, one of the most interesting examples of the homology between a woman's secret parts and her private closets or cabinets is to be found in Jacques Duval, *Des Hermaphrodits, accouchemens des femmes, et traitement qui est requis pour les relever en santé & bien élever leur enfans* (Rouen, 1612). Duval states in the

'Advertissement au lecteur' that he intends to offer 'a representation of the instruments hidden in the most secrets cabinets of women, in the use of which both men and women are fully transported with delight' ('representation de[s] utensiles reconces aux plus secret cabinets des femmes: en l'usage desquels les uns & les autres se donnent carriere de delectation') (my translation). Duval develops this homology throughout the treatise. At the beginning of the section of the book called *Des Hermaphrodits*, dedicated more specifically to childbirth, he states that it is his duty to 'expose the richness of their [women's] cabinets, as well as the richness of their doors and locks and keys with which one forces them open in order to procreate' ('l'exposé des richesses de leur cabinets, & des huis, portes, serrures & clefs dont on fait ouvertures pour engendrer') (Ibid., p. 158; my translation).

56 Thomas Laqueur, *Making Sex: Body and Gender From the Greeks To Freud* (Cambridge MA and London: Harvard University Press, 1990), pp. 5–6 and *passim*. All these aspects of the one-sex body/flesh emphasized by Laqueur are largely Galenic. See Galen, *On the Usefulness of the Parts of the Body*, trans. by Margaret T. May, 2 vols (Ithaca and New York: Cornell University Press, 1968), II, esp. pp. 630–8.

57 See Michael Neill, '"Hidden malady": Death, Discovery, and Indistinction in *The Changeling*', *Renaissance Drama*, 22 (1991), esp. pp. 101–3. Neill also refers to a study by Georges Duby and Philippe Braunstein, 'The Emergence of the Individual', in Philippe Ariès and George Duby (eds), *A History of Private Life*, trans. by Arthur Goldhammer, 5 vols (Cambridge MA and London: Belknap-Harvard University Press, 1987–92), II, 507–630.

58 Jonathan Dollimore, *Sexual Dissidence: Augustine to Wilde, Freud to Foucault* (Oxford: Clarendon Press, 1991), p. 253.

59 Othello threatens to 'tear [Desdemona] all to pieces' (III.iii.438) or 'chop her into messes' (IV.i.196). In Jonson's *Volpone*, Corvino addresses Celia as follows: 'I will make thee an anatomy / Dissect thee mine own self, and read a lecture / Upon thee to the city, and in public' (II.v.70–3). I cite from The New Mermaids edition of *Volpone*, ed. Philip Brockbank (London: Ernest Benn, 1968). For interesting comments on these lines and, more generally, on the connection between the emerging discourse of anatomy and early modern plays, see Howard Marchitello, 'Vesalius' *Fabrica* and Shakespeare's *Othello*: Anatomy, Gender and the Narrative Production of Meaning', *Criticism*, 35 (1993), 529–58.

60 See also IV.ii.37–44.

61 Leonard Tennenhouse, *Power On Display. The Politics of Shakespeare's Genres* (London and New York: Methuen, 1986), p. 120.

62 See Foucault, *Discipline and Punish*, pp. 3–69.

63 The underlying logic of Ferdinand's resolve is that 'she'll needs be mad' (IV.i.126) to confirm the 'madness' of her transgression.

64 For an analysis of this aspect, see Coddon, '*The Duchess of Malfi*: Tyranny and Spectacle in Jacobean drama', pp. 12–15.

65 For the system of resemblances as the governing paradigm of sixteenth-century *episteme*, see Michel Foucault, *The Order of Things. An Archeology of the Human Sciences* (London and New York: Tavistock, 1970 [1966]), pp. 17–45.

66 According to Barker, the most evident sign of these contradictions is that 'the body ... is so frequently presented in fragments, or in the process of its effective dismemberment' (*The Tremulous Private Body*, p. 24).

67 On dominant, residual and emergent, see Raymond Williams, *Marxism and Literature* (Oxford: Oxford University Press, 1977), pp. 121–7.

68 As pointed out earlier, this description is not, in any case, unambiguous or unmarked by anxiety.

69 Valerie Traub, 'The Psychomorphology of the Clitoris', *GLQ: A Journal of Lesbian and Gay Studies* (Special issue: *Pink Freud*, ed. Diana Fuss), 2, 1–2 (1995), 81–113 (p. 103n.). For a study that is closer to this sense of anatomy, see Sawday, *The Body Emblazoned*. For

anatomy as a performance that deconstructs and then reconstitutes the body as a 'body of knowledge', see Luke Wilson, 'William Harvey's *Prelectiones*: The Performance of the Body in the Renaissance Theater of Anatomy', *Representations*, 17 (1987), 62–95. For anatomy as a set of representational evasions of the violation of the body that operate by producing a 'normative' classical bodily form, see Glenn Harcourt, 'Andreas Vesalius and the Anatomy of Antique Sculpture', *Representations*, 17 (1987), 28–61. For anatomy as 'textualization' of bodies, see Barker, *The Tremulous Private Body*, pp. 73–85.

70 For Laqueur's indebtedness to Foucault's order of resemblances, see Laqueur, *Making Sex*, p. 10.

71 Ibid., p. 73.

72 Ibid., p. 70. Laqueur's emphasis.

73 Devon L. Hodges, *Renaissance Fictions of Anatomy* (Amherst: The University of Massachusetts Press, 1985), p. 2.

74 'The Translators Preface', in Guillemeau, *Child-Birth*, p. 3.

75 John Sadler, 'The Epistle Dedicatory', *The Sick Womans Private Looking-Glasse* (London, 1636) (repr. Amsterdam: Theatrum Orbis Terrarum, 1972).

76 'The Translators Preface', in Guillemeau, *Child-Birth*, p. 2.

77 Ibid., p. 3.

78 Eucharius Roesslin, *The Birth of Man-Kinde; Otherwise Named The Womans Book*, trans. by Thomas Raynalde (London, 1626 [1545]), p. 3. Roesslin's treatise, first published in German in 1513 as *Der swangern Frauwen und Hebammen Rosegarten* and then translated into Latin in 1532 as *De partu hominis* by Christian Egenolph, was first translated into English by Richard Jonas in 1540. It was then 'newly set forth, corrected, and augmented' by Thomas Raynalde in 1545 and went through numerous editions from 1545 to 1654. I cite from the 'Prologue to the Women Readers' in the 1626 edition. (The first 'Prologue' in English dates back to the 1560 edition.) See Jean Donnison, *Midwives and Medical Men: A History of Inter-Professional Rivalries and Women's Rights* (New York: Schocken Books, 1977), pp. 7–8; Audrey Eccles, *Obstetrics and Gynaecology in Tudor and Stuart England* (London and Canberra: Croom Helm, 1982), pp. 11–12; and Joan Larsen Klein's introductory remarks to an abridged version of the 1560 text in *Daughters, Wives and Widows*, pp. 177–9.

79 Roesslin, *The Birth of Man-Kinde*, p. 9.

80 Ibid., p. 16.

81 Jakob Rueff, *The Expert Midwife, or an Excellent and Most Necessary Treatise of the Generation and Birth of Man* (London, 1637), sig. A4–A5. This is a translation of Rueff's widely plagiarized *De conceptu et generatione hominis* (1554).

82 Ibid., p. 45.

83 Ibid., p. 44. At the end of *The Compleat Midwife's Practice Enlarged* (London, 1659), the four unidentified authors state: 'Perhaps it may be judged by some, to have been more decent that these things should have been delivered in the Latine, than in the vulgar Tongue, that so the secrets of nature, might not have been prostituted to every unworthy Reader, that makes use of such things onely for a mockery, and a May-game, and to promote idle and lascivious discourse.' The justification is that these 'secrets' are 'intended only for the use of sober, pious, and discreet Matron[s]', whose 'want of skill and knowledge in these mainly important Secrets, hath been the occasion of very many mistakes'. Therefore, 'the concealment of them [would have] been much more inexcusable than the publishing can be' (p. 309). Later in the century this line of argument was to be rejected. James McMath, in *The Expert Midwife: A Treatise of the Diseases of Women with Child and in Child-Bed* (Edinburgh, 1694), explains: 'I have of purpose omitted a Description of the Parts in a Woman destined to Generation, not being absolutely necessar[y] to this purpose, and lest it might seem execrable to the more chast[e] and shamefast, through Baudiness and Impurity of Words …: Nor am I of the mind with some, as to think there is no Debauchery in the thing, except it be in the abuse; for these parts, which even sinful Nature would [have] v[e]iled, who may uncover by Word or Deed and be guiltless [?]' (sig. A7).

84 See, for instance, Sadler's *The Sick Womans Private Looking-Glasse*: 'From the wombe comes convulsions, epilepsies, apoplexies, palseyes, hecticke fevers, dropsies, malignant ulcers.' This rhetorical amplification is in contrast with the following claim: 'I have stooped to your capacities in avoiding hard words and Rhetoricall phrases, desiring rather to informe your judgements with the truth, through a plaine manner, than to confound your understanding with a more rhetoricall discourse' (sig. A4).

85 Guillemeau, *Child-Birth*, p. 82. In this treatise the origin of women's 'practice of Physicke' is interestingly associated with the fact that women, 'finding themselves … troubled with divers diseases in their naturall parts, … durst not discover, and lay open their infirmities, to any but themselves' (Ibid., p. 80).

86 The struggle over midwifery as a domain of knowledge of the body traditionally associated with women, and the increasing regulation and subsequent marginalization of the midwife, have all been well documented by feminist historians. They have been taken as emblematic of the curtailment of women's professional activities in the early modern period. See especially the pioneering work of Alice Clark, *Working Life of Women in the Seventeenth Century* (London: Routledge & Kegan Paul, 1982 [1919]), esp. pp. 265–85. See also, amongst many works, Barbara Ehreinreich and Deirdre English, *Witches, Midwives, and Nurses: A History of Women Healers* (New York: Feminist Press, 1973); Hilda Smith, 'Gynecology and Ideology in Seventeenth-Century England', in Berenice A. Carroll (ed.), *Liberating Women's History. Theoretical and Critical Essays* (Urbana: University of Illinois Press, 1976), pp. 97–114. Here I only want to cite a passage from McMath's *The Expert Midwife* (1694), which is emblematic of the intensifying attempts, as one moves into the eighteenth-century, to redefine the role of the midwife: 'Natural Labour … is the proper work of the Mid-Wife, and which she alone most easily performs aright, being only to fit and attend Nature's pace and progress, receive the Child in her Lap, bring away the Burden [placenta], cut and tye the String, and perform some other things of smaller moment, which Physicians gave Mid-wives to do, as unnecessar[y] & indicent for them, and for the Matronal chastity (though some of Old absurdly assigned them more, and made it also their Office, to help the Delivery, and not by Medicaments only …, but Inchantements also' (sig. A5).

87 Peter Stallybrass, 'Patriarchal Territories: The Body Enclosed', in Margaret W. Ferguson, Maureen Quilligan, and Nancy J. Vickers (eds), *Rewriting the Renaissance: The Discourses of Sexual Difference in Early Modern Europe* (Chicago and London: Chicago University Press, 1986), pp. 123–42 (pp. 133–4).

88 Ferdinand's 'rogues' are split between a voice that 'publishes' and 'a covetous searching eye' that lends itself to a re-inscription in the paranoid atmosphere of espionage: they 'publish' to profit from a further divulging or from a withdrawing of additional information. See Russell Brown's edition of the play, p. 63n. Ferdinand's position is equally split, as the 'publishing' with which he associates himself is not only a 'prostituting' of the Duchess's body, but also of his bodily identity; or, to be more precise, an undermining of his sense of masculine honour. Indeed, as the scene progresses, what he sees as the Duchess's devastation of 'her honours' (II.v.17–21) becomes synonymous, as it does for Othello, with the shipwreck of his and other men's 'honour' (II.v.33–6).

89 This discovery will bring to an end any and every form of display: 'That known, I'll … fix her in a general eclipse' (II.v.78–9).

90 On the *mise-en-scène* of jealousy, I find Jacques Derrida's following observations extremely suggestive: 'Jealousy always comes from the night of the unconscious, the unknown, the other. Pure sight relieves all jealousy. Not seeing what one sees, seeing what one cannot see and what cannot present itself, that is the jealous operation. Jealousy has always to do with some trace, never with perception' (*Glas*, trans. by John P. Leavey, Jr., and Richard Rand [Lincoln: University of Nebraska Press, 1986], pp. 214–15.)

91 Jacques Lacan, *The Four Fundamental Concepts of Psycho-Analysis*, trans. by Alan Sheridan (Harmondsworth: Penguin, 1979), p.185. This is based on Lacan's 1964 seminar.

92 Ibid.

93 This framework always gravitates towards some form of prohibition. Ferdinand's refusal to see can be read as a token of this prohibition, concerning what cannot *directly* be brought to light.

94 Jean Laplanche and Jean-Bertrand Pontalis, 'Fantasy and the Origins of Sexuality', *International Journal of Psycho-Analysis*, 49, 1 (1968), 1–18 (p. 17).

95 Ibid.

96 '*Or* my imagination will carry me / To see her in the shameful act of sin ' (II.v.40–1) (my emphasis). I owe this suggestion to Sue Ainscough.

97 Of course, as far as Ferdinand is concerned, this would be a form of prohibited incestuous desire.

98 Mikkel Borch-Jacobsen, *The Freudian Subject*, trans. by Catherine Porter (Stanford CA: Stanford University Press, 1988 [1982]), p. 17.

99 Ibid, p. 18.

100 Ibid., p. 47. Or, in another formulation: '[I]f desire is satisfied in and through identification, it is not in the sense in which a desire somehow precedes gratification, since no desiring subject … precedes the mimetic identification: identification brings the desiring subject into being, and not the other way around' (Ibid.). Borch-Jacobsen also builds on René Girard's work, especially *Deceit, Desire, and the Novel: Self and Other in Literary Structure*, trans. by Yvonne Freccero (Baltimore MD: Johns Hopkins University Press, 1972). To Borch-Jacobsen, object-oriented desire is an *effect* of identification and mimesis: 'Mimesis informs desire, directs it, and, more broadly speaking, incites it. Mimesis is thus the matrix of desire and, by the same token, the matrix of rivalry, hatred, and (in the social order) violence' (Ibid., p. 27).

101 On the use of quasi-transcendental concepts in the work of Jacques Derrida, see Geoffrey Bennington and Jacques Derrida, *Jacques Derrida* (Paris: Seuil, 1991), pp. 248–63.

102 Butler, *Bodies That Matter*, esp. pp. 57–119.

103 Ibid., p. 99.

104 Ibid. Amongst the many analyses addressing the dichotomy identification versus desire, see John Fletcher, 'Freud and His Uses: Psychoanalysis and Gay Theory', in Simon Shepherd and Mick Wallis (eds), *Coming on Strong: Gay Politics and Culture* (London: Unwin Hyman, 1989), pp. 90–118.

105 Dollimore, *Sexual Dissidence*, p. 305.

106 Ibid.

107 Sigmund Freud, 'Some Neurotic Mechanisms in Jealousy, Paranoia and Homosexuality' (1922), in *The Standard Edition of the Complete Psychological Works of Sigmund Freud* (hereafter *SE*), ed. James Strachey, 24 vols (London: The Hogarth Press, 1953–74), XVIII, 221–32 (p. 223). In her study of early modern scenarios of male sexual jealousy, Katharine E. Maus, citing Freud, argues: 'the jealous onlooker participates vicariously in his own betrayal, indulging heterosexual and homosexual fantasies at the same moment, without ordinarily recognizing his motives or acknowledging the implications of those fantasies to himself' ('Horns of Dilemma: Jealousy, Gender, and Spectatorship in English Renaissance Drama', *English Literary History*, 54 [1987], 561–83 [p. 570]).

108 Dollimore, *Sexual Dissidence*, p. 304 (my emphasis).

109 Ibid. However, in other sections of his book Dollimore emphasizes the 'dis-coherence' of Freud's own statements on the relation between homosexuality and sociality. See especially Ibid., pp. 169–204. Borch-Jacobsen also clearly shows that Freud's statements on this subject are driven by the – unsuccessful – attempt to rigidly demarcate 'libidinal' (that is, unsublimated and homosexual) from 'non-libidinal' (that is, identificatory) bonds, as regards *both* the relation between men in a social group *and* the relation between the men and their leader qua 'ego ideal'. See Borch-Jacobsen, *The Freudian Subject*, esp. pp. 127–239. (This is mostly a deconstructive analysis of Freud's 'Group Psychology and the Analysis of the Ego' [1921], in *SE*, XVIII, 69–144.)

110 Dollimore, *Sexual Dissidence*, p. 304. Dollimore's remarks show his indebtedness to the groundbreaking work of Eve Kosofsky Sedgwick. Sedgwick analyses the *potentially* unbroken continuum between male social bonding, including bonds of rivalry, and men's desire for other men. This is a structure she designates as 'male homosocial desire'. She also points out that the 'sexual' in homo*sexual* desire and, more generally, what counts as sexual, is historically contingent. See Eve Kosofsky Sedgwick, *Between Men. English Literature and Male Homosocial Desire* (New York: Columbia University Press, 1985), pp. 1–2 and *passim*.

111 Amongst the many works on early modern culture which attempt to historicize the 'hetero/homosexual divide', see Alan Bray, *Homosexuality in Renaissance England* (London: Gay Men's Press, 1982) and 'Homosexuality and the Signs of Male Friendship in Elizabethan England', *History Workshop*, 29 (1990), 1–19. (The latter article is especially relevant to my argument, in that it emphasizes how variables such as class and status introduce discontinuity in the early modern invisible continuum between male homosocial bonds and male homoeroticism, paving the way for homophobia.) See also Bruce R. Smith, *Homosexual Desire in Shakespeare's England* (Chicago: University of Chicago Press, 1991); Jonathan Goldberg, *Sodometries: Renaissance Texts, Modern Sexualities* (Stanford CA: Stanford University Press, 1992); Traub, *Desire and Anxiety*, esp. pp. 91–116; the essays in Susan Zimmerman (ed.), *Erotic Politics: Desire on the Renaissance Stage* (New York and London: Routledge, 1992); the essays in Jonathan Goldberg (ed.), *Queering the Renaissance* (Durham and London: Duke University Press, 1994); Catherine Belsey, 'Cleopatra's Seduction' and Alan Sinfield, 'How to Read *The Merchant of Venice* without Being Heterosexist', both in Terence Hawkes (ed.), *Alternative Shakespeares: Vol. 2* (London and New York: Routledge, 1996), respectively pp. 38–62 and pp. 122–39.

112 The 'poniard' (I.i.331) that belonged to his father is another item of the masculine paraphernalia Ferdinand displays.

113 Stallybrass, 'Patriarchal Territories', p. 133.

114 Freud, *Jokes and Their Relation to the Unconscious* (1905), in *SE*, VIII, p. 98.

115 Ibid.

116 Ibid., p. 99.

117 Sedgwick, *Between Men*, p. 61.

118 See the Revels edition of the play, p. 16n.

119 For the theoretical aspect of this masculinization, explored in relation to a rather different context, see Mary Anne Doane, *Femmes Fatales: Feminism, Film Theory, Psychoanalysis* (London and New York: Routledge, 1991), pp. 28–31.

120 See the Revels edition of the play, p. 29n.

121 For the concept of 'transgressive reinscription', see Dollimore, *Sexual Dissidence*, p. 285.

122 One of the examples Foucault gives of the interpenetration between the deployment of alliance and that of sexuality is the development of the problematic of the 'flesh', which has to do with 'the body, sensation, the nature of pleasure, the more secret forms of enjoyment or acquiescence'. See Foucault, *The History of Sexuality: An Introduction*, p. 108.

123 Foucault, *Discipline and Punish*, p. 16. For a reading that antedates this disciplinary strategy, see Barker, *The Tremulous Private Body*. See also Steven Mullaney's reading of *Measure for Measure* in terms of the re-incorporation of subjects through their subjectivities in *The Place of the Stage: Licence, Play, and Power in Renaissance England* (Chicago and London: Chicago University Press, 1988), pp. 88–115.

124 Foucault, *The History of Sexuality: An Introduction*, p. 38.

125 Valerie Traub, 'The (In)significance of "Lesbian" Desire in Early Modern England', in Susan Zimmerman (ed.), *Erotic Politics: Desire on the Renaissance Stage* (New York and London: Routledge, 1992), pp. 150–69 (p. 163). For the 'anatomically "excessive" woman', see Chapter 5.

126 Ibid., p. 164.

127 III.ii.25–32.

128 For these speeches, see note 22.
129 Whigham, 'Sexual and Social Mobility in *The Duchess of Malfi*', p. 169. Yet, as Whigham adds, the Duke's 'frenetic iteration' of the 'ontological separation from those below' is the sign of 'a strategic failure' (Ibid.).
130 Ibid., p. 170.
131 Jacques Lacan, *Écrits: A Selection*, trans. by Alan Sheridan (London: Tavistock, 1977 [1966]), p. 18. For reflections on the mirror stage and the ego as a bodily ego (that is, the projection of a bodily surface) that are relevant to my argument here, see Butler, *Bodies That Matter*, esp. pp. 57–91.
132 Lacan, *Écrits: A Selection*, p. 2.
133 Ibid.
134 Ibid., p. 19.
135 Lacan's later elaborations of the Imaginary make clear that the *Gestalt* in which the child anticipates the control of his body is a *phallic* form. In this sense, the idealized 'body of hers' – an image of Ferdinand himself as psychically and bodily bound ego – corresponds to the imaginary phallus qua 'form' and 'erected image of the penis'. (See Jacques Lacan, *Le Séminaire, livre IV: La Relation d'objet 1956–7* [Paris: Editions du Seuil, 1994], p. 70.) Ferdinand's evocation of this body qua 'imaginary phallus' is intricately linked to his vociferous conjuring up of the whole panoply of fetishized phallic attributes – weapons, tails, tongues, bars, sledges, artificial hands, and so on. This is a conjuring up that anxiously acknowledges and jubilantly disavows that they are objects possessed by the other, in class and gender terms. They stand in for what is *missing* from the projected phallomorphic wholeness of his body.
136 Lacan, *Écrits: A Selection*, p. 4.
137 Ibid.
138 Freud, 'The "Uncanny"' (1919), in *SE*, XVII, 217–52 (p. 235).
139 Ibid.
140 For Lacan, it is more a matter of 'structural' co-simultaneity of the *heimlich* and *unheimlich* specular image, an image that in both its aspects takes precedence over the ego, unlike Freud's 'double'. For some observations on this, see Mikkel Borch-Jacobsen, *Lacan: The Absolute Master*, trans. by Douglas Brick (Stanford: Stanford University Press, 1991), pp. 43–72.
141 Emphasis mine.
142 Emphasis mine.
143 See also Lacan, *The Seminar of Jacques Lacan. Book VII: The Ethics of Psychoanalysis 1959–60*: 'We retreat … from assaulting the image of the other, because it was the image on which we were formed as an ego' (p. 195).
144 Emphasis mine.
145 On the gaze qua *objet a* and the illusion of the plenitude of the 'geometral' point of vision, see Lacan, *The Four Fundamental Concepts of Psycho-Analysis*, pp. 65–119. See also Chapter 2.
146 Clifford Leech, *Webster: The Duchess of Malfi* (London: Arnold, 1963), p. 57. For Ferdinand's identification with the Duchess's first husband, see the following speech: 'And thou hast ta'en that massy sheet of lead / That hid thy husband's bones, and folded it / About my heart' (III.ii.112–14).
147 The Duchess herself seems to envision this in the following lines: 'You are, in this, / Too strict: and were you not my princely brother / I would say too wilful' (III.ii.116–18).
148 On the 'heterosexual matrix', see Judith Butler, *Gender Trouble: Feminism and the Subversion of Identity* (London and New York: Routledge, 1990), p. 151n.
149 Borch-Jacobsen, *The Freudian Subject*, esp. pp. 5–8.
150 Ibid., p. 8.
151 Ferdinand can be said to approach what Lacan chooses to call 'extimacy' (*extimité*). Lacan describes it as 'this central place, this intimate exteriority or "extimacy," that is the Thing'

(translation slightly modified). (*The Seminar of Jacques Lacan. Book VII: The Ethics of Psychoanalysis 1959–60*, p. 139.) In this seminar, he also makes a distinction that is relevant to my argument here, between 'this fellow self whom we so easily turn into our reflection' (p. 197), and 'that which is most myself in myself, that which is at the heart of myself, and beyond me, insofar as the self stops at the level of the walls to which one can apply a label' (p. 198). That which is 'most myself in myself' thus escapes 'imaginary' reflection. It is 'beyond' the ego qua 'imaginary' construct. It is an intimate kernel ('at the heart of myself') *and* a foreign body ('beyond me'), an 'ex-timate object' that is intrinsically *unheimlich*. As Mladen Dolar explains, '*extimité* ... points neither to the interior nor to the exterior, but is located there where the most intimate interiority coincides with the exterior and becomes threatening, provoking horror and anxiety' ('"I Shall Be with You on Your Wedding Night": Lacan and the Uncanny', *October*, 58 [1991], 5–23 [p. 6]).

2 'Behind the back of life'

1 All references are to the Revels edition of the play, ed. N.W. Bawcutt (London: Methuen, 1958), and are included parenthetically in the text.
2 Frank Whigham, 'Reading Social Conflict in the Alimentary Tract: More on the Body in Renaissance Drama', *English Literary History*, 55, 2 (1988), 333–50 (p. 340).
3 The medical image of bleeding, noted by Whigham, is the focus of a few suggestive pages on the play by Gail Kern Paster, *The Body Embarrassed: Drama and the Disciplines of Shame in Early Modern England* (Ithaca and New York: Cornell University Press, 1993), pp. 88–90.
4 Leonard Tennenhouse, *Power On Display. The Politics of Shakespeare's Genres* (London and New York: Methuen, 1986), p. 118.
5 Ibid., p. 120.
6 Tennenhouse builds on Foucault's description of early modern public execution as one of the rituals through which the power of the king manifests itself in all its spectacularity. (Michel Foucault, *Discipline and Punish: The Birth of the Prison*, trans. by Alan Sheridan [New York: Pantheon, 1977], pp. 3–69.) He maintains that any and every form of transgression by the aristocratic female in Jacobean drama is homologous to 'the criminal's assault on the law'. In fact, it is 'an assault on the Crown' (*Power On Display*, p. 121), which calls for a violent reinscription of the asymmetry of power relations. If in public executions the king is 'never present in person but always present in the person of the law' (Ibid., p. 120), in the elaborate rituals of punishment of the transgressive aristocratic female of Jacobean drama he is symbolically present in the person of his aristocratic patriarchal representatives.
7 The 'penknife', as Michael Neill observes, is an 'instrument of *private* inscriptions' (my emphasis). See Michael Neill, '"Hidden malady": Death, Discovery, and Indistinction in *The Changeling*', *Renaissance Drama*, 22 (1991), 95–121 (p. 117). Paster notes the paradoxical role played by De Flores: 'The daughter's seducer and murderer, he also becomes the father's surgeon, practicing as it were upon the patriarchal body for its "better health"' (*The Body Embarrassed*, p. 89). For the juxtaposition of phlebotomy and sexual act, see also the speech by Charlemont in Tourneur's *The Atheist's Tragedy*, where he refers to Castabella's marriage with the impotent Rousard: 'O strange incontinence! Why, was thy blood / Increas'd to such a pleurisy of lust / That of necessity there must a vein / Be open'd, though by one that had no skill / To do 't?' (III.i.112–16). I cite from the Revels edition of the play, ed. Irving Ribner (London: Methuen, 1964).
8 Emphasis mine. The imagined or real threat of contamination De Flores represents for Tomazo's weapon, body and 'manhood' (V.ii.21) prompts an active will to shed blood. Tomazo will soon draw his sword and strike De Flores. Freud observes: 'The enmity which the persecuted paranoic sees in others is the reflection of his own hostile impulses

against them' ('Some Neurotic Mechanisms in Jealousy, Paranoia and Homosexuality', in *SE*, XVIII, 221–32 [p. 226]).

9 Tennenhouse, *Power On Display*, p. 120; p. 118.

10 Jacques Derrida, *Dissemination*, trans. by Barbara Johnson (Chicago: Chicago University Press, 1981, pp. 63–171). Michael Neill concludes that the 'cleansing' mobilized at the end of the play is 'tantamount to self-annihilating convulsion' ('"Hidden malady": Death, Discovery, and Indistinction in *The Changeling*', p. 116).

11 Tennenhouse, *Power On Display*, p. 120; p. 119.

12 See also Dollimore's analysis of the importance and strength of the homosocial bond even among antagonists in *Othello* (*Sexual Dissidence: Augustine to Wilde, Freud to Foucault* [Oxford: Clarendon Press, 1991], esp. pp. 157–62).

13 Emphasis mine.

14 Alsemero is even able to spot the exteriorized sign of De Flores's guilt, a speck of blood upon his band: 'What's this blood upon your band, De Flores …? ['T]is almost out, but 'tis perceiv'd, though' (V.iii.95; 99).

15 Emphasis mine.

16 Commenting on Freud's work on narcissism ('On Narcissism: An Introduction', in *SE*, XIV, 67–102), Jacques Lacan argues as follows: '*Verliebtheit* is fundamentally narcissistic. On the libidinal level, the object is only ever apprehended through the grid of the narcissistic relation' (*The Seminar of Jacques Lacan Book II. The Ego in Freud's Theory and the Technique of Psychoanalysis 1954–55*, trans. by Sylvana Tomaselli [Cambridge: Cambridge University Press, 1988], p. 167). This is not the place to discuss Freud's complex concept of narcissism. But see Borch-Jakobsen's extremely suggestive and persuasive analysis of the lack of 'a straightforward opposition between narcissism and object orientation [of the libido], between ego libido and object libido', which, in a sense, is already in Freud (Mikkel Borch-Jakobsen, *The Freudian Subject*, trans. by Catherine Porter [Stanford CA: Stanford University Press, 1988], pp. 94–126).

17 On this fantasy, see Lacan: '*We are but one.* Of course everybody knows that it has never happened for two to make one but nevertheless *we are but one*. It is from this that the idea of love originates. It is truly the crudest way of attributing to "sexual relation", this term that manifestly crumbles, its signified' (Jacques Lacan, *Le Séminaire, livre XX: Encore 1969–70* [Paris: Editions du Seuil, 1975], p. 46 [translation mine]).

18 For the fundamentally narcissistic character of the ideology of courtly love, see Jaques Lacan, *The Seminar of Jacques Lacan. Book VII: The Ethics of Psychoanalysis 1959–60*, trans. by Dennis Porter (New York and London: W.W. Norton, 1992), p. 151. See also Lacan, *Le Séminaire, livre XX: Encore 1969–70*, p. 65. It is in the latter seminar that Lacan cogently exposes the male fantasies of Woman as unbarred or absolute Other, the quasi-godly locus through which man attempts to disavow splitting and division. This is a locus that is supposed to act as a guarantee for the possibility of inscription of 'sexual relation' (Ibid., esp. pp. 61–82). For an analysis of how the ideology of courtly love permeates *The Changeling*, see Sara Eaton, 'Beatrice-Joanna and the Rhetoric of Love', *Theatre Journal*, 36 (1984), 371–82.

19 This is made explicit by Vermandero later on: 'Valencia speaks so nobly of you, sir, / I wish I had a daughter now for you' (III.iv.1–2).

20 *Contre-temps* is an allusion to Jacques Derrida, 'L'Aphorisme à contretemps', in *Psyché. Inventions de l'autre* (Paris: Galilée, 1987), pp. 519–33. This is a reading of Shakespeare's *Romeo and Juliet.*

21 Emphasis mine. On the significance of the castle within the play, and the aristocratic body of Beatrice as a 'castellated body', see Neill, '"Hidden malady": Death, Discovery, and Indistinction in *The Changeling*', esp. pp. 101–5.

22 Emphasis mine.

23 As I pointed out, Alsemero refers to Beatrice's father as follows: 'He means to feast me, and *poison* me beforehand' (I.i.207) (my emphasis).

24 As N.W. Bawcutt points out in the Revels edition of the play, it could be a shortened

form of 'forestall', or it could mean 'satiate, surfeit with'. He also notes that many editors emend it to 'stale', in the sense of 'make flat, deprive of zest' (p. 8n).

25 Jacques Lacan, *The Four Fundamental Concepts of Psycho-Analysis*, trans. by Alan Sheridan (Harmondsworth: Penguin, 1979), p. 73.

26 Ibid., p. 74. This is an 'order', as he notes, that is centred upon the specular image.

27 Ibid. For instance, Lacan asserts: 'I see only from one point, but in my existence I am looked at from all sides' (Ibid., p. 72). Later on he adds: 'I am not simply that punctiform being located at the geometral point from which the perspective is grasped' (Ibid., p. 96).

28 Ibid., p. 103. Lacan's emphasis.

29 Slavoj Žižek, 'Looking Awry', *October*, 50 (1989), 31–55 (p. 43). For an excellent study of the discrepancy between a Foucaultian and a Lacanian understanding of the gaze, in the context of film theory, see Joan Copjec, 'The Orthopsychic Subject: Film Theory and the Reception of Lacan', *October*, 49 (1989), 53–71. For another interesting analysis of the Lacanian gaze, see Mary Ann Doane, 'Remembering Women: Psychical and Historical Constructions in Film Theory', in her *Femmes Fatales: Feminism, Film Theory, Psychoanalysis* (London and New York: Routledge, 1991), pp. 76–95. Doane agrees with Copjec that film theory has often reduced vision to a 'geometric perspective', and thus failed to 'take into account other aspects of the gaze – its excess, its annihilation of subjectivity' (p. 86). These 'aspects' are more properly Lacanian, or, at least, characteristic of the Lacan of *The Four Fundamental Concepts of Psycho-Analysis*. However, she notes the paradox that a more faithful rendition of the Lacanian theory of the gaze works only by 'assuming the autonomy of the realm of the psychical – its freedom from both historical and ideological determinations' (Ibid.). She adds that this theory 'cannot be used to analyze sexual difference because it allows no differential analysis of mastery and subjection – everyone is subjected to a gaze which is outside' (Ibid.). For an analysis that employs Lacan's theory of the gaze in relation to early modern artifacts, see Barbara Freedman, *Staging the Gaze: Postmodernism, Psychoanalysis, and Shakespearean Comedy* (Ithaca NY and London: Cornell University Press, 1991). See also Philip Armstrong, 'Watching *Hamlet* Watching: Lacan, Shakespeare and the Mirror/Stage', in Terence Hawkes (ed.), *Alternative Shakespeares: Vol.2* (London and New York: Routledge, 1996), pp. 216–37.

30 Lacan, *The Four Fundamental Concepts of Psycho-Analysis*, p. 74.

31 See especially I.i.65–82 and II.i.13–14.

32 See Lacan, *The Four Fundamental Concepts of Psycho-Analysis*, pp. 263–76.

33 Lacan, *The Seminar of Jacques Lacan. Book VII: Ethics of Psychoanalysis 1959–60*, p. 71.

34 Slavoj Žižek, *The Sublime Object of Ideology* (London and New York: Verso, 1989), p. 180.

35 See also Neill, '"Hidden malady": Death, Discovery, and Indistinction in *The Changeling*', p. 107. According to Sara Eaton, this is an example of 'the underside of the Courtly Love tradition: the woman as monster, the Duessa' ('Beatrice-Joanna and the Rhetoric of Love', p. 374).

36 'Myself (I must confess) have the same frailty' (I.i.126).

37 Emphasis mine.

38 For the concept of 'extimacy' (*extimité*) and the 'ex-timate object', see Lacan, *The Seminar of Jacques Lacan. Book VII: Ethics of Psychoanalysis 1959–60*, p. 139. See also Chapter 1.

39 By using the word 'a(na)morphous', I intend to stress, at one and the same time, the notion of 'amorphousness' (that is, the lack of a distinct form) and the notion of 'anamorphosis' as emblematizing the excess of the gaze over vision and the de-centring of the subject of vision qua punctiform being. On anamorphosis, see Lacan, *The Four Fundamental Concepts of Psycho-Analysis*, pp. 79–119. The expression 'material correlative' is used by Slavoj Žižek in a related theoretical context. See his 'Grimaces of the Real, or When the Phallus Appears', *October*, 58 (1991), 45–68 (p. 55).

40 Žižek, *The Sublime Object of Ideology*, p. 180.

41 Ibid.

42 Emphasis mine.

43 As we shall see later, the 'distance' that is threatened with annihilation is also to be interpreted as a *class* distance and distinction.

44 Emphasis mine. To Lacan, one of the dimensions in which 'the power of the gaze is exercised directly' has to do with the evil eye, 'the *fascinum* …, that which has the effect of arresting movement and … of killing life' (*The Four Fundamental Concepts of Psycho-Analysis*, p. 118). The terms used here by De Flores, as well as those employed by Beatrice in II.i.89–91, recall this dimension.

45 Emphasis mine.

46 Emphasis mine.

47 Freud's definition of 'dirt' in 'Character and Anal Erotism' is 'matter in the wrong place' (Freud, 'Character and Anal Erotism', in *SE*, IX, p. 173). This is in English in the original.

48 Mary Douglas, *Purity and Danger: An Analysis of the Concepts of Pollution and Taboo* (London and New York: Routledge, 1991 [1966]), p. 160.

49 Ibid., pp. 160–1. For a study of abjection to which I refer, more or less implicitly, throughout the book, see Julia Kristeva, *Powers of Horrors: An Essay on Abjection*, trans. by Leon S. Roudiez (New York: Columbia University Press, 1982 [1980]).

50 In recent reappropriations of Lacan, such as Copjec and Žižek, the traumatic object or the Real of *jouissance* are once again de-historicized or equated with an *essential* nothingness. For a critique of these approaches, see, respectively, Doane, *Femmes Fatales*, esp. pp. 76–95 and Butler, 'Arguing with the Real', in *Bodies That Matter: On the Discursive Limits of 'Sex'* (London and New York: Routledge, 1993), pp. 187–222.

51 She hopes to 'rid [herself] … at one time' (II.ii.144–5) of both her 'loathings', as she also intends to provide the financial means for De Flores's flight from Alicante 'when the deed's done' (II.ii.141).

52 On the splitting of Beatrice's identity, see also Ania Loomba, *Gender, Race, Renaissance Drama* (Manchester and New York: Manchester University Press, 1989), pp. 96–7.

53 Lisa Jardine, *Reading Shakespeare Historically* (London and New York: Routledge, 1996), p. 125.

54 Ibid., p. 118.

55 Ibid., p. 116.

56 Ibid., p. 124. See also Jacques Derrida for 'the double exclusion that can be seen at work in all the great ethico-politico-philosophical discourses on friendship, namely … the exclusion of friendship between women and … the exclusion of friendship between a man and a woman' ('The Politics of Friendship', trans. by Gabriel Motzkin, *The Journal of Philosophy*, 85, 11 [1988]), 632–44 [p. 642]). For a paradigmatic early modern example of the understanding of friendship between a man and a woman, see Michel de Montaigne: 'The ordinary sufficiency of women cannot answer this conference and communication, the nurse of this sacred bond [of male friendship]: nor seeme their mindes strong enough to endure the pulling of a knot so hard, so fast, and durable' ('Of Friendship', in *The Essayes of Michael Lord of Montaigne*, trans. by John Florio [1603] [London and New York: Routledge, 1885], p. 85).

57 Jardine, *Reading Shakespeare Historically*, p. 115.

58 Ibid., p. 120.

59 Emphasis mine.

60 Ibid., p. 131.

61 Ibid.

62 In particular, the relation between Alsemero and Vermandero is transubstantiated into a blood relation.

63 Jardine, *Reading Shakespeare Historically*, p. 123.

64 This conviction has already been articulated in the first scene of the second act: 'Wrangling has prov'd the mistress of good pastime; / As children cry themselves

asleep, I ha' seen / Women have chid themselves abed to men' (II.i.86–8); and, more implicitly, at the end of I.i.

65 On the female body as castle, see Neill, '"Hidden malady": Death, Discovery, and Indistinction in *The Changeling*', esp. pp. 101–5. Vermandero's reaction at the end of the play is: 'An host of enemies enter'd my citadel / Could not amaze like this: Joanna! Beatrice! Joanna!' (V.iii.147–8).

66 On the gender connotations of woman's stillness and movement see, for example, Loomba, *Gender, Race, Renaissance Drama*, pp. 100–4.

67 Emphasis mine.

68 Jardine, *Reading Shakespeare Historically*, p. 129.

69 Ibid.

70 Ibid., p. 126.

71 Ibid., pp. 125–6.

72 Beatrice's invocation of the insurmountable 'distance' separating her from De Flores is the utmost sign of her attempt to displace abjection.

73 I am adapting from Freud's 'On Narcissism'. Of course, in this paper Freud does not speak yet of the super-ego, but of 'a special psychic agency which ... constantly watches the actual ego and measures it by that ideal [that is, the ego ideal]' ('On Narcissism: An Introduction', p. 89). Freud often emphasizes the cruel, dictatorial and compulsive character of the super-ego in *The Ego and the Id* (1923), in *SE*, XIX, 1–66. See also Lacan, *The Seminar of Jacques Lacan. Book VII: The Ethics of Psychoanalysis 1959–60*, trans. by Dennis Porter (New York and London: W.W. Norton, 1992), pp. 89–90.

74 It is almost as if the 'act' erased the metaphysical and political order of class distinctions only to lay bare the 'naturalness' of gender 'distinctions'. De Flores immediately perceives the emergence of this second set of 'distinctions' as the basis for some kind of mobility at the expense of Beatrice.

75 In Lacanian terms, that De Flores is simultaneously obscene and hypermoral is less of a contradiction than indicative of the 'normal' functioning of the super-ego, *concesso non dato*, of course, that anything to do with the super-ego can be defined as 'normal'. See especially Slavoj Žižek's analysis of the 'idiotic' and 'obscene' super-egoic law as a specific suspension of the Law that does not fail to keep the subject in check in *The Metastases of Enjoyment. Six Essays on Woman and Causality* (London and New York: Verso, 1994), esp. pp. 54–86.

76 For a theoretically related argument, in connection with the formations of identity in *Macbeth*, see Francis Barker, *The Culture of Violence: Essays on Tragedy and History* (Manchester: Manchester University Press, 1993), esp. pp. 54–55 and p. 63.

77 The 'work of secrecy' (III.ii.17) carried out by De Flores on a disarmed Alonzo from behind the latter's back looks very much like a form of anal aggression. In the 'reward scene', he glories in this 'performance', whilst claiming to be 'so warm yet in [his] service' (III.iv.56–7). Later on, he exclaims: 'Oh, this act / Has put me into spirit! I was greedy on't / As the parch'd earth of moisture, when the clouds weep' (III.iv.106–8).

78 See also Arthur L. Little, Jr, '"Transshaped" Women: Virginity and Hysteria in *The Changeling*', in James Redmond (ed.), *Madness in Drama* (Cambridge: Cambridge University Press, 1993), pp. 19–42.

79 Frank Whigham points out that the margins of Beatrice's body stand for the margins of the 'aristocratic body'. He cites the speech De Flores delivers at the end of the first scene of the play, after he picks up the glove Beatrice drops for Alsemero and is given the other as a token of her dis-favour. 'Now I know / She had rather wear my pelt tann'd in a pair / Of dancing pumps, than I should thrust my fingers / Into her sockets here' (I.i.231–4). He argues as follows: 'we ought to see the entire chain of glove/skin/pelt as marking an external boundary of the aristocratic body, already breached in prospect' ('Reading Social Conflict in the Alimentary Tract', p. 339.) However, this is not the only construction of Beatrice's body. Nor can it be taken as emblematic of all the others. Moreover, the fantasmatic dimension is crucial, also because, as I argue

later, De Flores *simulates*, to a large extent, the position of the class aspirant on behalf of Alsemero. Mary Douglas's work is behind Whigham's observations. To Douglas, 'the body is a model which can stand for any bounded system. Its boundaries can represent any boundaries which are threatened or precarious.' It is therefore a mistake 'to treat bodily margins in isolation from all other margins' (*Purity and Danger*, p. 115; p. 121).

80 From his very first aside, De Flores stresses that his desire is not an identification with the object of desire: 'I'll please myself with sight / Of her, at all opportunities, / If but to spite her anger; I know she had / Rather see me dead than living, and yet / She knows no cause for't, but a peevish will' (I.i.103–7).

81 Eve Kosofsky Sedgwick, *Between Men: English Literature and Male Homosocial Desire* (New York: Columbia University Press, 1985), p. 38.

82 Ibid., p. 57.

83 Penetration simultaneously interrupts her contiguity with herself, interestingly articulated in terms of friendship ('Can such friends divide, never to meet again…?). It is not by chance that Alsemero echoes some of her terms: 'I must now part and never meet again with any joy on earth' (I.i.198–9). At this stage of the play, he sees his position as compatible with the creation of male–female intimate bonds, even as he stresses the contingent unfeasibility of these bonds. Commenting on Beatrice's lines, Arthur L. Little usefully summarizes the double-edged construction of Beatrice's hymen as follows: 'Beatrice's virginity is a "toy", a thing that (for patriarchy) means everything and nothing …. [It] stays secondary to the male power structure whose social interchange is guaranteed by its presence' ('"Transshaped" Women: Virginity and Hysteria in *The Changeling*', p. 29).

84 See also Sedgwick: 'the male path through heterosexuality to homosocial satisfaction is a slippery and threatened one – although for most men, in at least most cultures, compulsory' (*Between Men*, p. 50).

85 Vermandero, on whose intense homosocial desire I have already commented, salutes Alonzo and Tomazo as follows: 'Y'are both welcome, / But an especial one belongs to you, sir, / To whose most noble name our love presents / The addition of a son, our son Alonzo' (II.i.96–9). Alonzo replies: 'The treasury of honour cannot bring forth / A title I should more rejoice in, sir' (II.i.100–1).

86 He seals his scenario with the following words: 'And how dangerous and shameful her restraint may go in time to, / It is not to be thought on without sufferings' (II.i.138–40). As pointed out earlier, De Flores, after watching the secret meeting between Alsemero and Beatrice in II.ii., takes the trouble to fantasize about the effects of Beatrice's further loss of 'restraint'.

87 Dollimore, *Sexual Dissidence*, p. 304.

88 Ibid., p. 305.

89 Emphasis mine.

90 Many critics have underlined differences between early modern and modern and late modern erotic systems. Male effeminacy is often referred to as an emblematic example of some of these differences. Phyllis Rackin usefully summarizes: 'Valuing sexual passion, the popular wisdom of contemporary culture associates it with the more valued gender, assuming that men feel it more often and more strongly. Despising lust as a mark of weakness and degradation, Renaissance thought gendered it feminine, attributed more of it to women, and regarded excessive lust in men as a mark of effeminacy. Reduced to its simplest terms, it is the difference between seeing heterosexual sex as the place where manhood is proved and affirmed in a conquest of the female and seeing it as the place where it is contaminated and lost in congress with her' ('Historical Difference/Sexual Difference', in Jean R. Brink [ed.], *Privileging Gender in Early Modern England: Sixteenth Century Essays & Studies Vol. XXIII* [Ann Arbor: Michigan University Press, 1993], pp. 37–63 [p. 47]). For an earlier account of early modern constructions of the excessive and/or non-reproductive contact with women as a threat to male identity – as more of a threat, in fact, than male homoeroticism – see Stephen Orgel, 'Nobody's Perfect: Or Why Did the English Stage Take Boys for

Women', *South Atlantic Quarterly*, 88 (1989), 7–29. These studies historicize the hetero/homosexual divide. But it is worth adding, with Jean Howard, that 'while heterosexuality was often stigmatized as dangerous and demeaning to men, the late sixteenth and early seventeenth centuries also saw increased cultural emphasis upon marriage, especially among the middling sort, as the affective focus of their lives', and that 'many texts from the period celebrate marriage and present women as the proper and "natural" objects of masculine erotic desire' ('Sex and Social Conflict: The Erotics of *The Roaring Girl*', in Susan Zimmerman (ed.), *Erotic Politics: Desire on the Renaissance Stage* [New York and London: Routledge, 1992], pp. 170–90 [p. 173]). See also Jean Howard, *The Stage and Social Struggle in Early Modern England* (London and New York: Routledge, 1994), pp. 93–128. For further reflections on male effeminacy, see Chapter 4. On the visibility and demonization of male–male erotic relations as 'sodomitical' only in relation to other social, ethnic and religious transgressions, see Alan Bray, *Homosexuality in Renaissance England* (London: Gay Men's Press, 1982), and his 'Homosexuality and Signs of Male Friendship in Elizabethan England', *History Workshop*, 29 (1990), 1–19. See also Jonathan Goldberg, *Sodometries: Renaissance Texts, Modern Sexualities* (Stanford CA: Stanford University Press, 1992).

91 In Tomazo's scenario, these exploits go as far as to include the rival's ability to reproduce himself without any direct contact with the woman.

92 This is Jasperino addressing Alsemero: 'Ashore you were wont to call your servants up, / And help to trap your horses for the speed; / At sea I have seen you weigh the anchor with 'em, / Hoist sails for fear to lose the foremost breath' (I.i.29–32).

93 To Beatrice, 'blood-guiltiness becomes a fouler visage' (II.ii.40) than Alsemero's. This decision is also made in the name of an intimate love bond that stands opposed to traditional aristocratic values, as especially shown by the following speech: 'Are not you ventured in the action, / That's all my joys and comforts …? / Say you prevail'd, y'are danger's and not mine then; / The law would claim you from me, or obscurity / Be made the grave to bury you alive' (II.ii.31–5). In this speech, Beatrice emphasizes that Alsemero (the 'you' of the speech) is *all* her 'joys and comforts'; that his chivalrous act would involve a 'danger' that is not shared; that the Law is alien to the 'law of the heart'.

94 This 'valour' is, to Alsemero, 'the honourablest piece 'bout man' (II.ii.27).

95 See also Neill, '"Hidden malady": Death, Discovery, and Indistinction in *The Changeling*', pp. 107–8.

96 Vermandero's 'magical' acquisition of a son bears witness to the male fantasy of a reproduction that is untainted by the passage through the female body. (On this fantasy, see Chapter 3.) The only potentially reproductive couple on stage at the end of the play is the couple of the subplot. Yet, there are numerous hints throughout the play suggesting that Alibius is an old and impotent man.

97 These lines show how the 'passage' through Beatrice's body on the way to homosocial satisfaction is re-articulated at the end of the play. This 'passage' has indeed become 'an easy passage' (V.iii.40).

98 This is Alsemero addressing Beatrice: 'There was a visor / O'er that cunning face, and that became you' (V.iii.46–7).

99 See also my discussion of Ferdinand's hostile reaction to the return of the image of his sister qua uncanny double in Chapter 1.

100 For reflections on the 'legitimate' violence of the dominant and the 'illegitimate' violence of the subordinated that are theoretically relevant here, see Alan Sinfield, *Faultlines: Cultural Materialism and the Politics of Dissident Reading* (Oxford: Clarendon Press, 1992), pp. 95–108, and Barker, *The Culture of Violence*, pp. 143–206.

101 In this latter sense, Beatrice's 'beauty' is not clearly separable from 'whoredom'. Nor is her 'so seeming-bottomless' [V.iii.1–6] loathing for De Flores clearly distinguishable from its opposite, and so forth.

102 The only 'change' he admits to is having 'chang'd embraces / With wantoness' (V.iii.200–1). 'That', he adds, 'was paid before' (V.iii.201), but by Diaphanta.

103 Alsemero's narrative does not seem to proceed without hesitation: 'In what part of this sad story shall I first begin?' (V.iii.87–8); 'I forgot my message' (V.iii.100).

104 See also Neill, '"Hidden malady": Death, Discovery, and Indistinction in *The Changeling*', p. 116.

105 I am using here Katharine Maus's more general study of early modern scenarios of male sexual jealousy. See Katharine Maus, 'Horns of Dilemma: Jealousy, Gender, and Spectatorship in English Renaissance Drama', *English Literary History*, 54 (1987), 561–83 (p. 571).

106 The play uses the word 'deformed' to connote both De Flores and Beatrice.

107 Borch-Jacobsen, *The Freudian Subject*, p. 21.

108 For instance, in Alsemero's *mise-en-scène*, Beatrice is quite unlike the 'turtle' she is for De Flores at the end of the third act: ''Las, how the turtle pants! Thou'lt love anon / What thou so fear'st and faint'st to venture on' (III.iv.170–1).

109 In Lacanian terms, it is strictly impossible for Alsemero to occupy a position of 'intimate exteriority'. This position can only signify the subversion of Alsemero's presence to himself as a spectating subject. Lacan's remarks on the distance dividing the 'subject' from the 'object' of its desire can be usefully juxtaposed to my reading: 'But this distance [from the object of desire] is not completely one; it is an intimate distance that is called proximity, which is not identical to the subject, which is literally close to it' (*The Seminar of Jacques Lacan. Book VII: The Ethics of Psychoanalysis 1959–60*, p. 76 [translation modified]). This 'intimate distance' is threateningly proximate.

110 Jacques Derrida, 'Fors', trans. by Barbara Johnson, *The Georgia Review*, 31, 1 (1977), 64–116 (p. 70; p. 80). Derrida's 'Fors' is a 'Foreword' to Nicolas Abraham and Maria Torok, *Cryptonymie: Le Verbier de l'Homme aux loups* (Paris: Aubier-Flammarion, 1976). It is also a more general account of Abraham and Torok's work. (This work has since been collected as Nicolas Abraham and Maria Torok, *L'Ecorce et le noyau* [Paris: Aubier-Flammarion, 1978].) For Abraham and Torok, introjection is a process that 'expands the self'. It does not 'retreat; it advances, propagates itself, assimilates, takes over' (Derrida, 'Fors', p. 70). Incorporation, instead, 'intervenes at the limit of introjection itself, when introjection, for any reason, fails' (Ibid, p. 71). Unlike introjection, which is 'gradual, slow, laborious, mediated, effective', incorporation is 'fantasmatic, unmediated, instantaneous, magical, sometimes hallucinatory' (Ibid.). The rejection of the intrinsically 'metaphoric' process of mourning, a process that should proceed by successive introjections, is a paradigmatic example of the magic and hallucinatory fantasy of incorporation. Derrida explains the paradoxical character of incorporation, as redefined by Abraham and Torok, as follows: 'With the real loss of the object having been rejected and the desire having been maintained but at the same time excluded from introjection …, incorporation is a kind of theft to reappropriate the pleasure-object. But that reappropriation is simultaneously rejected: which leads to the paradox of a foreign body preserved as foreign but by the same token excluded from a self which thenceforth deals not with the other, but only with itself. The more the self keeps the foreign element as a foreigner inside itself, the more it excludes it. The self *mimes* introjection. But this mimicry with its redoubtable logic depends on clandestinity.' (Ibid., p. 72.) Incorporation is thus an inherently unstable process. It is a way of keeping the other as other in all its integrity, but is also a refusal of the alterity of the other that always-already precedes the self. Derrida also underlines that the parasitic and cryptic enclave constructed 'inside' the Self as an 'outer' safe as a result of this process is subjected to 'the double pressure of contradictory forces: it is erected by its very ruin, held up by what never stops eating away at its foundation' (Ibid., p. 80). Derrida's strategic engraving of his name on the work of Abraham and Torok, which tries to force their work in a certain direction so as to make way for an anti-Lacanian psychoanalysis, can be interpreted *as* the cryptic incorporation he describes. For some

reflections on the relevance of the work of Abraham and Torok for an understanding of the problematics of the 'wounded name' in *Hamlet*, see Maurizio Calbi, '"A wounded name": *Hamlet* e il fantasma del nome', in Lidia Curti (ed.), *Ombre di un'ombra. Amleto e i suoi fantasmi* (Napoli: Istituto Universitario Orientale, 1994), pp. 189–222.

111 Heterosexual desire is here identified, in Sedgwick's words, as a 'machine for depriving males of self-identity' (*Between Men*, p. 36). Due to his position as the *actual* outsider and class aspirant, Alsemero is not only contingently, but almost by definition, subjected to these anxieties. On the unstable position of the class aspirant, see Peter Stallybrass, 'Patriarchal Territories: The Body Enclosed', in Margaret W. Ferguson, Maureen Quilligan, and Nancy J. Vickers (eds), *Rewriting the Renaissance: The Discourses of Sexual Difference in Early Modern Europe* (Chicago and London: Chicago University Press, 1986), pp. 123–42 (p. 134).

112 Dollimore, *Sexual Dissidence*, p. 159.

113 In a sense, De Flores's is an act performed by a man on a man. On the 'other man' as the most significant 'other' within male hetero/sexuality, see also Dollimore, *Sexual Dissidence*, esp. pp. 302–6.

114 Derrida, 'Fors', p. 70.

3 'A meer chaos'

1 On Beatrice as 'the changeling' of Middleton and Rowley's play, see Dale B.J. Randall, 'Some Observations on the Theme of Chastity in *The Changeling*', *English Literary Renaissance*, 14, 3 (1984), 347–66; and Lois E. Bueler, 'The Rhetoric of Change in *The Changeling*', *English Literary Renaissance*, 14, 1 (1984), 95–113.

2 This 'sign' is the 'mole cinque-spotted' (II.ii.38) on Imogen's breast. References to the play are from William Shakespeare, *The Complete Works*, ed. Peter Alexander (London and Glasgow: Collins, 1951).

3 Janet Adelman observes that Posthumus's 'parthenogenesis fantasy … makes bastardy contingent not on the mother's infidelity but on her mere participation in the act of procreation. The gap between the opening question – "Is there no way for men to be, but women / Must be half-workers?" – and the answer – "We are all bastards" – contains a submerged *if*: if there is no way for men to come into being without the half-work of women, then we are all bastards' (*Suffocating Mothers: Fantasies of Maternal Origin in Shakespeare's Plays, Hamlet to The Tempest* [New York and London: Routledge, 1992], p. 212).

4 Posthumus's is a vain attempt. However, as Adelman suggests, the fantasy of male parthenogenesis is not so much unfulfilled as displaced from the 'marriage plot' (that is, the Posthumus–Imogen plot) to the 'Cymbeline plot'. It reaches its apex with Cymbeline's 're-delivery' of his sons, which significantly takes place after the Queen's death: 'O, what am I? / A mother to the birth of three? Ne'er mother / Rejoic'd deliverance more' (V.v.368–70). Another interesting early modern exemplification of the impossibility of separating the woman's 'part' from the man's, albeit with rather different connotations, is in Marston's *Antonio's Revenge*. Here is Antonio, before stabbing Julio, Piero's son: 'O that I knew which joint, which side, which limb, / Were father all, and had no mother in't / That I might rip it, vein by vein, and carve revenge / In bleeding rases! But since 'tis mix'd together, / Have at adventure, pell-mell, no reverse!' (III.i.164–8.) I cite from John Marston, *Antonio's Revenge*, ed. G.K. Hunter (London: Edward Arnold, 1966).

5 I cite from the Arden edition of the play, ed. Harold Jenkins (London: Methuen, 1982).

6 Patricia Parker, '*Othello* and *Hamlet*: Dilation, Spying, and the "Secret Place" of Woman', *Representations*, 44 (1993), 60–95 (p. 81).

7 Jacques Guillemeau, *Child-Birth or, The Happy Deliverie of Women* (London, 1612) (repr. Amsterdam: Theatrum Orbis Terrarum, 1972). p. 13; James McMath, *The Expert*

Midwife: A Treatise of the Diseases of Women with Child and in Child-Bed (Edinburgh, 1694), p. 16.

8 Helkiah Crooke, *Microcosmographia. A Description of the Body of Man* (London, 1615), p. 298.

9 Thomas Laqueur, *Making Sex: Body and Gender From the Greeks To Freud* (Cambridge MA and London: Harvard University Press, 1990), p. 5. Here Laqueur is specifically referring to bodies as inverted and hierarchically structured versions of one another. However, he adds later on that reproductive fluids are 'but the higher stages in the concoction of food', and thus 'cannot be imagined as sexually specific, morphologically distinct, entities'. They are 'hierarchically ordered versions of one another according to their supposed power' (Ibid., p. 38). For a critique of Laqueur's assumption of the interchangeability of bodily fluids as symptomatic of the lack of definite boundaries between the sexes, see Gail Kern Paster, *The Body Embarrassed: Drama and the Disciplines of Shame in Early Modern England* (Ithaca and New York: Cornell University Press, 1993), esp. pp. 79–84. In particular, she emphasizes that the blood of the menstruating woman 'was readily classifiable as superfluity and waste' (Ibid., p. 79).

10 I am speaking of false conceptions and/or moles because not all early modern treatises differentiate false conceptions from moles. In these treatises, 'mole' (or 'mola') is etymologically related to the Greek μνλη (a millstone), because of its hardness, or to the Persian *moli* (a deformed thing).

11 Guillemeau, *Child-Birth*, p. 13.

12 *The Compleat Midwife's Practice Enlarged* (London, 1659), p. 84; p. 87. This text was first published in 1656. I am referring to the second edition, corrected and 'enlarged', and containing, as the title page has it, 'a full supply of those rare secrets of Mr Culpeper'. However, in the 'Preface' the authors launch an attack on Nicholas Culpeper's *A Directory for Midwives* (London, 1651). Jane Sharp also speaks of a 'membranous' mole, and discusses the 'pendent' mole in much the same terms as *The Compleat Midwife's Practice*, as a 'piece of flesh hanging within the inward neck of the womb … growing dayly downward in form like a bell' (*The Midwives Book* [London, 1671], p. 114). She also states that there are so many different kinds of moles that 'it is not possible to set them down according to their varieties' (Ibid., p. 107). Jane Sharp's is the first English midwifery treatise written by a woman. See Elaine Hobby's illuminating edition of this text (New York: Oxford University Press, 1999). See also Elaine Hobby, '"Secrets of the Female Sex": Jane Sharp, The Reproductive Female Body, and Early Modern Midwifery Manuals', *Women's Writing*, 8, 2 (2001), 201–12.

13 Ambroise Paré, *The Workes*, trans. by Thomas Johnson (London, 1634), p. 925. As the title page specifies, this is 'translated out of Latine and compared with the French'. The first Latin version of his works dates back to 1549. The first French version dates back to 1573.

14 Crooke, *Microcosmographia*, p. 297.

15 Ibid., p. 298.

16 Ibid., p. 297.

17 Ibid.

18 Ibid., p. 297; p. 298. Crooke adds that although 'it dayly groweth and encreaseth, that commeth not by true nutrition but by apposition onely' (p. 298).

19 Ibid.

20 Ibid., p. 297.

21 Ibid. That the child was nourished in the womb by menstrual blood was a commonly held notion. See Patricia Crawford, 'Attitudes to Menstruation in Seventeenth-Century England', *Past and Present*, 91 (1981), 47–73.

22 Guillemeau, *Child-Birth*, p. 14.

23 Paré, *The Workes*, p. 925.

24 Ibid. Similarly, François Mauriceau points out that 'the abundance of the gross and corrupt menstrual blood … gives not leisure to Nature to perfect, what she hath with

great pains begun, and so troubling its work, bringing thither confusion and disorder, there is made of the seeds and blood a meer chaos, called a mole' (*The Diseases of Women with Child, and in Child-Bed*, trans. by Hugh Chamberlen [London, 1683], p. 54). On the Chamberlen family, the inventors of the forceps, see J.H. Aveling, *The Chamberlens and the Midwifery Forceps* (London: Churchill, 1882).

25 'Vanquishing' and 'overcoming' are Paré's metaphors (*The Workes*, p. 925).

26 Jakob Rueff, *The Expert Midwife, or an Excellent and Most Necessary Treatise of the Generation and Birth of Man* (London, 1637), p. 139.

27 Ibid.

28 Scipione Mercurio, *La Commare o riccoglitrice* (Venice, 1601), p. 242.

29 For Aristotle, the cause of the *mola* is the 'weakness of heat ... because it looks as though Nature in these cases suffers from some inability, and is unable to complete the work and to bring the process of formation to its consummation'. This is the reason why 'the *mola* lasts on into old age or at any rate for a considerable time, for in its nature it is neither a finished product nor yet something wholly alien' (*Generation of Animals*, trans. by A.L. Peck, in Aristotle, *Works*, XIII, Loeb Classical Library [London: Heinemann, 1942], p. 465 [IV.vii.776a 1–9]). Aristotle's definition of the *mola* as 'neither a finished product nor yet something wholly alien' recalls some of his statements on the female as being 'as it were a deformity, though one which occurs in the ordinary course of nature' (Ibid., p. 461 [IV.vi.775a 15–17]). As is well known, Aristotle's first example of 'monstrosity', of how 'Nature has ... strayed from the generic type', is 'when a female is formed instead of a male' (Ibid., p. 401 [IV.iii.767b 8–10]). The production of female offspring emblematizes the lack of resemblance between parents and children, which is already a form of monstrosity. The French *accoucheur* Cosme Viardel defines the mole as a 'monstrous generation that deviates from [Nature's] original aim, which was that of forming a perfect animal' (Cosme Viardel, *Observations sur la practique des accouchements naturels, contre nature & monstreux* [Paris, 1671], p. 50 [my translation]). These are terms that recall the Aristotelian definition of woman. Amongst the many analyses of Aristotle's conception of woman, see especially Sylviane Agacinski, 'Le tout premier écart', in Philippe Lacoue-Labarthe and Jean-Luc Nancy (eds), *Les fins de l'homme* (Paris: Galilée, 1981), pp. 117–32; and Luce Irigaray, *Speculum of the Other Woman*, trans. by Gillian C. Gill (Ithaca NY: Cornell University Press, 1985, pp. 160–7).

30 Mercurio, *La Commare*, p. 244. For Mercurio, therefore, continent women or virgins cannot produce a *mola*. Avicenna's opinion, as reported by Paré and Sadler, is quite different. To Paré, Avicenna maintains that the cause of the mole is an 'unfruitfull' male seed, which 'onely puffes up or makes the womans seed to swell or leaven into a greater bigness, but not into any perfect shape or forme' (*The Workes*, p. 925). According to Sadler, Avicenna believes that a *mola* is produced when 'the womans seed goes into the wombe and not the mans' (John Sadler, *The Sick Womans Private Looking-Glasse* [London, 1636] [repr. Amsterdam: Theatrum Orbis Terrarum], p. 124).

31 Giovanni Marinelli, *Le medicine partenenti alle infermità delle donne* (Venice, 1563), p. 193 (translation mine).

32 Ibid. That women may inseminate themselves is an opinion Helkiah Crooke, amongst others, rejects, attributing it to Plutarch (*Microcosmographia*, p. 298). Some treatises make a distinction between 'dead moles' (that is, bags full of blood and seed produced by virgins and widows, with no contribution from the man) and 'living moles', for the production of which the male seed, however weak and defective, is essential. For Jane Sharp, the latter have 'some sense, or feeling or true motion', and 'can never be produced but mans seed must be a part of their beginning'. As to the former, 'if you cast it into the water, the skin coagulates like a clod of seed, and the blood runs away' (*The Midwives Book*, p. 108; p.109). In other treatises, the distinction between dead and living moles roughly corresponds to the distinction between false conceptions and moles. Referring to Hippocrates, Guillemeau stresses that 'the dead are like to the false burthens, so called, because women carry them not long, as being but lightly tyed and

fastened to the sides of the Matrice'. Instead, 'the quicke and living Moles are they which wholy cleave to the wombe, and continue with the woman even to her death' (*Child-Birth*, p. 14).

33 Laqueur, *Making Sex*, p. 58.

34 Ibid. However, Laqueur only considers the medical tradition that attributes the *mola* to female self-insemination.

35 Paré, *The Workes*, p. 885. I am citing from Paré's treatise because it contains a standard account of a 'normal' conception, typically conflating Aristotelian and Galenic notions.

36 Laqueur, *Making Sex*, p. 58.

37 Ibid., p. 59. See also Louis A. Montrose, '"Shaping Fantasies": Figurations of Gender and Power in Elizabethan Culture', in Stephen Greenblatt (ed.), *Representing the English Renaissance* (Berkeley: University of California Press, 1988), pp. 31–64 (pp. 42–45).

38 Laqueur, *Making Sex*, p. 59. Emphasis mine.

39 Patricia Parker, 'Gender Ideology, Gender Change: The Case of Marie Germain', *Critical Inquiry*, 19 (1993), 337–64 (p. 340). Parker focuses on Laqueur's interpretation of narratives of gender transformations from female to male. Yet her trenchant critique of the methodological assumptions underlying Laqueur's approach can be applied to other aspects of the one-sex model. She objects to Laqueur's uncritical reiteration of what medical authorities are never tired of repeating: these transformations 'work only up the great chain of being' (Thomas Laqueur, 'Orgasm, Generation, and the Politics of Reproductive Biology', *Representations*, 14 [1986], 1–41 [p. 13]), from less perfect to more perfect, hence women are nothing but men turned outside in who in 'normal' circumstances lack sufficient heat to extrude the penises they bear within, and endlessly desire the token of nature's perfection (that is, the phallus). Without denying the importance of this teleology of gender in the early modern period, Parker argues that the failure on Laqueur's part to submit this teleological model to a 'symptomatic reading' results in the homogenization of the complex and contradictory textual field of anatomical and gynaecological discourses, as well as in dubious generalizations about gender or gender change that also overlook 'the shifting and often incongruent relation' between these discourses and 'theological, political, literary, and other representations of women' ('Gender Ideology, Gender Change', p. 339). By contextualizing an anecdote on gender change reported by Montaigne and used by Laqueur, she persuasively shows how the 'rhetoric of insistence' governing early modern writings on gender transformation covers up anxiety about 'a form of … *renversement* [of the teleology of gender], the imperfection and defect … of male impotence' (Ibid., p. 343).

40 Laqueur, *Making Sex*, p. 58.

41 Rueff, *The Expert Midwife*, pp. 139–40.

42 See also Luce Irigaray: 'Being deprived of a womb [is] the most intolerable deprivation of man, since his contribution to gestation … is hence asserted as less than evident, as open to doubt. An indecision to be attenuated both by man's "active" role in intercourse and by the fact that he will mark the product of copulation *with his own name*' (*Speculum of the Other Woman*, p. 23).

43 Rueff, *The Expert Midwife*, p. 9.

44 Guillemeau, *Child-Birth*, p. 13.

45 Paré, *The Workes*, p. 925.

46 'Light behaviour' does not necessarily imply adultery or pre-marital sex. It could be a more general reference to the breaking of the taboo of sexual intercourse during menstruation; a transgression for which Paré may be blaming the woman more than the man. On menstruation, the Levitical taboo and monstrous conceptions, see Ottavia Niccoli, '"Menstruum quasi monstruum": Monstrous Births and Menstrual Taboo in the Sixteenth Century', trans. by Mary M. Gallucci, in Edward Muir and Guido Ruggiero (eds), *Sex and Gender in Historical Perspective* (Baltimore MD: Johns Hopkins University Press, 1990), pp. 1–25; Crawford, 'Attitudes to Menstruation in

Seventeenth-Century England', esp. pp. 57–65; Paster, *The Body Embarrassed*, pp. 168–71.

47 On the interimplication of anatomy and gynaecology's ocular drive and judicial discourses, see Chapter 1.

48 Paré, *The Workes*, p. 928.

49 Ibid., p. 926.

50 Ibid.

51 Ibid., p. 925. It is worth mentioning in this context that Paré finds her 'right testicle' bigger than the other. A large right testicle was often associated with lasciviousness. On anatomy-as-performance see Luke Wilson, 'William Harvey's *Prelectiones*: The Performance of the Body in the Renaissance Theater of Anatomy', *Representations*, 17 (1987), 62–95; Giovanna Ferrari, 'Public Anatomy Lessons and the Carnival in Bologna', *Past and Present*, 117 (1987), 50–106; and Jonathan Sawday, *The Body Emblazoned: Dissection and the Human Body in Renaissance Culture* (London and New York: Routledge, 1995). See also Andrew Cunnigham, 'The Kinds of Anatomy', *Medical History*, 19 (1975), 1–19.

52 Paré, *The Workes*, p. 926. Medical discussions of the *mola*, including Paré's, are often replete with the 'signs' that differentiate the *mola* from a 'true birth'. One of the differentiating signs is the type of movement occurring inside the womb. For Guillemeau, 'in true conception … the mother feeleth the child move every way … without any helpe. But in false conception, though there be some motion, it is not animall, but proceedeth rather from the expulsive facultie of the Mother than of the Mole, which having no living soule endevoureth not of itself to come forth, neither provoketh the wombe as the child doth, who having need of aire to breath in, seekes after it' (*Child-Birth*, p. 16). Interestingly, Guillemeau attributes some kind of agency to the womb in relation to the *mola*, but almost entirely denies any such agency to it in relation to the process of 'legitimate' birth. Birth is invariably interpreted at the time as the act of the child; the act of the male child, in turn, is seen as more vigorous than that of the female child. See Jean Donnison, *Midwives and Medical Men: A History of Inter-Professional Rivalries and Women's Rights* (New York: Schocken Books, 1977), pp. 11–12. On birth as the accomplishment of the fetus, as opposed to the mother's, and, more generally, on the contest over the meanings of childbirth in contemporary medical discourses, see Paula A. Treichler, 'Feminism, Medicine, and the Meaning of Childbirth', in Mary Jacobus, Evelyn Fox Keller and Sally Shuttleworth (eds), *Body/Politics: Women and the Discourses of Science* (London and New York: Routledge, 1990), pp. 113–38 (esp. pp. 116–23 and pp. 135–6n.). For contemporary medical metaphors of birth, see also Emily Martin, *The Woman in the Body: A Cultural Analysis of Reproduction* (Milton Keynes: Open University Press, 1989), pp. 54–68 and pp. 139–65.

53 Paré, *The Workes*, p. 928.

54 Ibid., p. 925.

55 Ibid., p. 4. On the fashioning and disciplining of the body, and the correction of bodily excess through tools, including surgical tools, see Michel de Certeau, 'Des outils pour écrire le corps', *Traverses* (Special issue: *Panoplies du corps*), 14–15 (1979), 3–14 (esp. p. 11). On the art of the surgeon, see Marie-Christine Pouchelle, 'Espaces cosmiques et dispositifs mécaniques. Le Corps et les outils au XIII et XIV siècles', *Traverses* (Special issue: *Panoplies du corps*), 14–15 (1979), 93–104. She explores medieval surgery, but her description of the self-fashioning of the surgeon as a demiurge or thaumaturge – to a large extent, an imaginary construct that is related to his anxiety about his professional identity – is applicable to the early modern period. On Paré's claim about the pre-eminence of the surgeon and surgery, see Jean Céard, *La Nature et les prodiges. L'Insolite au XVI siècle* (Genève: Droz, 1977), pp. 301–7. Guillemeau's 'Epistle Introductory to the Reader' to *Child-Birth* exemplifies the surgeon's resolution to see himself as more than a craftsman, although in a way that is more specifically related to the increasing intervention by surgeons in the field of midwifery. To Guillemeau, midwifery, because of its 'Antiquitie, Necessitie, and

Dexterity', is 'the most laudable and commendable' practice to which a surgeon can devote himself. As for its antiquity, 'the first worke in Chirurgery, that ever was in the worlde, was the cutting of the Navell which ... Adam practiced uppon his first borne'. The reference to the antiquity of the surgeon's work becomes one of the means of ideological legitimation of his intervention in the field of midwifery. 'Natural' births are part of a 'feminine nature' that is subjected to the 'art' of the male surgeon. Guillemeau's treatise is designed for the instruction of 'the young chirurgion'.

56 'Culture of dissection' is Jonathan Sawday's expression in his *The Body Emblazoned*. See especially pp. 1–15.

57 As shown in Chapter 1, Laqueur is at pains to demonstrate that the emergence of the aggressive science of anatomy, with its emphasis on looking and touching, does not reveal new 'truths' about the body. To Laqueur, in fact, 'advances in anatomy and anatomical illustration ... made the body ever more a representation of one flesh and of one corporeal economy' (*Making Sex*, p. 114). For criticism of this view, see Sawday, *The Body Emblazoned*, esp. pp. 213–29; Valerie Traub, 'The Psychomorphology of the Clitoris', *GLQ: A Journal of Lesbian and Gay Studies*, 2, 1–2 (1995), 81–113; and, *avant la lettre*, Francis Barker, *The Tremulous Private Body: Essays on Subjection* (London and New York: Methuen, 1984), pp. 73–85. See also Evelyn Fox-Keller, *Reflections on Gender and Science* (New Haven and London: Yale University Press, 1985), pp. 33–66.

58 See Chapter 1, note 86. Pivotal to this encroachment is the publication of midwifery treatises translated into the vernacular, starting with Roesslin's *The Birth of Man-Kinde* (1540). As Elizabeth D. Harvey points out, although these midwifery treatises are professedly designed to help midwives by supplying information in English to which they might not have access, they are 'both a vehicle for [this encroachment] and a symptom of it' (*Ventriloquized Voices: Feminist Theory and Renaissance Texts* [London and New York: Routledge, 1992], p. 79). See also Ibid., pp. 89–93. Thomas Raynalde's 'Prologue' to his translation of Roesslin's treatise (1545) presents an idyllic picture of what is in fact a complex struggle. In this 'Prologue', Raynalde hopes that the book 'may supply the room and place of a good Midwife'. He continues by asserting that since 'the first setting forth of this booke' (he is probably referring to Richard Jonas's 1540 translation of Roesslin), there have been 'right many honourable Ladies, & other Worshipfull Gentlewomen, which have not disdained the oftener by the occasion of this booke to frequent and haunt women in their labours, carrying with them this booke in their handes, and causing such part of it as doth chiefely concerne the same purpose, to be read before the midwife, and the rest of the women then being present; whereby ofttimes ... the laboring woman hath beene greatly comforted, and alleviated of her throngs and travaile' ('Prologue', pp. 14–15). Nonetheless, this idyllic picture is coupled with the indictment of envious and malicious midwives who have attempted to disparage the book out of a sense of false modesty: 'For verily there is no science, but that it hath his Apes, Owles, Beares and Asses' ('Prologue', p. 15).

59 Sadler, *The Sick Womans Private Looking-Glasse*, p. 132.

60 Harvey, *Ventriloquized Voices*, p. 87. Interestingly, in Mercurio's *La Commare o riccoglitrice*, the description of the extraction of the *mola*, which takes place at the end of the second book, is defined as a 'garland' (*ghirlanda*), as some kind of 'crowning achievement' of this book. The *commare* (the midwife) is invited to sit, relax and listen to this 'pleasant' description, which is meant to 'instruct and delight' (p. 211). In other words, her role is seen as even less active than the one played in other 'praternatural' deliveries such as Caesarean sections and the extraction of the dead fetus piecemeal; deliveries during which the use of surgical instruments is of paramount importance. (In the course of Caesarean sections, the *commare* is asked to help the woman evacuate, and then to hold her tight with other valiant women or men, while the surgeon marks with ink the place where he is about to cut [p. 193]. As for the extraction of a dead fetus, her only task is that of veiling the woman, so as to prevent the latter from seeing this horrible sight [p. 185].)

61 See Jean Donnison, *Midwives and Medical Men*, pp. 2–3. *The Birth of Man-Kinde* presents a rare example of advice to midwives about the use of surgical instruments in the removal of 'dead births': 'And first the woman must bee laid along upright, the middle part of her body lying higher than all the rest, accompanied of women assisting her about and to keepe her down. … Then let the midwife anointe her left hand with oil of white lilies, or other that may make it supple and smooth, and holding out her fingers, shutting together her hande, let her put it into the matrix to feele and perceive after what fashion the dead birth lieth in the mother's wombe so that she may the better put in hooks and such other instruments to plucke it out withall' (Roesslin, *The Birth of Man-Kinde*, p. 146).

62 Judith Butler, 'Imitation and Gender Insubordination', in Henry Abelove, Michèle Aina Barale and David M. Halperin (eds), *The Lesbian and Gay Studies Reader* (London and New York: Routledge, 1993), pp. 307–20 (p. 313). Butler, of course, intimates that this 'imitation' is never entirely successful. For further reflection on early modern masculinity, see Chapter 4.

63 My understanding of prosthetic extensions is indebted to Rosi Braidotti, *Nomadic Subjects: Embodiment and Sexual Difference in Contemporary Feminist Theory* (New York: Columbia University Press, 1994), esp. pp. 42–44 and p. 63.

64 Jacques Lacan, 'Desire and the Interpretation of Desire in *Hamlet*', trans. by James Hulbert, in Shoshana Felman (ed.), *Literature and Psychoanalysis. The Question of Reading: Otherwise* (Baltimore MD and London: The Johns Hopkins University Press, 1982), pp. 11–52 (p. 52). See also Jacques Lacan, 'The Signification of the Phallus', in *Écrits: A Selection*, trans. by Alan Sheridan (London: Tavistock, 1977), pp. 281–91, where he characterizes the 'masculine' position as man's vain display of the phallus he does *not* have. I am not arguing that Butler's groundbreaking work can be reduced to a Lacanian understanding of the phallus. For Butler's most sustained reflections on the Lacanian phallus, see Judith Butler, *Bodies That Matter. On the Discursive Limits of 'Sex'* (London and New York: Routledge, 1993), pp. 78–79 and pp. 101–11.

65 This can be juxtaposed to Sawday's following observation on the 'drive for knowledge' structuring anatomical discourses: 'The "thing" – the secret place, the core of bodily pleasure or knowledge of the body – always escapes representation' (*The Body Emblazoned*, p. 12). In Lacanian terms, this 'thing' is the 'Thing' that does not cease *not* writing itself. See also Joan Copjec, 'The Orthopsychic Subject: Film Theory and the Reception of Lacan', *October*, 49 (1989), 53–71 (esp. pp. 69–70).

66 Paré, *The Workes*, p. 128.

67 The midwifery treatise that most straightforwardly abides by the Aristotelian idea of the production of woman as somewhat of an aberration is perhaps *The Compleat Midwife's Practice Enlarged*, which contains a chapter on 'What course is to be taken that male children be brought into the world, not a female'. The author goes as far as to complain that the equilibrium between the sexes is being seriously disrupted, as well as the 'method' and 'design' of Nature . One is faced with a kind of cataclysmic mutation: more women 'are daily brought forth into the world than men' (*The Compleat Midwife's Practice Enlarged*, p. 289). See Hilda Smith, 'Gynecology and Ideology in Seventeenth-Century England', in Berenice A. Carroll (ed.), *Liberating Women's History. Theoretical and Critical Essays* (Urbana: University of Illinois Press, 1976), pp. 97–114, for observations on this treatise. Theoretically useful on this aspect is Braidotti, 'Mothers, Monsters, and Machines', in *Nomadic Subjects*, pp. 75–94. In parts of Roesslin's *The Birth of Man-Kinde*, a somewhat different voice emerges: 'although that man bee as principall mover and cause of generation, yet … the woman doth conferre and contribute much more … than doth the man. And doubtless, if a man would demande to whom the childe oweth most his generation, ye [women] may worthily make answer that to the mother, whether ye regard the pains in bearing, other else the conference of most matter in begetting' (*The Birth of Man-Kinde*, p. 17).

68 Paré, *The Workes*, p. 932.

69 Culpeper, *A Directory for Midwives*, p. 120; p. 121. Culpeper was an indefatigable author

and translator of medical texts. His work, reprinted many times, was aimed at a popular audience. For his alignment with radical critics of the medical establishment, see Christopher Hill, 'The Medical Profession and its Critics', in *Change and Continuity in Seventeenth-Century England* (London: Weidenfeld and Nicolson, 1974), pp. 157–78. On the medical profession more generally, and its relation with the socio-political changes of the period, see Harold J. Cook, *The Decline of the Old Medical Regime in Stuart London* (Ithaca NY and London: Cornell University Press, 1986). Culpeper's treatise is pervaded by a rhetoric of truth, and is replete with attacks on the College of Physicians. One example might suffice: 'I could have written you deeper notions in Physick than you shall find in this book; but I write for children, and Milk is fittest food for them. … The College hath wrap't [these notions] up in the Blankets of Ignorance' ('Epistle' to *A Directory for Midwives*, sig. A4v). In the 'Epistle' he also calls the members of the College 'a company of lazy Doctors'. The treatise is also permeated by denunciations of Galenic medicine. To Culpeper, Galen only ever dissected apes. This is why he wrote 'such an Apish Anatomy' (*A Directory for Midwives*, p. 33). Unlike Galen, he himself 'saw one woman opened that died in Child-bed, not delivered' (Ibid., p. 55). His claims to truth partially derive from this fact. Yet his treatise does not differentiate itself dramatically from other sixteenth- and seventeenth-century works.

70 Ibid., p. 121. This is the reason why 'whores have so seldom children'. This is also why 'women after long absence of their husbands, when they come again, usually soon conceive' (Ibid.).

71 Nicholas Fontanus, *The Womans Doctour: or, An Exact and Distinct Explanation of All Such Diseases as Are Peculiar to That Sex* (London, 1652), p. 130.

72 Ibid., p. 133. Instead, women with a 'temperate matrix' are 'fresh coloured, and of a rosie complexion, gentle of behaviour, affable in their carriage, merry and pleasant in their conversation, not dull and drowsie, and full of pensiveness' (Ibid., p. 130). On the barrenness of prostitutes, see Thomas Laqueur, 'The Social Evil, the Solitary Vice and Pouring Tea', in Michel Feher, Ramona Naddaff and Nadia Tazi (eds), *Fragments for a History of the Human Body. Part Three*, (New York: Zone, 1989), pp. 334–43.

73 Crooke, *Microcosmographia*, p. 234. He also points out that when the 'orifice' of the womb (the cervix) is 'too much loosened or opened above measure … by reason of too frequent copulation as in Harlots, it bringeth barrennesse' (Ibid.). Crooke is not untypical in referring to the vagina as the *collum uteri* (neck of the womb) or *cervix uteri*. Laqueur argues that 'the absence of a precise nomenclature for the female genitals, and for the reproductive system generally, is the linguistic equivalent of the propensity to *see* the female body *as* a version of the male'. It testifies to 'the absence of an imperative to create incommensurable categories through images or words' (*Making Sex*, p. 96).

74 Paré, *The Workes*, p. 931.

75 Sadler, *The Sick Womans Private Looking-Glasse*, p. 3.

76 To be a receptacle is opposed to fluidity. This falls within the scope of what Irigaray identifies as the 'dominant representation of the maternal figure as volume'; a representation that 'may lead us to forget that woman's ability to enclose is enhanced by her fluidity, and vice versa' (Irigaray, *Speculum of the Other Woman*, p. 239).

77 Sadler, *The Sick Womans Private Looking-Glasse*, p. 122.

78 *The Compleat Midwife's Practice Enlarged*, p. 83.

79 Ibid.

80 Crooke defines superfetation as 'a second conception, when a woman already with child accompanying with a man conceiveth again'. He also calls it an 'iterated conception' (*Microcosmographia*, p. 314). See also Aristotle, *Generation of Animals*, pp. 447–57 (IV.v.–vi. 773a33–774b27).

81 *The Compleat Midwife's Practice Enlarged*, p. 83. Emphasis mine.

82 As shown by Paré's reference to women's 'light behaviour' and Rueff's emphasis on 'lasciviousness', it is the woman's desire rather than the man's that is more often held most responsible for this disruption of the reproductive design. Although not in the

context of the discussion of the mole, the authors of *The Compleat Midwife's Practice Enlarged* point out that excessive copulation can alter the female sexual structure: 'in women with often copulation, they are oftentimes worn out, sometimes they are wholly worn out, and the inner side of the neck appears smooth, as it happens to whores' (Ibid. p. 28). On this alteration, which is not comparable to any of the effects of copulation on men's structure, see Smith, 'Gynecology and Ideology in Seventeenth-Century England', p. 105.

83 Culpeper, *A Directory for Midwives*, p. 121.

84 Paré, *The Workes*, p. 928. Like most early modern treatises, Paré's points out that the *mola* inexorably absorbs vital nourishment.

85 Laqueur points out that female erotic pleasure is frankly acknowledged and causally related to successful procreation. See Laqueur, 'Orgasm, Generation, and the Politics of Reproductive Biology', esp. p. 4. According to some critics, this is excessively optimistic. See, for instance, Paster, *The Body Embarrassed*, esp. p. 167. See also Chapter 5.

86 Fontanus, *The Womans Doctour*, p. 6.

87 Ibid., p. 4.

88 Ibid., p. 54. As shown earlier, some authors associate this retention with self-insemination and the production of the *mola*.

89 Sadler, *The Sick Womans Private Looking-Glasse*, p. 61.

90 Edward Jorden, *A Briefe Discourse of a Disease Called the Suffocation of the Mother* (London, 1603), p. 19. To Jorden, the 'suffocation of the Mother' is *not* to be seen as a prodigy. It is attributable to natural causes: 'The Symptoms of this disease are sayd to be monstrous and terrible to beholde, and of such varietie as they can hardly be comprehended within any method or boundes. Insomuch as they which are ignorant of the strange affects which naturall causes may produce, and of the manifold examples which our profession of Phisicke doth minister in this kind, have sought above the Moone for supernaturall causes: ascribing these accidents either to diabolicall possession, to withcraft, or to the immediate finger of the Almightie (Ibid., p. 2). This disease may no longer be seen as a prodigy (that is, as 'monstrous and terrible to beholde'). Yet the performance of the physician administering the cure is nothing short of prodigious. Jorden, for instance, tells the story of a fellow physician curing 'a maide of 18. years of age, which had every day two or three such strange fits'. He 'prescribed such remedies as are usuall in this case, and within few dayes recovered her, *to the great admiration of the beholders*' (Ibid., p. 4) (emphasis mine). For a study of the discursive shift 'from final causes (divine will) to proximate ones (physical explanations and the natural order)' in relation to monsters, which preludes to the medicalization and pathologization of monstrosity, see Katharine Park and Lorraine J. Daston, 'Unnatural Conceptions: The Study of Monsters in France and England, *Past and Present*, 92 (1981), 20–54. See also Céard, *La Nature et les prodiges*, esp. pp. 437–79. I return to the representation of monstrosity in Chapter 4.

91 Sadler, *The Sick Womans Private Looking-Glasse*, p. 110; Fontanus, *The Womans Doctour*, p. 6.

92 Jorden, *A Briefe Discourse*, p. 5.

93 Ibid., p. 18.

94 Sadler, *The Sick Womans Private Looking-Glasse*, p. 62.

95 Fontanus, *The Womans Doctour*, p. 52. For the straying womb, see Plato, *Timaeus*, trans. by R.G. Bury, in *Works*, VII, Loeb Classical Library (London: Heinemann, 1929), pp. 249–51 (91b–d).

96 Fontanus, *The Womans Doctour*, p. 52; p. 53.

97 Ibid., p. 53. Interestingly, in terms of the metonymic contiguity between the deformed womb and the *mola*, Fontanus scorns the French physician Fernelius, who perpetuates the 'fantastical conceit' of the wandering womb. Fernelius alleges that 'in these diseases he hath touched [the womb] upwards', but he is clearly wrong. He has probably mistaken 'a gross windy swelling of a roundish figure, and somewhat resembling the matrix' for 'the true matrix' (Ibid.). Is this 'windy swelling' a mole?

98 Fontanus, *The Womans Doctour*, p. 6.

99 Ibid., p. 150.

100 See Laqueur, 'Orgasm, Generation, and the Politics of Reproductive Biology', pp. 4–12, and Laqueur, *Making Sex*, pp. 43–52 and p. 64. As a seventeenth-century French treatise succinctly puts it, 'one can do no good in this matter without taking pleasure' (Jacques Duval, *Des Hermaphrodits, accouchemens des femmes, et traitement qui est requis pour les relever en santé & bien élever leur enfans* [Rouen, 1612], p. 36 [translation mine]).

101 Crooke, *Microcosmographia*, p. 216. For Crooke's ambivalent rejection of what he calls the 'proportion' of male and female sexual parts, see Laqueur, *Making Sex*, pp. 90–1. In the first of the 'Controversies' appended to the fifth book of *Microcosmographia*, Crooke offers a lengthy discussion of sexual difference, attacking both Aristotle and Galen. He objects to Aristotle's definition of woman as 'nothing else but an error or aberration of nature'; to his referring to woman as 'παραβασιζ by a metaphor taken from travellers which misse of their way, and yet at length attain their iournies end' (Ibid., p. 271). Yet, the objection to Aristotle is, in a sense, Aristotelian: 'The perfection of all naturall things is to be esteemed and measured by the end: now it was necessary that woman would be formed or else nature must have missed of her scope because she intended a perfect generation, which without woman cannot be accomplished.' Appealing to 'the truth of anatomy', Crooke also disputes Galen's idea that 'the necke of the wombe is nothing else but the virile member turned inward and the bottom of the wombe nothing but the scrotum or cod inverted.' He concludes by stressing that 'we must not think that the female is an imperfect male differing only in the position of the genitals', and that 'neither yet must we think that the sexes do differ in essential form and perfection, but in the structure and temperature of the parts of generation' (Ibid., p. 272). However, as he elaborates on this, he returns to a position that is partly Aristotelian and partly Galenic. The sexes differ in structure because 'the female generateth in herself, the male not in himself, but in the female', and in temperature because the female 'was to suggest and minister matter for the nourishment of the infant' (Ibid.). In fact, 'the temper of her whole body is colder than that of the man' (Ibid.), as also borne out by the fact that women 'want heat to thrust forth [their testicles]' (Ibid., p. 276).

102 Ibid., p. 262. Emphasis mine.

103 Ibid., p. 295. Emphasis mine.

104 Paré, *The Workes*, p. 887. Emphasis mine.

105 Duval, *Des Hermaphrodits*, p. 109. I am using the translation of this passage in Jacques Gélis, *History of Childbirth: Fertility, Pregnancy and Birth in Early Modern Europe*, trans. by Rosemary Morris (Cambridge: Polity Press, 1991), p. 60. See also Irigaray: 'Woman is neither open nor closed, form is never complete in her. The incompleteness in her form, her morphology, allows her to continually become something else. Perhaps this is what is meant by her insatiable (hysterical) thirst for satisfaction' (*Speculum of the Other Woman*, p. 229).

106 Sadler, *The Sick Womans Private Looking-Glasse*, p. 12.

107 Ibid.

108 Taking her cue from the representations of the wandering womb in *King Lear*, Janet Adelman suggests that these representations 'might … partly destabilize the hierarchical tidiness and stability implicit in the Galenic model' (*Suffocating Mothers*, p. 301n.). She adds that 'the body in which a womb can wander … may figure not a comfortable homology with the male but rather a fearful interior' (Ibid.). She also argues that woman's womb is 'the epitome of the woman who refuses to stay in her proper place' (Ibid, p. 114). On the ambivalence of the figure of the wandering womb, see also Paster, *The Body Embarrassed*, p. 175. She maintains, more generally, that 'reproductive writing uses physiology … to reinforce the construction of the female body as dangerously open' (Ibid., p. 181), and threatening to 'a dominant ideological configuration that always valorizes enclosure of the female body' (Ibid., p. 189). See

also Jonathan Sawday: 'The cultural history of the body suggests that a body which *escapes* its boundary … tends to be constructed … as female, whatever the biological sex' (*The Body Emblazoned*, p. 9). To Sawday, in early modern anatomical discourses the womb is the focus of fear: 'Like disease, the uterus operated according to its own laws, travelled at its own pace, hid itself from the searching gaze of the natural scientist, and demonstrated its presence by a token: blood' (Ibid., p. 10). Later in his study, he criticizes the one-sex view by focusing on the representations of the uterus in medical and poetical texts (Ibid., pp. 214–29).

109 Butler, *Bodies That Matter*, p. 16.

110 In Lacanian terms, this corresponds to the womb's capacity to *be* the phallus. This is *not* to be taken in Laqueur's sense, as an example of the structural homology between female and male genitalia – a homology whereby the former are the latter's inverted and reassuring double – but quite in the opposite sense, as signifying the womb's ability to be a threatening and uncanny double. Butler usefully summarizes Lacan's position: 'He "has"; she "reflects his having" and has the power to offer or withdraw that guarantee; therefore, she "is" the phallus, castrated, potentially threatening castration' (*Bodies That Matter*, p. 103). Butler goes on to show that this 'hierarchized and differentiated specular relation … is itself established through the exclusion and abjection of [other] domain[s] of relations' (Ibid.). This same logic applies to the treatises I have analysed.

111 Crooke, *Microcosmographia*, p. 262; p. 295.

112 Lacan, 'The Signification of the Phallus', in *Écrits: A Selection*, esp. pp. 289–90. Patricia Parker brilliantly emphasizes that in early modern texts the 'exaltation of the virile part is countered by the threat of impotence both as a "castrative gesture" and as a "sign of lack"', and that 'medical models of female imperfection and passivity are matched by fear of an inability to satisfy an insatiable female demand' ('Gender Ideology, Gender Change', p. 346). In other words, the representation of the womb as 'lack' is an anxious and largely unsuccessful attempt to defer man's implication in an abjecting castration.

113 Duval, *Des Hermaphrodits*, p. 35 (translation mine). Related to this fear is the representation of the 'vulva or valva' as a 'large door … [that] once opened cannot be closed again and grows more and more spacious, because one finds a great many workmen who take the trouble of opening and dilating it, but not so many who are willing to close and reseal it' (Ibid., p. 88) (translation mine).

114 Paré, *The Workes*, p. 887.

115 Michel de Montaigne, 'Of Idlenesse', in *The Essayes of Michael Lord of Montaigne*, trans. by John Florio (London and New York: Routledge, 1885), p. 13.

116 In relation to the analogy womb/mind in reproductive discourses, Laqueur observes that since 'normal conception is, in a sense, the male having an idea in the woman's body, then abnormal conception, the mola, is a conceit for her having an ill-gotten and inadequate idea of her own' (*Making Sex*, p. 59). It would be worth analysing, in the context of this analogy, the 'fable' William Harvey devises in *De generatione animalium* (1651), based as it is on the double meaning of 'conception'. (See William Harvey, *De generatione animalium*, in *The Works of William Harvey*, trans. by Robert Willis [London: Sydenham Society, 1847], esp. pp. 575–80.) For an extremely suggestive association between uterus and mind, and its relation to the fashioning of femininity, see Erasmus' *Institutio matrimonii christiani* (1526): 'Just as in generation a woman does not produce anything perfect without intercourse with an healthy man, and without this she produces nothing but unformed matter that is no more than a mass of bad humours, so also if a husband does not take care to cultivate his wife's spirits, what else can one hope for?' (This is cited in Constance Jordan, *Renaissance Feminism: Literary Texts and Political Models* [Ithaca NY and London: Cornell University Press, 1990], p. 63.) Thus, without 'proper cultivation', there is no hope of well-formed concepts and conceptions. Erasmus' 'mass of bad humours' does not seem to me to be a reference to the menses, as Jordan suggests, but to some kind of 'humorall' mole. See Guillemeau, *Child-Birth*, p. 13; p. 15.

117 Crooke, *Microcosmographia*, p. 270.

118 Duval, *Des Hermaphrodits*, p. 102 (translation mine). Duval often associates defloration and penetration with the 'cultivation' (*culture*) of a woman's 'garden' or 'natural field' (Ibid., p. 102; p. 57). *Culture* is the prerogative of the male.

119 Sharp, *The Midwives Book*, p. 33. It is worth pointing out that the *mola* is sometimes said to lead 'a life ... vegitative', in the manner of a weed (Sadler, *The Sick Womans Private Looking-Glasse*, p. 126). It is also worth noting that in *The Tempest* Caliban is called a 'moon-calf' (II.ii.99), a synonym for *mola*; and that, to Prospero, the exercise of restraint acts as a guarantee for a 'legitimate' conception. Ferdinand's 'breaking' of Miranda's 'virgin-knot before / All sanctimonious ceremonies' would 'bestrew / The union of [Ferdinand and Miranda's] bed with weeds so loathly' (IV.i.15–16; 20–21); 'weeds' like Caliban, who is 'not honour'd with / A human shape (I.ii.283–4). References to *The Tempest* are from William Shakespeare, *The Complete Works*.

120 See Judith Butler, 'Sexual Inversions', in Domna C. Stanton (ed.), *Discourses of Sexuality: From Aristotle to Aids* (Ann Arbor: The University of Michigan Press, 1992), pp. 344–61. In a reading that is critical of Foucault's use of the concepts of prohibition and production in *The History of Sexuality: An Introduction* (trans. by Robert Hurley [Harmondsworth: Penguin Books, 1981]), she argues that there is only 'a production that is *at the same time* constraint', a 'constraining production' (p. 350). See also my 'Introduction'.

121 For instance, Crooke maintains, referring to Aristotle, that 'the seeds of the parents containing in them the idea or forme of the singular parts of the body are never actuated, never exhibit their power or efficacy unless they be sown and, as it were, buried in the fruitful field or garden of nature, the womb of the woman' (*Microcosmographia*, p. 270). However, the power of the womb is acknowledged but also disavowed. The male remains 'the first principle of the worke, and ... affordeth the greater part of the formative power or faculty'. The female 'affordeth the place wherein the seede is conceived and the matter whereby the conception is nourished and sustained'. This 'place', in turn, only 'helpeth to add vigour and efficacy' to 'the spirit of the seed' (Ibid.). Thus, the womb qua mark of the female is an 'ex-orbitant *trait*' (see also Agacinski, 'Le tout premier écart', esp. pp. 125 and p. 129), the *conditio sine qua non* of reproduction that matters less. *The Compleat Midwife's Practice Enlarged* presents some interesting examples of the construction of the womb as a less-(than)-significant *and* crucial entity. This treatise speaks of different 'actions of the womb', but then underlines that its 'chiefest action ... and most proper to it, is the retention of the seed' (*The Compleat Midwife's Practice Enlarged*, p. 42). One may add that the construction of the womb as less-(than)-significant is inextricably bound with the fact that inception, and the formative power of the male in inception, are valued over and above gestation. See also Margreta de Grazia, 'Imprints: Shakespeare, Gutenberg and Descartes', in Terence Hawkes (ed.), *Alternative Shakespeares: Vol. 2* (London and New York: Routledge, 1996), pp. 63–94 (esp. p. 80).

122 Montaigne, 'Of Idlenesse', in *The Essayes*, p. 13.

123 Given the conclusion to 'Of Idlenesse', as well as Montaigne's more general unrelenting highlighting of the contradictory and self-divided concept of the 'natural', as perhaps most notoriously articulated in 'Of the Caniballes', it is worth re-marking the question of just how 'wilde' and 'unprofitable' the products of female self-insemination are. To use the language of the latter essay, they are 'fruits ... which nature of her selfe and of her ordinarie progresse hath produced' ('Of the Caniballes', in *The Essayes*, p. 94). However, this problematization of distinctions does not erase the fact that Montaigne's self-impregnation is an appropriation and transubstantiation of female reproductive power. For the production of books as offspring, a 'spiritual' engendering in which Montaigne sees himself as both father and mother, see, for instance, 'Of the Affections of Fathers to their Children', in *The Essayes*, esp. pp. 200–2. Midwifery treatises often exploit the metaphorical connection between books and

offspring. Culpeper and Crooke present some interesting variations on the theme. In *A Directory for Midwives*, Culpeper observes: 'If [the book] be childish, it is like its Mother: Before you dispraise my work, put forth your own like a Man' ('To the Reader', sig. A4v). He adds: 'I have viewed over this work, and acknowledg[ed] it as my own Child begotten in me by the Eternal Providence of God, Errors mentioned in the Errata excepted; if it be good, let the Father [God] have the praise, its corruption it hath from its Mother [himself]' (Ibid.). He returns to his 'Errors' in a facetious way in the 'Errata Corrigenda' at the end of the treatise: 'Although it seems very improbable to Nature, that a Generation should be gotten by absence; yet hath my absence from the Press beget a generation of Errours'. Is this the death of the author *avant la lettre*? Introducing 'The History of the Infant', the fifth book of his *Microcosmographia*, Crooke comments as follows: '[A]t the first sight I conceived that my selfe also in this my conception should find pleasure. But it hap[pe]neth all otherwise with me than it is in naturall generation, where the infant is begotten in pleasure though brought forth in paine. For this I assure thee was begotten with much paine & travail, and if thy gentle hand help not in the birth, that also will be very irksome' (*Microcosmographia*, p. 257).

124 Butler, *Bodies That Matter*, p. 35; p. 38. Butler's emphasis.

125 As Hélène Cixous notes, women are bearers of 'the greatest norm, that of reproduction', but they also 'embody … the anomaly'. See Hélène Cixous and Catherine Clément, *The Newly Born Woman*, trans. by Betsy Wing (Minneapolis: University of Minnesota Press, 1986), pp. 7–8.

4 'Strange flesh' and 'unshap't bodies'

1 Rosi Braidotti, 'Signs of Wonder and Traces of Doubt: On Teratology and Embodied Differences', in Nina Lykke and Rosi Braidotti (eds), *Between Monsters and Goddesses and Cyborgs. Feminist Confrontations with Science, Medicine and Cyberspace* (London and New Jersey: Zed Books, 1996), pp. 135–52 (p. 141).

2 Jacques Guillemeau, *Child-Birth or, The Happy Deliverie of Women* (London, 1612) (repr. Amsterdam: Theatrum Orbis Terrarum, 1972), p. 26.

3 Paré's teratological treatise was first translated into English as a section of his monumental *Workes*. See Ambroise Paré, *The Workes*, trans. by Thomas Johnson (London, 1634), pp. 961–1026. For the complex textual history of this treatise, see Ambroise Paré, *On Monsters and Marvels*, ed. Janis L. Pallister (Chicago: University of Chicago Press, 1982), pp. viii–xv. By 'naturalization' I mean, following Park and Daston, the shift of discursive emphasis in teratological literature from 'final causes (divine will) to proximate ones (physical explanations and the natural order)'. See Katharine Park and Lorraine J. Daston, 'Unnatural Conceptions: The Study of Monsters in France and England', *Past and Present*, 92 (1981), pp. 20–54 (p. 35). See also Jean Céard, *La Nature et les prodiges. L'Insolite au XVI siècle* (Genève: Droz, 1977), especially pp. 437–79.

4 Paré, *The Workes* (London, 1634), p. 979.

5 Phyllis Rackin, 'Historical Difference / Sexual Difference', in Jean R. Brink (ed.), *Privileging Gender in Early Modern England: Sixteenth Century Essays & Studies Vol. XXIII* (Ann Arbor: Michigan University Press, 1993), pp. 37–63 (p. 39).

6 Helkiah Crooke, *Microcosmographia. A Description of the Body of Man* (London, 1615).

7 I owe much to Karen Newman's reading of Crooke's title page. See Karen Newman, *Fashioning Femininity and English Renaissance Drama* (Chicago and London: The University of Chicago Press, 1991), pp. 3–4.

8 I appropriate Judith Butler's distinction between bodies that matter, on the masculine side, and bodies that do not matter, on the feminine side. I hasten to add that this is a reiterable and highly unstable distinction, which in the material I analyse often re-presents itself as a distinction between a 'masculine' form that is not a body – what I call

a figure of 'dis-embodiment' – and a formless matter that is not quite a body (that is, a 'body proper'). See Judith Butler, *Bodies That Matter: On the Discursive Limits of 'Sex'* (London and New York: Routledge, 1993), esp. pp. 27–55 and *passim*. As will become clearer in the course of this chapter, this is different from arguing that femininity is yet another name for the body/flesh.

9 See also Chapter 1 on ocularity and Chapter 3 on early modern reproductive discourses.

10 Karen Newman rightly points out the instability of the images in Crooke's title page. She argues that the 'hierarchized polarities – male / female, active / passive, culture / nature ' through which they present themselves can be made to speak otherwise (*Fashioning Femininity*, p. 11). In this chapter, I pursue her argument on the ambiguity of the apparently neutral and 'normative' male body by tracing the uneven routes of masculinity as a figure that is supposed to matter only as an icon of 'dis-embodiment'.

11 Mark Breitenberg, *Anxious Masculinity in Early Modern England* (Cambridge: Cambridge University Press, 1996), p. 11.

12 Judith Butler, *Gender Trouble: Feminism and the Subversion of Identity* (London and New York: Routledge, 1990), esp. 134–41.

13 Laura Levine, *Men in Women's Clothing: Anti-theatricality and Effeminization 1579–1642* (Cambridge: Cambridge University Press, 1994), p. 8.

14 Ibid.

15 Ibid., p. 153n.

16 Butler, *Bodies That Matter*, p. x.

17 Levine, *Men in Women's Clothing*, p. 55.

18 For a lucid discussion of the relevance of Butler's work to the field of early modern studies, see Linda Charnes, 'Styles That Matter: On The Discursive Limits of Ideology Critique', *Shakespeare Studies*, 24 (1996), 118–47.

19 *Antony and Cleopatra* is quoted from the Arden Edition, ed. M.R. Ridley (London: Methuen, 1954). References are included parenthetically in the text.

20 Antony identifies this as 'penetrative shame' (IV.xiv.75).

21 My brief reading of the play is also offered as an alternative to interpretations of masculinity such as Coppelia Kahn, *Roman Shakespeare: Warriors, Wounds, and Women* (London and New York: Routledge, 1997).

22 A rather different interpretation of masculinity could be put forward on the basis of Jacques Derrida's observations on the masculine leader as the one who must necessarily eat flesh, and the intrinsic relation between the virile subject of sacrifice and symbolic anthropophagy. See Jacques Derrida, '"Eating Well," Or the Calculation of the Subject: An Interview with Jacques Derrida', in Eduardo Cavava, Peter Connor and Jean-Luc Nancy (eds), *Who Comes After the Subject?* (London and New York: Routledge, 1991), pp. 96–119.

23 *Coriolanus* is cited from the Arden Edition, ed. Philip Brockbank (London: Methuen, 1976). References are included parenthetically in the text.

24 Cynthia Marshall, '*Coriolanus*, Gender, and the Theatrical Construction of Interiority', in Valerie Traub, M. Lindsay Kaplan and Dympna Callaghan (eds), *Feminist Readings of Early Modern Culture* (Cambridge: Cambridge University Press, 1996), pp. 93–118 (p. 109).

25 Bruce Smith, *Shakespeare and Masculinity* (Oxford: Oxford University Press, 2000), p. 104.

26 Breitenberg, *Anxious Masculinity in Early Modern England*, p. 21.

27 See Ania Loomba, *Gender, Race, Renaissance Drama* (Manchester and New York: Manchester University Press, 1989), pp. 48–62 (p. 48). My interpretation of *Othello* is much indebted to her groundbreaking work on the intersection of race, gender and status in the play.

28 All references to *Othello* are from the New Arden Edition, ed. M.R. Ridley (London and New York, Methuen, 1965), and are included parenthetically in the text.

29 It could be argued that effeminacy, just like sodomy, emerges as a charge against men only as a way of signifying a wider undermining of boundaries, including, and most importantly for my purposes here, ethnic and racial boundaries.

30 That Othello is willing to exchange his 'unhoused free condition' for the domestic pleasure of the *oikos* is one of the elements that differentiates him from stereotypical representations of the Moor such as Aaron's in *Titus Andronicus* or Eleazar's in the anonymous *Lust's Dominion* (1600). Eleazar, for instance, speaks as proudly as Othello of his origins: 'Although my flesh be tawny, in my veines, / Runs blood as red, and royal as the best / And proud'st in Spain' (I.ii.9–11), but he is outside any circuit of exchange. (*Lust's Dominion* is cited from *Literature Online*, University of Salerno, 16 June 2002, http://lion.chadwyck.co.uk.) Yet, as Lyotard reminds us, and as *Othello* shows, the *oikos* is never a place of safety. It is, rather, 'the place of tragedy'. See Jean François Lyotard, *Political Writings*, trans. by Bill Readings and Kevin Paul Geiman (Minneapolis: University of Minnesota Press, 1991), p. 97.

31 Daniel J. Viktus, 'Turning Turk in *Othello*: The Conversion and Damnation of the Moor', *Shakespeare Quarterly* 48, 2 (1997), 145–76 (p. 147).

32 Edward Kellett, *A Return from Argier. A Sermon Preached at Minhead in the Country of Somerset the 16. of March, 1627 at the re-admission of a relapsed Christian into our Church* (London, 1628), Early English Books Online, University of Salerno Library, 16 June 2004, http://eebo.chadwyck.com, p. 74. The pamphlet is divided into two sections. The first section contains the sermon by Edward Kellett. The second section includes the sermon by Henry Byam from which I am citing (pp. 48–78).

33 Nicholas de Nicholay, *Navigations, Peregrinations and Voyages, Made into Turkie*, trans. by T. Washington (London, 1585), p. 8. The 'original Turk' is no better than his supplementary renegade double. In his *Discours of the Turkes* (1617), Thomas Shirley junior, who had been in Turkish captivity, characterizes the Turks as follows: 'Theyre manner of living in private & in generalle is moste unciville & vicious; & firste, for theyre vices they are all pagans & infidelles, Sodomittes, liars, & drunkardes, & for theyre Sodommerye they use it soe publiquelye & impudentelye as an honest Christian woulde shame to companye with his wyffe as they doe with theyre buggeringe boyes.' See Thomas Shirley, *Discours of the Turkes*, ed. E. Denison Ross (London: Royal Historical Society, 1936), p. 2.

34 The expression 'turning Turk' often recurs in the drama of the period. The spectre of conversion to Islam is so widespread that it becomes the central theme of plays such as *A Christian Turn'd Turke* (1612) by Robert Daborne, fictionalizing the life of the famous English renegade John Ward, and *The Renegado* (1624) by Philip Massinger. See Nabil Matar, 'The Renegade in English Seventeenth-Century Imagination', *Studies in English Literature* 33 (1993), 489–505.

35 Kellett, *A Return from Argier*, p. 23.

36 Edward Aston, *The Manners, Lawes and Customes of All Nations* (London, 1611), p. 137, cit. in Viktus, 'Turning Turk in *Othello*', 156.

37 Nicholas de Nicholay, *Navigations, Peregrinations and Voyages, Made into Turkie*, p. 100.

38 Ibid.

39 It is not by chance that Brabantio's warning will become part of Iago's repertoire of seductive strategies later on: 'She did deceive her father, marrying you' (III.iii.210).

40 See also Newman, *Fashioning Femininity*, pp. 71–93, for a reading of the monstrous conjunction of blackness and femininity in and around *Othello*.

41 Othello kills Desdemona, as well as himself, acting and speaking on behalf of 'all men', adopting a universalistic construct of man that *de facto* excludes him as a non- white and non-Christian man. See Loomba, *Gender, Race, Renaissance Drama*, pp. 59–60.

42 Leo Africanus, *A Geographical Historie of Africa*, trans. by John Pory (London, 1600) (repr. Amsterdam: Theatrum Orbis Terrarum and Da Capo Press, 1969), pp. 314–15. His description of the women of Cairo is by no means unique. Leo often points out the deceitfulness of women of North Africa. This passage can be fruitfully read in conjunction with Othello's affirmation that his 'wife is fair, feeds well, loves company, / Is free of speech, sings, plays, and dances well' (III.iii.188–9). It can also be associated with the following lines: 'Haply, for I am black, / And have not those soft parts of

Conversation / That chamberers have: or for I am declin'd / Into the vale of years … / She's gone. I am abus'd, and my relief / Must be to loathe her: O curse of Marriage, / That we can call these delicate creatures ours, / And not their appetites!' (III.iii.267–74).

43 See Ania Loomba, '"Delicious traffick": Racial and Religious Difference on Early Modern Stages', in Catherine M.S. Alexander and Stanley Wells (eds), *Shakespeare and Race* (Cambridge: Cambridge University Press, 2000), pp. 203–24 (p. 204). In addition to the critical works I have already referred to, dealing with the complex cultural negotiations between East and West and representations of the Islamic 'other', the following are compulsory reading: Nabil Matar, *Turks, Moors, and Englishmen in the Age of Discovery* (New York: Columbia University Press, 1999); Lisa Jardine and Jerry Brotton, *Global Interests: Renaissance Art Between East and West* (London: Reaktion Books, 2000); Jerry Brotton, *The Renaissance Bazaar: From the Silk Road to Michelangelo* (Oxford: Oxford University Press, 2003); Gerald MacLean, *Rise of Oriental Travel. English Visitors to the Ottoman Empire, 1580–1720* (Houndsmill and New York: Palgrave, 2004).

44 Africanus, *A Geographical Historie of Africa*, p. 2.

45 This eulogy becomes more complicated in other sections of the text, but I cannot dwell on this here.

46 Africanus, *A Geographical Historie of Africa*, p. 42.

47 Ibid., p. 284–5.

48 Much more work is needed on this aspect. I maintain, following Viktus, that Othello, as emblematic of the representation of the Moor in early modern culture, is 'a hybrid who might be associated … with a whole set of related terms – *Moor, Turk, Ottomite, Saracen, Mahometan, Egyptian, Judean, Indian* – all constructed and positioned in opposition to Christian faith and virtue' (Viktus, 'Turning Turk in *Othello*', pp. 159–60). Yet I also want to suggest, for further research, that the proto-colonial fantasy of the infinite malleability of the other, which is part of Othello's *imaginaire*, often seems to find its articulation only in relation to the representation of the black other. This gendered fantasy of inscription on the *tabula rasa* of a virgin territory and body becomes, in relation to representation of the Ottoman 'other', a fear of being sodomized. (See also the examples I have cited referring to Muslim people's supposed sexual propensities, and Matar, *Turks, Moors, and Englishmen in the Age of Discovery*, esp. pp. 3–18; pp. 109–28.) One must consider, moreover, that in early modern discourses there persists the myth of the intractability of the body of the black woman. She is often seen as exemplifying the age-old proverb 'To wash an Ethiop white'. The Muslim (and Jewish) woman is often figured, instead, as eminently susceptible to conversion, and thus willing to reinsert her body in the circuit of exchange. Cf. Ania Loomba, '"Delicious traffick"', p. 211; pp. 214–19.

49 By 'sodomitical', I am not simply referring to the way the sexual act between Othello and Desdemona is visualized. Sodomy, as many studies of early modern erotic systems have pointed out, after Foucault, is also a way of naming the unnamable. It signifies the breakdown of the early modern *dispositif* of alliance. See especially Alan Bray, *Homosexuality in Renaissance England* (London: Gay Men's Press, 1982), and Jonathan Goldberg, *Sodometries: Renaissance Texts, Modern Sexualities* (Stanford: Stanford University Press, 1992).

50 Ambroise Paré, *On Monsters and Marvels*, p. 67 (emphasis mine). Cf. Paré, *The Workes*, p. 982.

51 Martin Orkin, '*Othello* and the "Plain Face" of Racism', *Shakespeare Quarterly*, 38 (1987), 166–88 (p. 170). See also Ian Smith, 'Barbarian Errors: Performing Race in Early Modern England', *Shakespeare Quarterly*, 49 (1998), 168–86, an essay arguing that the play disrupts and interrogates the binaries of early modern racial hierarchies by means of rhetorical inversion.

52 Indeed, he hastens to add: 'Yet, the dishonesty lies in the deed and not in the words.' For his problems with censorship, see Paré, *On Monsters and Marvels*, pp. X–XI; p. 188n.

53 Jonathan Dollimore, *Sexual Dissidence: Augustine to Wilde, Freud to Foucault* (Oxford: Clarendon Press, 1991), p. 161.

54 Samuel Chew, *The Crescent and the Rose: Islam and England during the Renaissance* (New York: Octagon Books, 1974 [1937]), pp. 486–8; Viktus, 'Turning Turk in *Othello*', p. 147.

55 All references to the play are to Thomas Goffe, *The Couragious Turke, or, Amurath the First* (London: Richard Meighen, 1632), *Literature Online*, University of Salerno, 16 June 2004, <http://lion.chadwyck.co.uk>, and are included parenthetically in the text.

56 Amurath seems to be aware that effeminacy is not merely the sign of the breakdown of the boundaries of gender: 'The Christians now will scoffe at Mahomet; / Perchance they sent this wretch [i.e. Eumorphe] thus to inchant me!' (I.iii.50–1). This is another example of early modern effeminacy appearing as such only when other types of transgressions are involved – just like sodomy.

57 On the feminine leaking body, see Gail Kern Paster, *The Body Embarrassed: Drama and the Disciplines of Shame in Early Modern England* (Ithaca and New York: Cornell University Press, 1993), esp. 23–63.

58 It is not by chance that Alexander the Great is introduced here. He is one of the Renaissance icons of masculine struggle against effeminizing love. One only needs to think of Alexander's 'conquest' of himself – his subduing of his passion for Campaspe – in John Lily's *Alexander and Campaspe* (1584).

59 My emphasis.

60 In spite of this rhetoric of hypermasculinity, a wound will be fatal to Amurath later on in the play.

61 For some reflections on the logic of displacement of this hyperbolic masculinity on to the demonized 'Turk', see Maurizio Calbi, '"Unshap't Bodies": Masculinity Travels East', in *1453–1699: Cultural Encounters Between East and West*, ed. Matthew Dimmock and Matthew Birchwood (Cambridge: Cambridge Scholars Press, 2005). For the contradictory representation of masculinity within early modern discourses on the Levant, see also Daniel J. Viktus, 'Trafficking with the Turk: English Travelers in the Ottoman Empire During the Early Seventeenth Century', in Ivo Kamps and Jyotsna Singh (eds), *Travel Knowledge. European 'Discoveries' in the Early Modern Period*, (Houndsmill and New York: Palgrave, 2001), pp. 35–52.

5 'Un-pleasurable' detours

1 Helkiah Crooke, *Microcosmographia. A Description of the Body of Man* (London, 1615), p. 238.

2 Ibid.

3 Ibid., p. 200.

4 Ibid.

5 Ibid., p. 238.

6 Ibid., p. 200. See also Michel Foucault, *The Use of Pleasure*, trans. by Robert Hurley (New York: Pantheon, 1985), pp. 133–6.

7 The ejection of sperm, the most vital substance of the body, is often associated with death. See Michel Foucault *The Care of the Self*, trans. by Robert Hurley (New York: Pantheon, 1986), pp. 112–13; and, more generally, pp. 112–23; see also Foucault, *The Use of Pleasure*, esp. pp. 125–39. Early modern texts are replete with puns on 'die' and 'death'.

8 On the concept of restricted economy, see Jacques Derrida's reading of Bataille in his *Writing and Difference*, trans. by Alan Bass (London: Routledge and Kegan Paul, 1978); and Jacques Derrida, *Donner le temps* (Paris: Galilée, 1991). Writing on Hegel, in a way that is extremely suggestive for my argument here, Derrida ponders as follows: 'The parents … reg(u)ard their child as their own death. And in reg(u)arding that disappearance, that death, they retard it, appropriate it; they maintain in the monumental presence of their seed – in the name – the living sign that they are dead, not that *they are dead*, but that *dead they are*, which is another thing. Ideality is death, to be sure, but to be dead – this is the whole question of dissemination – is that *to be* dead or to be *dead*? The ever so slight difference of stress, conceptually imperceptible, the inner fragility of each attribute produces the oscillation between the presence of being as death and the death of being as presence …. [Their] own proper death, when

contemplated in the child, is the death that is denied, the death that *is*, that is to say, denied' (Jacques Derrida, *Glas*, trans. By John P. Leavey, Jr. and Richard Rand [Lincoln: University of Nebraska Press, 1986], p. 133).

9 'Transposed' is used by Crooke, *Microcosmographia*, p. 200.

10 On male homosocial desire, see Eve Kosofsky Sedgwick, *Between Men: English Literature and Male Homosocial Desire* (New York: Columbia University Press, 1985), esp. pp. 1–66. See also Chapter 2.

11 Crooke, *Microcosmographia*, p. 238.

12 Ibid., p. 200.

13 Michel Foucault, *The History of Sexuality: An Introduction*, trans. by Robert Hurley (Harmondsworth: Penguin Books, 1981), p. 106.

14 The following lines by Edward II, addressed to the peers, emblematize the extent to which his desire is a declining of his political duties as a king: 'If this content you not, / Make several kingdoms of this monarchy / And share it equally amongst you all, / So I may have some nook or corner left / To frolic with my Gaveston' (I. iv. 69–73). (Christopher Marlowe's *Edward II* is cited from from the New Mermaids edition of the play, ed. Moelwyn Merchant [London, Ernest Benn, 1967].) I am juxtaposing the erotic bond between Brachiano and Vittoria and the liaison between Edward II and Gaveston to suggest that the gender of the object of desire is uninfluential. For a study of Marlowe's play that is extremely attentive to the historicity of configurations of the erotic within and without the play, see Jonathan Goldberg, *Sodometries: Renaissance Texts, Modern Sexualities* (Stanford: Stanford University Press, 1992), pp. 105–26. Alan Bray refers to Marlowe's play in the course of his argument on the uncanny overlapping of seemingly opposed figures such as the 'masculine friend' and the 'sodomite'. See Alan Bray, 'Homosexuality and the Signs of Male Friendship in Elizabethan England', *History Workshop*, 29 (1990), 1–19 (pp. 8–13). See also Catherine Belsey, 'Desire's Excess and the English Renaissance Theatre: *Edward II, Troilus and Cressida, Othello*', in Susan Zimmerman (ed.), *Erotic Politics: Desire on the Renaissance Stage* (New York and London: Routledge, 1992), pp. 84–102. Belsey's Lacanian emphasis that desire is in excess of both the 'subject' and 'object' of desire is not incompatible with the attempts by critics such as Goldberg to historicize the regime of dichotomous object-choice.

15 References to the play are from the New Mermaids edition, ed. Elizabeth M. Brennan (London: Ernest Benn, 1966).

16 Jonathan Dollimore, *Sexual Dissidence: Augustine to Wilde, Freud to Foucault* (Oxford: Clarendon Press, 1991), p. 305.

17 Bruce R. Smith usefully summarizes: 'An "effeminate" man is one who desires women only too much – or, rather, he experiences sexual desire, gender of the object unspecified – in just the extreme terms that women supposedly do' ('L[o]cating the Sexual Subject', in Terence Hawkes (ed.), *Alternative Shakespeares: Vol.2* [London and New York: Routledge, 1996], pp. 95–121 [p. 101]). See also Chapter 2 and Chapter 4.

18 Marcelia's reply starts with the following words: 'My worthiest lord, / The only object I behold with pleasure; / My pride, my glory, in a word *my all*' (I.iii.51–3) (emphasis mine). References to the play are from *The Selected Plays of Philip Massinger* (Cambridge: Cambridge University Press, 1978), and are included parenthetically in the text.

19 Vittoria is also to be his 'friend' and 'child' (I.ii.257).

20 This is to stress that there is no effeminacy *as such*. See also Chapter 4. For more general considerations on the figure of invasion in relation to Shakespeare's high tragedies, see Francis Barker, *The Culture of Violence: Essays on Tragedy and History* (Manchester: Manchester University Press, 1993), pp. 3–92.

21 Sforza is probably embracing Marcelia whilst saying: 'Supported thus'.

22 That Francisco, the Duke's 'especial favourite', as the *dramatis personae* has it, is an upstart is often emphasized in the course of the play. He is also referred to as a 'mushroom' (II.i.86), a common epithet for upstarts.

23 See Franco Moretti, 'The Great Eclipse: Tragic Form as the Deconsecration of Sovereignty', in *Signs Taken for Wonders: Essays in the Sociology of Literature*, trans. by Susan Fischer, David Forgacs and David Miller (London and New York: Verso, 1988), pp. 42–82 (p. 75).

24 All references to the play are from the New Mermaids edition, ed. Roma Gill (London: Ernest Benn, 1968), and are included parenthetically in the text.

25 Slavoj Žižek, 'Looking Awry', *October*, 50 (1989), 31–55 (esp. p. 34).

26 As will be shown shortly, this pleasure principle also unstably governs the restricted economy of 'increase' (I.iii.47) Leantio (Bianca's husband) so heavily invests in. Interestingly, incestuous desire, as represented in the play, exceeds this restricted economy because it saves too much. It is the reverse side of the 'prodigal expense' signified by a love that is *ir*respective of linear and placid 'increase', but has similar effects. Livia describes her brother Ippolito's desire for his niece Isabella as a 'turn[ing]' of his 'point to [his] own blood' (II.i.7); a desire that is 'confined … in a narrower prison than was made for't' (II.i.10–11); a 'spar[ing]' of 'free means' (II.i.16) and 'ill husbandry' (II.i.13). 'Prodigal expense' is Levidulcia's expression in Tourneur's *The Atheist's Tragedy*. I cite from Irving Ribner's edition of the play (London: Methuen, 1964).

27 Belsey, 'Desire's Excess and the English Renaissance Theatre: *Edward II, Troilus and Cressida, Othello*', p. 90.

28 According to Moretti, the final masque in *Women Beware Women* is a paradigmatic example of the 'elusive allegory' that is so typical of Jacobean tragedy as a whole ('The Great Eclipse', p. 78). Referring to Tourneur's *The Revenger's Tragedy*, Jonathan Dollimore shows how the function of the masque as 'an ideological legitimation of the power structure' is 'contradicted because of, and through, a process of double inversion: crucially, antimasque displaces masque rather than vice-versa' (*Radical Tragedy: Religion, Ideology and Power in the Drama of Shakespeare and his Contemporaries* [Hemel Hempstead: Harvester, 1984], p. 27). That the 'ideal masque', as Dollimore adds, 'is merely an aesthetic, ritualised execution of antimasque violence' (Ibid.) is also true of the masque in *Women Beware Women* and other Jacobean plays. Even the clearly celebratory and seemingly unproblematic masque for the wedding between Amintor and Evadne in Beaumont and Fletcher's *The Maid's Tragedy* turns out to be, in retrospect, nothing but a parody of itself. Speaking in an aside to Evadne at the end of the masque, the king orders: 'We will not see you laid' (I.ii.285). Thus, one soon realizes that the king, the centre of the 'deployment of alliance', is in fact the lover of the bride, some kind of Lacanian *père-jouissance*. I am referring to the Revels edition of the play, ed. T.W. Craik (Manchester: Manchester University Press, 1988). For reflections on the obscene figure of *père-jouissance*, a figure that is a re-reading by Lacan of the Freudian myth of the 'primal father' of *Totem and Taboo*, see Slavoj Žižek, *Looking Awry: An Introduction to Jacques Lacan Through Popular Culture* (London and Cambridge MA: MIT Press, 1991), esp. pp. 23–5.

29 Belsey, 'Desire's Excess and the English Renaissance Theatre: *Edward II, Troilus and Cressida, Othello*', p. 95.

30 Ibid., p. 96.

31 Ibid.

32 On companionate marriages, see Chapter 1.

33 Anthony B. Dawson notes that through 'the clash between the Duke and Leantio over Bianca, Middleton represents the ethos of aristocratic display crushing the opposing ethos of bourgeois thrift and secrecy' ('*Women Beware Women* and the Economy of Rape', *Studies in English Literature*, 27 [1987], 303–20 [p. 308]). Yet, as previously mentioned, the Duke's desire seems to me to be in excess of 'aristocratic display'.

34 On the vexed question of whether there is a new legitimation of married sexual pleasure in the period, in connection with the emergence of the model of companionate marriage, see Belsey, 'Desire's Excess and the English Renaissance

Theatre: *Edward II, Troilus and Cressida, Othello*', pp. 95–8; p. 100n. Here Belsey questions Greenblatt's idea of the continuity between the Church fathers' celebration of celibacy and the Reformers' attitude to pleasure in marriage, as articulated in Stephen Greenblatt, *Renaissance Self-Fashioning: From More to Shakespeare* (Chicago: University of Chicago Press, 1980), pp. 240–52. See also Mary Beth Rose, *The Expense of Spirit: Love and Sexuality in English Renaissance Drama* (Ithaca NY and London: Cornell University Press, 1988), and, more generally, Jean-Louis Flandrin, 'La vie sexuelle des gens mariés dans l'ancienne societé: de la doctrine de l'Eglise à la réalité des comportements', in *Communications: Sexualités occidentales*, 35 (Paris: Seuil, 1982), pp. 102–15. Flandrin usefully draws attention to the distinction between pleasure in marriage and the pursuit of pleasure for pleasure's sake in marriage (Ibid. p. 103). It is worth citing, in this context, from the Puritan preacher and writer William Perkins (1558–1602): 'The end of marriage is fourfold: the first is the procreation of children. … The second is the procreation of an holy seed whereby … there may always be a holy company of men that may worship and serve God in the church from age to age. The third is that after the fall of mankind, it might be a sovereign means to avoid fornication and consequently to subdue and slake the burning lusts of the flesh. *And for this cause, some schoolmen do err, who hold that the secret coming together of man and wife cannot be without sin unless it be done for the procreation of children* … The fourth end is that the parties married may thereby perform the duties of their callings in better and more comfortable manner' (William Perkins, *Christian Economy*, trans. by Thomas Pickering, in Joan Larsen Klein [ed.], *Daughters, Wives and Widows: Writings by Men about Women and Marriage in England, 1500–1640* [Urbana and Chicago: University of Illinois Press, 1992, pp. 158–9] [my emphasis]). Therefore, Perkins accepts some kind of non-procreative pleasure in 'the secred coming together of man and wife'. However, this pleasure is not necessarily identifiable with the pursuit of pleasure for pleasure's sake within marriage.

35 That differences of status affect the reproductive body is a commonplace in midwifery treatises. In Culpeper, this turns into an indictment of the upper-class woman's body. To Culpeper, those women who 'live idely (as most of our City Dames do) have so few children, and those they have seldom live …, whereas poor men and women that labor hard have many children usually, and they are strong and lusty' (Nicholas Culpeper, *A Directory for Midwives: or, A Guide for Women, in their Conception, Bearing, And Suckling their Children* [London, 1651], p. 115). On this *topos*, see Gail Kern Paster, *The Body Embarrassed: Drama and the Disciplines of Shame in Early Modern England* (Ithaca and New York: Cornell University Press, 1993), pp. 171–2.

36 As Leantio admits, this is the 'one sin', apart from the original sin, he is 'guilty of' (I.i.35). He rejoices in this 'one sin', and even claims he has obtained his 'pardon for't' through marriage (I.i.44). But anxiety does not disappear.

37 This self-(re)fashioning corresponds to a veritable rebirth: 'I'll call this place the place of my birth now / And rightly too, for here my love was born, / And that's the birthday of a woman's joys' (I.i.139–41). As they denote some kind of agency on her part, Bianca's lines do not achieve the desired effect. That Bianca has 'forsook' her 'friends, fortunes and … country', and chosen Leantio, somehow means, to Leantio, that she can continue to choose. Ania Loomba underlines the 'double bind' in which Bianca is caught: 'Leantio demands from Bianca that she both defy the stability of her initial positioning and guarantee her subsequent stillness' (*Gender, Race, Renaissance Drama* [Manchester and New York: Manchester University Press, 1989], p. 102).

38 Foucault, *The History of Sexuality: An Introduction*, p. 107.

39 Moretti, 'The Great Eclipse', p. 74.

40 Bianca's is a shifting to a subject-position that is almost the same as the one she relinquishes at the beginning of the play, but not quite. She never simply regains her upper-class body and identity. She is not unproblematically re-inserted in the circuit of exchange and power she has 'forsook'. This is perhaps best emblematized by one of her

last utterances before dying: 'What make I here? these are all strangers to me' (V.ii.204). Moreover, although the 'deployment of alliance' is finally re-activated with her remarriage, the wedlock is never quite sanctified. The Cardinal (the Duke's brother) breaks off the ceremony, seeing this bond as a 'garment / Of leprosy and foulness' (IV.iii.16–17). Additionally, the celebratory masque in honour of the wedding turns out to be not quite what was expected.

41 Signifiers such as 'strange', 'stranger', 'alteration', and so forth permeate this scene.

42 See also Catherine Belsey: 'it is … possible to see, in the period before liberalism becomes synonymous with common sense, explorations of some of the flaws in … the liberal concept of marriage' (*The Subject of Tragedy: Identity and Difference in Renaissance Drama* [London and New York: Methuen, 1985], p. 192).

43 Referring to Leantio's intention to lock Bianca up, Dawson observes, perhaps a little reductively, that this is an attempt 'to keep her in the bourgeois world' ('*Women Beware Women* and the Economy of Rape', p. 309). In an analysis of *The Revenger's Tragedy*, Peter Stallybrass points out that 'total possession is, paradoxically, premised upon the absence of that which is desired' ('Reading the Body: *The Revenger's Tragedy* and the Jacobean Theater of Consumption', *Renaissance Drama*, 18 (1987), 121–48 [p. 130]).

44 As shown by Leantio's desire to obliterate the object of desire, these two trajectories may not be so distinct from one another as they appear at first sight.

45 The first to claim to have discovered the clitoris is the Italian anatomist Realdo Colombo: 'Since no one else has discerned these projections [*processus*] and their working, if it is permissible to give a name to things discovered by me, it should be called the love or sweetness of Venus [*amor Veneris, vel dulcedo appelletur*]' (Realdo Colombo, *De re anatomica* [Venice, 1559], p. 243). (I am using the translation of this passage in Thomas Laqueur, 'Amor Veneris, vel Dulcedo Appelletur', in Michel Feher, Ramona Naddaff and Nadia Tazi (eds), *Fragments for a History of the Human Body. Part Three* [New York: Zone, 1989], pp. 91–131 [p. 103]). A few years later, Gabriele Falloppia emphasizes that this part of female anatomy 'is hidden even from the anatomists', and continues: 'I was the first who detected [it] … and any others who speak or write about this, be assured that they learned of the thing itself either from me or from my followers' (Gabriele Falloppia, *Observationes anatomicae* [Venice, 1561], p. 194, cit. in Laqueur, 'Amor Veneris, vel Dulcedo Appelletur', p. 108). Andreas Vesalius denied the existence of this organ, except as a pathological structure. See Katharine Park, 'The Rediscovery of the Clitoris: French Medicine and the Tribade, 1570–1620', in David Hillman and Carla Mazzio (eds), *The Body in Parts: Fantasies of Corporeality in Early Modern Europe* (New York and London: Routledge, 1997), p. 177. Park also points out that Falloppia's *Observationes* was written before the publication of Colombo's *De re anatomica*, around 1550, but not published until 1561.

46 Crooke, *Microcosmographia*, p. 200; p. 238.

47 This is, of course, Luce Irigaray's expression, specifically used in her analysis of Freud's notions of femininity in *Speculum of the Other Woman*, (N.B. B18.3). trans. by Gillian C. Gill (Ithaca NY: Cornell University Press, 1985).

48 Crooke, *Microcosmographia*, p. 238.

49 On Crooke's questioning of the Galenic homology, see Chapter 3, note 101. Thomas Laqueur discusses Crooke in 'Orgasm, Generation, and the Politics of Reproductive Biology', *Representations*, 14 (1986), 1–41 (pp. 15–16); 'Amor Veneris, vel Dulcedo Appelletur', p. 112; and *Making Sex: Body and Gender From the Greeks To Freud* (Cambridge MA, and London: Harvard University Press, 1990), pp. 90–1.

50 Crooke, *Microcosmographia*, p. 272. Laqueur, *Making Sex*, p. 6.

51 I am saying 'implicitly' because Crooke explicitly rejects the clitoris as an alternative candidate for the 'neck of the womb' in his discussion of the Galenic model of introverted homology in the fourth book of *Microcosmographia*, called 'Of the Natural Parts Belonging to Generation'. In the context of this discussion, he stresses only those elements that set the clitoris and the penis apart. For instance, he asserts that the clitoris

is 'a small body, not continued at all with the bladder, but placed in the height of the lap. [It] hath no passage for the emission of the seed; but the virile member is long and hath a passage for the seed' (*Microcosmographia*, p. 250). As shown in Chapter 3, in the course of another discussion of the Galenic model, he appeals to 'the truth of anatomy' to underline that '[t]hose things which Galen urgeth concerning the similitude of the parts of generation and their differing only in site and position, many men do esteeme very absurd' (Ibid., p. 272). Crooke seems to be more concerned with showing the absurdity of the Galenic 'similitude' than with arguing that there is an *essential* difference between the clitoris and penis, or between the vagina and the penis: 'We [must not] think that the sexes do differ in essential form and perfection' (Ibid.). In a sense, therefore, Laqueur is right: Crooke does not argue that there is a radical dimorphism between the sexes. But he is right because he seems to me to pose the question in the wrong terms, in terms, that is, of the incommensurability between the incommensurability of the sexes and their structural homology. Thus, to Laqueur, any implicit and/or explicit denial – or, rather, to be more precise, any non-affirmation – of the incommensurability between the sexes becomes *ipso facto* a *reassuring* homology or an *unproblematic* affirmation of the fundamental identity between the sexes.

52 Jane Sharp, *The Midwives Book* (London, 1671), p. 40.

53 Ibid., p. 43.

54 Ibid.

55 *The Compleat Midwife's Practice Enlarged* (London, 1659), p. 62.

56 Crooke, *Microcosmographia*, p. 234.

57 Ibid. Emphasis mine.

58 Luce Irigaray, *This Sex Which Is Not One*, trans. by Catherine Porter (Ithaca and New York: Cornell University Press, 1985), p. 23. Emphasis mine. Irigaray would probably argue that the 'vertical' one-sex model (in which female sexual organs are a turned-inward version of those of the male) and the 'horizontal' two-sexes model (in which woman is the 'opposite' sex) are two sides of the same coin, as can be inferred from the following passage: 'And her sexual organ, which is not *one* organ, is counted as *none*. The negative, the underside, the reverse of the only visible and morphologically designatable organ (even if the passage from erection to detumescence does pose some problems): the penis' (Ibid., p. 26). The resilience of the one-sex model would require a different study. As I was browsing through *FHM*, a fashion magazine mostly addressed to men, to take a break from work, I found an article on 'Performance Sex' stating that 'the vulva is like an inverted penis inside a woman's body with the clitoris corresponding to the glans' (John McVicar, 'Performance Sex', *FHM*, 51 [March 1994], p. 44). On a different occasion, I came across a book by Dr David Delvin, a medical consultant to the British Family Planning Association. He argues that 'quite a few of [sex organs] are the exact equivalent of each other in males and females', adding that 'perhaps the most important point to note ... is that woman's clitoris is the exact match of the man's penis. *That's why this is really the sexiest part of a woman, and why everybody should know precisely where it is*' (*The Complete Guide to Sex and Loving* [London: Ebury Press, 1990], p. 21) (Delvin's emphasis).

59 Colombo, *De re anatomica*, p. 243.

60 Irigaray observes: 'But *woman has sex organs more or less everywhere*. She finds pleasure almost everywhere. ... [T]he geography of her pleasure is far more diversified, more multiple in its differences, more complex, more subtle, than is commonly imagined – in an imaginary rather too narrowly focused on sameness.' (*This Sex Which Is Not One*, p. 28). In her groundbreaking article 'The Psychomorphology of the Clitoris', Valerie Traub argues that the 'geography of pleasure' Irigaray describes and enacts in her writing – what Traub calls 'a labial logic characterized by multiplicity, movement and tactility [that] disperses the singularity of the signifier into a plurality of pleasure and erotic zones' – does not escape 'the anatomical essentialism that links body part(s) to erotic desire' ('The Psychomorphology of the Clitoris', *GLQ: A Journal of Lesbian and Gay*

Studies [Special issue: *Pink Freud*, ed. Diana Fuss] 2, 1–2 [1995], 81–113 [p. 101]). To Traub, therefore, the 'lips that speak together' (Irigaray, *This Sex Which Is Not One*, pp. 205–18) fail to articulate – in fact, they repress – the history they come from. This is a history that furthers the assumption that bodily parts and erotic desires and practices are commensurate to one another. One of the crucial sites of origin of this history is early modern anatomy's incorporation and production of the clitoris *as an organ*, as a body part emblematizing *in toto* female (homo)erotic power. I fundamentally agree with Traub's argument that the discourse of anatomy is not a neutral description of pre-existing bodily structures, but, rather, 'a discipline of knowledge that inscribes a bodily schema' ('The Psychomorphology of the Clitoris', p. 103n.). I also agree that this discipline increasingly tends towards the production of a normative bodily form, as well as of a normative, essential mode of erotic behaviour; a production that abjects other pleasures and desires, not least by making them metonymically contiguous with, and indissociable from, a deformed bodily part (the enlarged clitoris). However, does Irigaray reiterate, even if only unwittingly, the commensurability between bodily parts and the erotic that governs the essentializing discourse of anatomy? For a reading of Irigaray that implicitly questions this interpretation, see Jane Gallop, *Thinking Through the Body* (New York: Columbia University Press, 1988), esp. pp. 92–9. See also Margaret Whitford, *Luce Irigaray: Philosophy in the Feminine* (London, Routledge, 1991). For the more general question of essentialism in Irigaray, see, for instance, Naomi Schor, 'This Essentialism Which Is Not One: Coming to Grips with Irigaray', *Differences*, 2 (1989), 38–58.

61 Colombo, *De re anatomica*, p. 243. Laqueur translates *processus* as 'projection' or 'protuberance' (see note 45). Crooke probably has Colombo's *processus* in mind when he speaks of the clitoris as a 'production' (*Microcosmographia*, p. 238).

62 The original is: '[I]lla praecipue sedes est delectationis mulierum, dum venerem exercent' (Colombo, *De re anatomica*, p. 243).

63 Crooke, *Microcosmographia*, p. 238.

64 *The Compleat Midwife's Practice Enlarged*, p. 61.

65 Nicholas Venette, *Conjugal Love; or, The Pleasures of the Marriage Bed* (London, 1750) (repr. New York and London: Garland, 1984), pp. 18–19. This is a translation of Venette's *Tableau de l'amour conjugal.* It is designated as the 'twentieth edition'. First published in the second half of the seventeenth century, Venette's *Tableau de l'amour conjugal* went through many editions and translations in the late seventeenth century and in the eighteenth century.

66 Culpeper, *A Directory for Midwives*, p. 28.

67 On the ideology of reproduction, an extremely useful text is Pierre Darmon, *Le mythe de la procréation à l'âge baroque* (Paris: Pawert, 1977).

68 Colombo uses the second person singular of the verbs for 'rubbing' and 'touching' (*confricabis* and *attrectabis*), which establishes some kind of intimacy with the paradigmatically male reader of the text (*De re anatomica*, p. 243).

69 Ibid. I am using the translation of this passage in Park, 'The Rediscovery of the Clitoris', p. 177. For the French physician Jacques Duval, if a woman allows a man to touch this bodily part, she becomes entirely subjected (*submise*) to his will, and so much so that she is somehow forced to have sexual intercourse with him (*forcée au deduit venereén*) (*Des Hermaphrodits, accouchemens des femmes, et traitement qui est requis pour les relever en santé & bien élever leur enfans* [Rouen, 1612], p. 63). Duval's emphasis on women's 'subjection' is yet another example of the contraction of the body erotic.

70 Crooke, *Microcosmographia*, p. 238.

71 Ibid.

72 For more general theoretical reflections on 'woman's *norm* as clitorally ex-centric from the reproductive orbit', and its effacement by a 'uterine social organization', see Gayatri Chakravorty Spivak, 'French Feminism in an International Frame', in *In Other Worlds: Essays in Cultural Politics* (London and New York: Methuen, 1987), pp. 150–3.

73 Traub, 'The Psychomorphology of the Clitoris', p. 96.

74 Crooke, *Microcosmographia*, p. 238. The 'touch of cloaths' is probably a reference to the sixth-century Byzantine doctor Aetius. See Laqueur, 'Amor Veneris, vel Dulcedo Appelletur', p. 114. To Crooke, many authors have mentioned the 'abuse' of this part by 'Tribades'. Yet, as Katharine Park persuasively shows, the link between an *enlarged* clitoris and female homoerotic practices was relatively recent at the time when Crooke was writing. Hypertrophy of the clitoris (and clitoridectomy) and female homoerotic practices were two separated topics in ancient texts. They were brought together in *Chirurgie françoise* (1570), a work by Jacques Daléchamps, who seems to 'have authorized his construction by projecting it back onto those texts' (Park, 'The Rediscovery of the Clitoris', p. 176). This connection soon became standard in French and other European medical treatises.

75 Thomas Bartholin, *Bartholinus Anatomy: Made from the Precepts of his Father, and from the Observations of all Modern Anatomists, Together with His Own* (London, 1668), p. 76. This is a translation of Thomas Bartholin's 1641 revisions of his father Kaspar's notorious text, *Institutiones anatomicae* (1611). See Laqueur, *Making Sex*, p. 263n. *Bartholinus Anatomy* was published by Nicholas Culpeper and Abdiah Cole.

76 Traub notes that there is an 'unspoken assumption of "tribadism's" national otherness' in Crooke's account ('The Psychomorphology of the Clitoris', p. 95). She also argues that Sharp's 'is not simply a conventional English effort to refer the origin of unwelcome behaviors and diseases to other countries' (Ibid., p. 90). It is also a response to 'the discursive amplification of the threat posed by this evergrowing "prick"' (Ibid., p. 96). (According to Traub, as one moves into the second half of the seventeenth century, one witnesses a proliferation of treatises in which the clitoris seems to get bigger and bigger in size.) It is this 'amplification' that motivates Sharp 'to resurrect the colonialist imperative, rise to the defense of Englishwomen, and exile the "tribade" from England' (Ibid.).

77 Sharp, *The Midwives Book*, p. 44. Later on, she adds: 'I told you the clitoris is so long in some women that it is seen to hang forth at their privities, and not only the clitoris that lieth behind the wings, but the wings also' (Ibid., p. 47). To 'keep it close', as Traub points out, 'could refer to keeping either genitals hidden or erotic practices secret' ('The Psychomorphology of the Clitoris', p. 89). In turn, this 'may correlate with an increasing privatization of erotic behaviour that accompanied its amplified discursivity' (Ibid., p. 106n.). On Sharp's passage, see also Cath Sharrock, 'Hermaphroditism; or "The Erection of a New Doctrine": Theories of Female Sexuality in Eighteenth-Century England', *Paragraph*, 17 (1994), 38–48 (pp. 44–45).

78 Laqueur, 'Amor Veneris, vel Dulcedo Appelletur', p. 119. He stresses the same point earlier on: the discovery of the clitoris 'provided a second register on which to play the old tune of hierarchical ordering of two genders in the one flesh' (Ibid, p. 105). In *Making Sex* he states that 'the old isomorphism dwelt in peace with the strange new homologue [the clitoris] from another conceptual galaxy' (p. 65).

79 Ibid., p. 118.

80 Ibid.

81 Laqueur, 'Orgasm, Generation, and the Politics of Reproductive Biology', p. 14.

82 Sharp, *The Midwives Book*, p. 43; p. 45; p. 43.

83 This expression is Culpeper's. See *A Directory for Midwives*, p. 28.

84 See also Judith Butler, *Bodies That Matter: On the Discursive Limits of 'Sex'* (London and New York: Routledge, 1993), esp. pp. 84–91.

85 Dollimore, *Sexual Dissidence*, p. 284.

86 Valerie Traub, 'The (In)significance of "Lesbian" Desire in Early Modern England', in Susan Zimmerman (ed.), *Erotic Politics: Desire on the Renaissance Stage* (New York and London: Routledge, 1992), pp. 150–69 (p. 155).

87 Bartholin, *Bartholinus Anatomy*, p. 76.

88 Colombo, *De re anatomica*, p. 243. I am using Laqueur's translation of this passage in 'Amor Veneris, vel Dulcedo Appelletur', p. 103. The original is: 'Hanc eandem uteri partem dum Venerem appetunt mulieres, & tanquam aestro percitae virum appetunt

ad libidinem concitatae: si attinges, duriusculam & oblongam redditam esse comperies; adeo ut nescio quam virilis mentulae speciem prae se ferat.'

89 Bartholin, *Bartholinus Anatomy*, p. 75. Emphasis mine. Bartholin dismisses both Colombo and Falloppia's claims about priority in the discovery of the clitoris, pointing out that it had already been described by many ancient writers, such as Avicenna, Albucasis, Aetius of Amida and Paulus Aegineta. For a discussion of earlier medical references to that which some anatomists will later claim to have discovered, see Danielle Jacquart and Claude Thomasset, *Sexualité et savoir médical au moyen âge* (Paris: Presses Universitaires de France, 1985), esp. pp. 63–6. See also Park, 'The Rediscovery of the Clitoris', pp. 175–6.

90 For Traub, 'by the early seventeenth century, under the auspices of anatomy, a paradigm of desire is transmuted into a paradigm of bodily structure: it is not the "tribade's" inconstant mind or sinful soul but her uniquely female yet masculinized morphology that propels her to engage in illicit behaviour' ('The Psychomorphology of the Clitoris', p. 94). Traub reads *Bartholinus Anatomy* as a text that significantly contributes to this transmutation (Ibid., p. 95).

91 'In some women [the clitoris] grows as big as the yard of a man: so that some women abuse the same, and make use thereof in place of a Mans Yard, exercising carnal copulation one with another, and they are termed Confricatrices [and] Rubsters' (Bartholin, *Bartholinus Anatomy*, p. 76).

92 Ibid., p. 77.

93 For reflections on the problematic relationship between the original and its misplaced copies in medical discourses of a later period, see Sharrock, 'Hermaphroditism; or "The Erection of a New Doctrine"', esp. pp. 41–2.

94 Bartholin, *Bartholinus Anatomy*, p. 77. This description is entirely conventional in all other respects.

95 Among the sixteenth- and seventeenth-century treatises I have consulted, *Bartholinus Anatomy* undoubtedly presents the most vehement rejection of the Galenic model of sexual difference. Bartholin concedes that 'some of [the genitals in women] agree after a sort with those in Men', such as the 'spermatick vessels', 'the stones' and the 'vasa deferentia'. Yet, he underlines that 'others are wholly different, as the Womb with its Bottom, Orifice, and Neck, the Hymen, the Myrtle-shaped Caruncles, the Vulva with its Wings, the Clitoris, and the little Hillock' (Ibid., p. 62). He continues: 'For we must not think with Galen, Archangelus, Falloppius … that these Female Genital Members differ from those of Men only in Situation. Which Opinion was hatched by those who accounted a Woman to be only an imperfect Man; and that her Genital Members could not be thrust out by reason of the coldness of her temper … Howbeit, the generative Parts in Women differ from those of in Men not only in Situation, but in their universal Fabrick, in respect of Number, Surface, Magnitude, Cavity, Figure, Office' (Ibid.). He also remarks on the absurdity of the similitude between male and female sexual organs: 'Some liken the Womb to the Cod of a Man, and some to the Nut of the Yard. Some will have the Neck of the Womb to answer the Mans Yard, *and others will have the Clitoris*' (Ibid.) (emphasis mine). It is in the light of these observations on the clitoris (as 'wholly different', as a body part that is extremely unlike man's 'Yard') that Bartholin's later descriptions seem puzzling: the clitoris 'resembles a Mans Yard in Situation, Substance, Composition, Repletion with Spirits and Erection. And also because it hath som[e]what like the Nut and Fore-skin of a Mans Yard' (Ibid., p. 76). (Its 'Head', he specifies, has a 'hole as a Mans Yard, but not thoroughfar', and is 'like the Fraenulum or Bridle on the Nut of a Mans Yard' [Ibid., p. 77].) Predictably, Laqueur points out that in spite of his 'astute … critique' of Galenic isomorphisms, Bartholin 'was caught up in a way of looking that kept him tied to the images of one sex …, with not one but two female penises to accommodate' (*Making Sex*, p. 92; p. 93). However, I want to suggest that Bartholin's 'return' to homology can be read as a mechanism of defence against the *specific* erotic threat posed by the clitoris; as an

attempt to reduce the latter to a reassuring double that is only partially infused with erotic power, and that is somehow differentiated from the enlarged clitoris as a signifier of nonreproductive practices.

96 Traub, 'The Psychomorphology of the Clitoris', p. 98.

97 Venette, *Conjugal Love*, p. 116. Venette continually returns to the happiness of 'a married state' and its pleasures: 'Whereas irregular love makes us stupid, love that is prudently managed causes health, inspires courage, and renders us agreeable ... Those lawful sensualities load us with all sorts of good things, rendering our souls satisfied, and encreasing the strength of our body' (Ibid., p. 147).

98 Ibid., p. 19. In saying that the clitoris 'grows with age', Venette is probably thinking about the deleterious effects of female masturbation. Later in the treatise, he hints at these erotic practices: 'Many young men, who are allowed much liberty, injure themselves greatly by premature connection with the sex; and some of the fair are as much to blame for other practices, which may easily be guessed; but I shall avoid to name, not wishing to instruct those who are yet ignorant in the *mysteries of iniquity*' (Ibid., pp. 84–5). (As far as 'young men' are concerned, he has mostly in mind 'the mercenary harlot' [Ibid., p. 85].) In another context, speaking of both 'male and female youths', he refers to 'that unnatural effeminacy, called self pollution, which is the bane and destruction of all those who exercise themselves in so beastly a practice' (Ibid., p. 48).

99 The 'abuse' of the 'nymphae' or 'wings' overlaps, in some treatises, with the 'abuse' of the clitoris. On practical advice for excision, Traub cites from Nicholas Culpeper's *Fourth Book of Practical Physick*, published in 1684 with *A Directory for Midwives* ('The Psychomorphology of the Clitoris', pp. 108–9n.). On the 'promotion of clitoridectomy' as a sign of the 'commitment to sexual binarism' and the policing of sexual boundaries by early modern French medical writers, see Park, 'The Rediscovery of the Citoris', pp. 183–4.

100 Crooke, *Microcosmographia*, p. 237.

101 Sharp, *The Midwives Book*, p. 47.

102 Venette, *Conjugal Love*, p. 70.

103 Ibid., p. 71. Bartholin approvingly refers to the excision of the clitoris practised by ancient and Eastern nations, but is puzzled by the cutting of the 'nymphs' (*Bartholinus Anatomy*, p. 77).

104 *The Compleat Midwife's Practice Enlarged*, p. 61.

105 'Tentigo' is often employed to designate the 'head' of the clitoris. See, for instance, Crooke, *Microcosmographia*, p. 238.

106 *The Compleat Midwife's Practice Enlarged*, p. 195.

107 Jacques Lacan, *Le Séminaire, livre XX: Encore 1969–70* (Paris: Editions du Seuil, 1975), p. 10. The most immediate context of this assertion is Lacan's discussion of the Law's partitioning and redistribution of *jouissance.*

108 Laqueur, 'Orgasm, Generation, and the Politics of Reproductive Biology', p. 2.

109 See Lacan, *Le Séminaire, livre XX: Encore 1969–70*, esp. pp. 54–7.

110 Ibid., pp. 68–9.

Bibliography

Abelove, Henry, Barale, Michèle Aina and Halperin, David M., eds, *The Lesbian and Gay Studies Reader* (London and New York: Routledge, 1993).

Abraham, Nicolas and Torok, Maria, *Cryptonymie: Le Verbier de l'Homme aux loups* (Paris: Aubier-Flammarion, 1976).

——, *L'Ecorce et le noyau* (Paris: Aubier-Flammarion, 1978).

Adelman, Janet, *Suffocating Mothers: Fantasies of Maternal Origin in Shakespeare's Plays, Hamlet to The Tempest* (New York and London: Routledge, 1992).

Africanus, Leo, *A Geographical Historie of Africa*, trans. by John Pory (London, 1600) (repr. Amsterdam: Theatrum Orbis Terrarum and Da Capo Press, 1969).

Agacinski, Sylviane, 'Le tout premier écart', in Philippe Lacoue-Labarthe and Jean-Luc Nancy (eds), *Les fins de l'homme* (Paris: Galilée, 1981), pp. 117–32.

Agnew, Jean-Christophe, *Worlds Apart: The Market and the Theatre in Anglo-American Thought, 1550–1750* (Cambridge: Cambridge University Press, 1986).

Althusser, Louis, 'Ideology and Ideological State Apparatuses', in *Lenin and Philosophy and Other Essays*, trans. by Ben Brewster (London: New Left Books, 1971), pp. 127–86.

Archer, J.M., *Sovereignty and Intelligence: Spying and Court Culture in the English Renaissance* (Stanford: Stanford University Press, 1993).

Ariès, Philippe and Duby, George, eds, *A History of Private Life*, trans. by Arthur Goldhammer, 5 vols (Cambridge MA and London: Belknap-Harvard University Press, 1987–92).

Aristotle, *Generation of Animals*, trans. by A.L. Peck, in Aristotle, *Works*, XIII, Loeb Classical Library (London: Heinemann, 1942).

Armstrong, Nancy and Tennenhouse, Leonard, eds, *The Violence of Representation: Literature and the History of Violence* (London and New York: Routledge, 1989).

Armstrong, Philip, 'Watching *Hamlet* Watching: Lacan, Shakespeare and the Mirror/Stage', in Terence Hawkes (ed.), *Alternative Shakespeares: Vol. 2* (London and New York: Routledge, 1996), pp. 216–37.

Aston, Edward, *The Manners, Lawes and Customes of all Nations* (London, 1611).

Aveling, J.H., *The Chamberlens and the Midwifery Forceps* (London: Churchill, 1882).

Bakhtin, Mikhail, *Rabelais and his World*, trans. by Hélène Iswolsky (Cambridge MA: MIT Press, 1968).

Banister, John, *Historie of Man* (London, 1578).

Barker, Francis, *The Tremulous Private Body: Essays on Subjection* (London and New York: Methuen, 1984).

——, *The Culture of Violence: Essays on Tragedy and History* (Manchester: Manchester University Press, 1993).

Bartholin, Thomas, *Bartholinus Anatomy: Made from the Precepts of his Father, and from the Observations of all Modern Anatomists, Together with His Own* (London, 1668).

Beaumont, Francis and Fletcher, John, *The Maid's Tragedy*, ed. T.W. Craik (Manchester: Manchester University Press, 1988).

Belsey, Catherine, *The Subject of Tragedy: Identity and Difference in Renaissance Drama* (London and New York: Methuen, 1985).

——, 'Desire's Excess and the English Renaissance Theatre: *Edward II, Troilus and Cressida, Othello*', in Susan Zimmerman (ed.), *Erotic Politics: Desire on the Renaissance Stage* (New York and London: Routledge, 1992), pp. 84–102.

——, 'Cleopatra's Seduction', in Terence Hawkes (ed.), *Alternative Shakespeares: Vol. 2* (London and New York: Routledge, 1996), pp. 38–62.

Bennington, Geoffrey and Derrida, Jacques, *Jacques Derrida* (Paris: Seuil, 1991).

Bhabha, Homi, 'Of Mimicry and Man: The Ambivalence of Colonial Discourse', *October*, 28 (1984), 125–33.

Borch-Jacobsen, Mikkel, *The Freudian Subject*, trans. by Catherine Porter (Stanford CA: Stanford University Press, 1988 [1982]).

——, *Lacan: The Absolute Master*, trans. by Douglas Brick (Stanford CA: Stanford University Press, 1991).

Braidotti, Rosi, 'Organs Without Bodies', *Differences*, 1 (1989), 147–61.

——, *Nomadic Subjects: Embodiment and Sexual Difference in Contemporary Feminist Theory* (New York: Columbia University Press, 1994).

——, 'Signs of Wonder and Traces of Doubt: On Teratology and Embodied Differences', in Nina Lykke and Rosi Braidotti (eds), *Between Monsters and Goddesses and Cyborgs. Feminist Confrontations with Science, Medicine and Cyberspace* (London and New Jersey: Zed Books, 1996), pp. 135–52.

Bray, Alan, *Homosexuality in Renaissance England* (London: Gay Men's Press, 1982).

——, 'Homosexuality and the Signs of Male Friendship in Elizabethan England', *History Workshop*, 29 (1990), 1–19.

Breitenberg, Mark, *Anxious Masculinity in Early Modern England* (Cambridge: Cambridge University Press, 1996).

Brink, Jean R., ed., *Privileging Gender in Early Modern England: Sixteenth Century Essays & Studies Vol. XXIII* (Ann Arbor: Michigan University Press, 1993).

Brotton, Jerry, *The Renaissance Bazaar: From the Silk Road to Michelangelo* (Oxford: Oxford University Press, 2003).

Bueler, Lois E., 'The Rhetoric of Change in *The Changeling*', *English Literary Renaissance*, 14, 1 (1984), 95–113.

Butler, Judith, *Gender Trouble: Feminism and the Subversion of Identity* (London and New York: Routledge, 1990).

——, 'Sexual Inversions', in Domna C. Stanton (ed.), *Discourses of Sexuality: From Aristotle to Aids* (Ann Arbor: The University of Michigan Press, 1992), pp. 344–61.

——, *Bodies That Matter: On the Discursive Limits of 'Sex'* (London and New York: Routledge, 1993).

——, 'Imitation and Gender Insubordination', in Henry Abelove, Michèle Aina Barale and David M. Halperin (eds), *The Lesbian and Gay Studies Reader* (London and New York: Routledge, 1993), pp. 307–20.

Bynum, Caroline, 'Why All the Fuss about the Body? A Medievalist's Perspective', *Critical Inquiry*, 22 (1995), 1–33.

Calbi, Maurizio, '"A wounded name": *Hamlet* e il fantasma del nome', in Lidia Curti (ed.), *Ombre di un'ombra. Amleto e i suoi fantasmi* (Napoli: Istituto Universitario Orientale, 1994), pp. 189–222.

——, 'Being a Guest But Not Quite … White: *Othello* and Hybrid Hospitality in the Mediterranean', *Anglistica-AION*: *Shakespeare and the Genres of Hospitality*, ed. Lidia Curti and Silvana Carotenuto, 6, 2 (2002)–7, 1 (2003), 27–42.

——, '"Unshap't Bodies": Masculinity Travels East', in Matthew Dimmock and Matthew Birchwood (eds), *1453–1699: Cultural Encounters Between East and West* (Cambridge: Cambridge Scholars Press, 2005).

Callaghan, Dympna, '"And All Is Semblative a Woman's Part": Body Politics and *Twelfth Night*', *Textual Practice*, 7, 3 (1993), 428–52.

Carroll, Berenice A., ed., *Liberating Women's History. Theoretical and Critical Essays* (Urbana: University of Illinois Press, 1976).

Céard, Jean, *La Nature et les prodiges. L'Insolite au XVI siècle* (Genève: Droz, 1977).

Charnes, Linda, 'Styles That Matter: On The Discursive Limits of Ideology Critique', *Shakespeare Studies*, 24 (1996), 118–47.

Chew, Samuel, *The Crescent and the Rose: Islam and England during the Renaissance* (New York: Octagon Books, 1974 [1937]).

Cixous, Hélène and Clément, Catherine, *The Newly Born Woman*, trans. by Betsy Wing (Minneapolis: University of Minnesota Press, 1986 [1975]).

Clark, Alice, *Working Life of Women in the Seventeenth Century* (London: Routledge & Kegan Paul, 1982 [1919]).

Clark, G.N., *A History of the Royal College of Physicians,* 3 vols (Oxford: Clarendon Press, 1964).

Coddon, Karin S., '*The Duchess of Malfi*: Tyranny and Spectacle in Jacobean Drama', in James Redmond (ed.), *Madness in Drama* (Cambridge: Cambridge University Press, 1993), pp. 1–17.

Colombo, Realdo, *De re anatomica* (Venice, 1559).

The Compleat Midwife's Practice Enlarged (London, 1659 [1656]).

Cook, Harold J., *The Decline of the Old Medical Regime in Stuart London* (Ithaca NY and London: Cornell University Press, 1986).

Copjec, Joan, 'The Orthopsychic Subject: Film Theory and the Reception of Lacan', *October*, 49 (1989), 53–71.

Crawford, Patricia, 'Attitudes to Menstruation in Seventeenth-Century England', *Past and Present*, 91 (1981), 47–73.

Crooke, Helkiah, *Microcosmographia. A Description of the Body of Man* (London, 1615).

Culpeper, Nicholas, *A Directory for Midwives: or, A Guide for Women, in their Conception, Bearing, And Suckling their Children* (London, 1651).

Cunnigham, Andrew, 'The Kinds of Anatomy', *Medical History*, 19 (1975), 1–19.

Daborne, Robert, *A Christian Turn'd Turke*, in Daniel J. Viktus, (ed.) *Three Turk Plays from Early Modern England* (New York: Columbia University Press, 2000).

Darmon, Pierre, *Le Mythe de la procréation à l'âge baroque* (Paris: Pawert, 1977).

Davies, Kathleen M., 'The Sacred Conditions of Equality – How Original Were Puritan Doctrines of Marriage?', *Social History*, 5 (1977), 563–80.

Dawson, Anthony B., '*Women Beware Women* and the Economy of Rape', *Studies in English Literature*, 27 (1987), 303–20.

de Certeau, Michel, 'Des outils pour écrire le corps', *Traverses* (Special issue: *Panoplies du corps*), 14–15 (1979), 3–14.

de Grazia, Margreta, 'Imprints: Shakespeare, Gutenberg and Descartes', in Terence Hawkes (ed.), *Alternative Shakespeares: Vol. 2* (London and New York: Routledge, 1996), pp. 63–94.

Delvin, David, *The Complete Guide to Sex and Loving* (London: Ebury Press, 1990).

de Nicholay, Nicholas, *Navigations, Peregrinations and Voyages, Made into Turkie*, trans. by T. Washington (London, 1585).

Derrida, Jacques, *Of Grammatology*, trans. by Gayatri Chakravorty Spivak (Baltimore MD and London: The Johns Hopkins University Press, 1976 [1967]).
——, *Writing and Difference*, trans. by Alan Bass (London: Routledge and Kegan Paul, 1978 [1967]).
——, *Dissemination*, trans. by Barbara Johnson (Chicago: Chicago University Press, 1981 [1972]).
——, *Margins of Philosophy*, trans. by Alan Bass (Chicago: University of Chicago Press, 1982 [1972]).
——, *Glas*, trans. by John P. Leavey, Jr, and Richard Rand (Lincoln: University of Nebraska Press, 1986 [1974]).
——, 'Fors', trans. by Barbara Johnson, *The Georgia Review*, 31, 1 (1977 [1976]), 64–116.
——, 'L'Aphorisme à contretemps', in *Psyché. Inventions de l'autre* (Paris: Galilée, 1987), pp. 519–33.
——, *The Post Card: From Socrates to Freud and Beyond*, trans. by Alan Bass (Chicago: The University of Chicago Press, 1987 [1980]).
——, 'The Politics of Friendship', trans. by Gabriel Motzkin, *The Journal of Philosophy*, 85, 11 (1988), 632–44.
——, *Donner le temps* (Paris: Galilée, 1991).
——, '"Eating Well", Or the Calculation of the Subject: An Interview with Jacques Derrida', in Eduardo Cavava, Peter Connor, and Jean-Luc Nancy (eds), *Who Comes After the Subject?*, (London and New York: Routledge, 1991), pp. 96–119.
——, '"To Do Justice to Freud"': The History of Madness in the Age of Psychoanalysis', trans. by Pascale-Anne Brault and Michael Naas, *Critical Inquiry*, 20 (1994 [1992]), 227–66.
DiGangi, Mario, 'Pleasure and Danger: Measuring Female Sexuality in *Measure for Measure*', *English Literary History*, 60 (1993), 589–609.
Doane, Mary Ann, *Femmes Fatales: Feminism, Film Theory, Psychoanalysis* (London and New York: Routledge, 1991).
Dolar, Mladen, '"I Shall Be with You on Your Wedding Night": Lacan and the Uncanny', *October*, 58 (1991), 5–23.
Dollimore, Jonathan, *Radical Tragedy: Religion, Ideology and Power in the Drama of Shakespeare and his Contemporaries* (Hemel Hempstead: Harvester, 1984).
——, 'Transgression and Surveillance in *Measure for Measure*', in Jonathan Dollimore and Alan Sinfield (eds), *Political Shakespeare: New Essays in Cultural Materialism*, (Manchester: Manchester University Press, 1985), pp. 72–87.
——, *Sexual Dissidence: Augustine to Wilde, Freud to Foucault* (Oxford: Clarendon Press, 1991).
——, and Sinfield, Alan, eds, *Political Shakespeare: New Essays in Cultural Materialism* (Manchester: Manchester University Press, 1985).
Donnison, Jean, *Midwives and Medical Men: A History of Inter-Professional Rivalries and Women's Rights* (New York: Schocken Books, 1977).
Douglas, Mary, *Purity and Danger: An Analysis of the Concepts of Pollution and Taboo* (London and New York: Routledge, 1991 [1966]).
Duby, Georges and Braunstein, Philippe, 'The Emergence of the Individual', in Philippe Ariès and George Duby (eds), *A History of Private Life*, trans. by Arthur Goldhammer, 5 vols (Cambridge MA and London: Belknap-Harvard University Press, 1987–92), II, 507–630.
Duval, Jacques, *Des Hermaphrodits, accouchemens des femmes, et traitement qui est requis pour les relever en santé & bien élever leur enfans* (Rouen, 1612).
Eaton, Sara, 'Beatrice-Joanna and the Rhetoric of Love', *Theatre Journal*, 36 (1984), 371–82.
Eccles, Audrey, *Obstetrics and Gynaecology in Tudor and Stuart England* (London and Canberra: Croom Helm, 1982).

Ehrenreich, Barbara and English, Deirdre, *Witches, Midwives, and Nurses: A History of Women Healers* (New York: Feminist Press, 1973).

Elam, Keir, '"In What Chapter of His Bosom?": Reading Shakespeare's Bodies', in Terence Hawkes (ed.), *Alternative Shakespeares: Vol. 2* (London and New York: Routledge, 1996), pp. 140–63.

——, 'The Fertile Eunuch: *Twelfth Night*, Early Modern Intercourse and the Fruits of Castration', *Shakespeare Quarterly*, 47, 1 (1996), pp. 1–36.

Epstein, Julia and Straub, Kristina, eds, *Body Guards: The Cultural Politics of Gender Ambiguity* (London and New York: Routledge, 1991).

Falloppia, Gabriele, *Observationes anatomicae* (Venice, 1561).

Feher, Michel, Naddaff, Ramona and Tazi, Nadia, eds, *Fragments for a History of the Human Body. Part Three* (New York: Zone, 1989).

Felman, Shoshana, ed., *Literature and Psychoanalysis. The Question of Reading: Otherwise* (Baltimore MD and London: The Johns Hopkins University Press, 1982).

Ferguson, Margaret W., Quilligan, Maureen and Vickers, Nancy J., eds, *Rewriting the Renaissance: The Discourses of Sexual Difference in Early Modern Europe* (Chicago and London: Chicago University Press, 1986).

Ferrari, Giovanna, 'Public Anatomy Lessons and the Carnival in Bologna', *Past and Present*, 117 (1987), 50–106.

Flandrin, Jean-Louis, 'La vie sexuelle des gens mariés dans l'ancienne société: de la doctrine de l'Église à la réalité des comportements', in *Communications: Sexualités occidentales*, 35 (Paris: Seuil, 1982), pp. 102–15.

Fletcher, John, 'Freud and His Uses: Psychoanalysis and Gay Theory', in Simon Shepherd and Mick Wallis (eds), *Coming on Strong: Gay Politics and Culture* (London: Unwin Hyman, 1989).

Fontanus, Nicholas, *The Womans Doctour: or, An Exact and Distinct Explanation of All Such Diseases as Are Peculiar to That Sex* (London, 1652).

Foucault, Michel, *Madness and Civilization: A History of Insanity in the Age of Reason*, trans. by Richard Howard (New York: Vintage/Random House, 1973 [1961]).

——, *The Order of Things. An Archeology of the Human Sciences* (London and New York: Tavistock, 1970 [1966]).

——, 'Nietzsche, Genealogy, History', in *Language, Counter-Memory, Practice. Selected Essays and Interviews*, ed. Donald F. Bouchard (Ithaca and New York: Cornell University Press, 1977 [1971]), pp. 139–64.

——, *Discipline and Punish: The Birth of the Prison*, trans. by Alan Sheridan (New York: Pantheon, 1977 [1975]).

——, *The History of Sexuality: An Introduction*, trans. by Robert Hurley (Harmondsworth: Penguin Books, 1981 [1976]).

——, *The Use of Pleasure*, trans. by Robert Hurley (New York: Pantheon, 1985 [1984]).

——, *The Care of the Self*, trans. by Robert Hurley (New York: Pantheon, 1986 [1984]).

Fox-Keller, Evelyn, *Reflections on Gender and Science* (New Haven and London: Yale University Press, 1985).

Freedman, Barbara, *Staging the Gaze: Postmodernism, Psychoanalysis, and Shakespearean Comedy* (Ithaca NY and London: Cornell University Press, 1991).

Freud, Sigmund, *Jokes and Their Relation to the Unconscious* (1905), in *The Standard Edition of the Complete Psychological Works of Sigmund Freud* (hereafter *SE*), ed. James Strachey, 24 vols (London: The Hogarth Press, 1953–74), VIII.

——, 'Character and Anal Erotism' (1908), in *SE*, IX, 167–75.

——, 'On Narcissism: An Introduction' (1914), in *SE*, XIV, 67–102.

——, 'The "Uncanny"' (1919), in *SE*, XVII, 217–52.

——, 'Group Psychology and the Analysis of the Ego' (1921), in *SE*, XVIII, 69–144.

——, 'Some Neurotic Mechanisms in Jealousy, Paranoia and Homosexuality' (1922), in *SE*, XVIII, 221–32.

——, *The Ego and the Id* (1923), in *SE*, XIX, 1–66.

Galen, *On the Usefulness of the Parts of the Body*, trans. by Margaret T. May, 2 vols (Ithaca NY: Cornell University Press, 1968).

Gallop, Jane, *Thinking Through the Body* (New York: Columbia University Press, 1988).

Gélis, Jacques, *History of Childbirth: Fertility, Pregnancy and Birth in Early Modern Europe*, trans. by Rosemary Morris (Cambridge: Polity Press, 1991 [1984]).

Girard, René, *Deceit, Desire, and the Novel: Self and Other in Literary Structure*, trans. by Yvonne Freccero (Baltimore MD: Johns Hopkins University Press, 1972).

Goffe, Thomas, *The Courageous Turke, or, Amurath the First* (London: Richard Meighen, 1632), Literature Online, University of Salerno, 16 June 2004, <http://lion.chadwyck.co.uk>.

Goldberg, Jonathan, *Sodometries: Renaissance Texts, Modern Sexualities* (Stanford CA: Stanford University Press, 1992).

——, ed., *Queering the Renaissance* (Durham and London: Duke University Press, 1994).

Greenblatt, Stephen, *Renaissance Self-Fashioning: From More to Shakespeare* (Chicago: University of Chicago Press, 1980).

——, *Shakespearean Negotiations: The Circulation of Social Energy in Renaissance England* (Oxford: Clarendon Press, 1988).

——, ed., *Representing the English Renaissance* (Berkeley: University of California Press, 1988).

Guillemeau, Jacques, *Child-Birth or, The Happy Deliverie of Women* (London, 1612 [1609]) (repr. Amsterdam: Theatrum Orbis Terrarum, 1972).

Haller, William and Malleville, 'The Puritan Art of Love', *Huntington Library Quarterly*, 5 (1941–42), 235–72.

Harcourt, Glenn, 'Andreas Vesalius and the Anatomy of Antique Sculpture', *Representations*, 17 (1987), 28–61.

Harvey, Elizabeth D., *Ventriloquized Voices: Feminist Theory and Renaissance Texts* (London and New York: Routledge, 1992).

Harvey, William, *The Works of William Harvey*, trans. by Robert Willis (London: Sydenham Society, 1847).

Hawkes, Terence, ed., *Alternative Shakespeares: Vol. 2* (London and New York: Routledge, 1996).

Haynes, Alan, *Invisible Power: The Elizabethan Secret Services 1570–1603* (Stroud: Alan Sutton, 1992).

Henderson, Andrea, 'Death on the Stage, Death of the Stage: The Antitheatricality of *The Duchess of Malfi*', *Educational Theatre Journal*, 48 (1987), 194–207.

Hill, Christopher, 'The Medical Profession and its Critics', in *Change and Continuity in Seventeenth-Century England* (London: Weidenfeld and Nicolson, 1974), pp. 157–78.

Hillman, David and Mazzio, Carla, eds, *The Body in Parts: Fantasies of Corporeality in Early Modern Europe* (New York and London: Routledge, 1997).

Hobby, Elaine, '"Secrets of the Female Sex": Jane Sharp, The Reproductive Female Body, and Early Modern Midwifery Manuals', *Women's Writing*, 8, 2 (2001), 201–12.

Hodges, Devon L., *Renaissance Fictions of Anatomy* (Amherst: The University of Massachusetts Press, 1985).

Howard, Jean, 'Sex and Social Conflict: The Erotics of *The Roaring Girl*', in Susan Zimmerman (ed.), *Erotic Politics: Desire on the Renaissance Stage* (New York and London: Routledge, 1992), pp. 170–90.

——, *The Stage and Social Struggle in Early Modern England* (London and New York: Routledge, 1994).

Irigaray, Luce, *Speculum of the Other Woman*, trans. by Gillian C. Gill (Ithaca NY: Cornell University Press, 1985 [1974]).

——, *This Sex Which Is Not One*, trans. by Catherine Porter (Ithaca and New York: Cornell University Press, 1985 [1977]).

Jacobus, Mary, Fox Keller, Evelyn and Shuttleworth, Sally, eds, *Body/Politics: Women and the Discourses of Science* (London and New York: Routledge, 1990).

Jacquart, Danielle and Thomasset, Claude, *Sexualité and savoir médical au moyen âge* (Paris, Presses Universitaires de France, 1985).

Jankowski, Theodora, 'Defining/Confining the Duchess: Negotiating the Female Body in John Webster's *The Duchess of Malfi*', *Studies in Philology*, 87 (1990), 221–45.

Jardine, Lisa, *Still Harping on Daughters: Women and Drama in the Age of Shakespeare* (Hemel Hempstead: Harvester, 1983).

——, *Reading Shakespeare Historically* (London and New York: Routledge, 1996).

——, and Brotton, Jerry, *Global Interests: Renaissance Art Between East and West* (London: Reaktion Books, 2000).

Jones, Ann Rosalind and Stallybrass, Peter, 'Fetishizing Gender: Constructing the Hermaphrodite in Renaissance Europe', in Julia Epstein and Kristina Straub (eds), *Body Guards: The Cultural Politics of Gender Ambiguity* (London and New York: Routledge, 1991), pp. 80–111.

Jonson, Ben, *Volpone*, ed. Philip Brockbank (London: Ernest Benn, 1968).

Jordan, Constance, *Renaissance Feminism: Literary Texts and Political Models* (Ithaca NY and London: Cornell University Press, 1990).

Jorden, Edward, *A Briefe Discourse of a Disease Called the Suffocation of the Mother* (London, 1603) (repr. Amsterdam: Theatrum Orbis Terrarum, 1971).

Kahn, Coppelia, *Roman Shakespeare: Warriors, Wounds, and Women* (London and New York: Routledge, 1997).

Kamps, Ivo and Singh, Jyotsna, eds, *Travel Knowledge. European 'Discoveries' in the Early Modern Period* (Houndsmill and New York: Palgrave, 2001).

Kellett, Edward, *A Return from Argier. A Sermon Preached at Minhead in the Country of Somerset the 16. of March, 1627 at the re-admission of a relapsed Christian into our Church* (London, 1628), Early English Books Online, University of Salerno Library, 16 June 2004, <http://eebo.chadwyck.com>.

Klein, Joan Larsen, ed., *Daughters, Wives and Widows: Writings by Men about Women and Marriage in England, 1500–1640* (Urbana and Chicago: University of Illinois Press, 1992).

Kristeva, Julia, *Powers of Horrors: An Essay on Abjection*, trans. by Leon S. Roudiez (New York: Columbia University Press, 1982 [1980]).

Lacan, Jacques, *Écrits: A Selection*, trans. by Alan Sheridan (London: Tavistock, 1977 [1966]).

——, *The Four Fundamental Concepts of Psycho-Analysis*, trans. by Alan Sheridan (Harmondsworth: Penguin, 1979 [1973]).

——, 'Desire and the Interpretation of Desire in *Hamlet*', trans. by James Hulbert, in Shoshana Felman (ed.), *Literature and Psychoanalysis. The Question of Reading: Otherwise* (Baltimore MD and London: The Johns Hopkins University Press, 1982), pp. 11–52.

——, *The Seminar of Jacques Lacan, Book II: The Ego in Freud's Theory and the Technique of Psychoanalysis 1954–55*, trans. by Sylvana Tomaselli (Cambridge: Cambridge University Press, 1988 [1978]).

——, *Le Séminaire, livre IV: La Relation d'objet 1956–57* (Paris: Editions du Seuil, 1994).

——, *Le Séminaire, livre VII: L'Ethique de la psychanalyse 1959–60* (Paris: Editions du Seuil, 1986).

——, *The Seminar of Jacques Lacan. Book VII: The Ethics of Psychoanalysis 1959–60*, trans. by Dennis Porter (New York and London: W.W. Norton, 1992) [1986]).

——, *Le Séminaire, livre XX: Encore 1969–70* (Paris: Editions du Seuil, 1975).

Lacoue-Labarthe, Philippe and Nancy, Jean-Luc, eds, *Les Fins de l'homme* (Paris: Galilée, 1981).

Laplanche, Jean, and Pontalis, Jean-Bertrand, 'Fantasy and the Origins of Sexuality', *International Journal of Psycho-Analysis*, 49, 1 (1968 [1964]), 1–18.

Laqueur, Thomas, 'Orgasm, Generation, and the Politics of Reproductive Biology', *Representations*, 14 (1986), 1–41.

——, 'Amor Veneris, vel Dulcedo Appelletur', in Michel Feher, Ramona Naddaff and Nadia Tazi (eds), *Fragments for a History of the Human Body. Part Three* (New York: Zone, 1989), pp. 91–131.

——, 'The Social Evil, the Solitary Vice and Pouring Tea', in Michel Feher, Ramona Naddaff and Nadia Tazi (eds), *Fragments for a History of the Human Body. Part Three* (New York: Zone, 1989), pp. 334–43.

——, *Making Sex: Body and Gender From the Greeks To Freud* (Cambridge MA and London: Harvard University Press, 1990).

Leech, Clifford, *Webster: The Duchess of Malfi* (London: Arnold, 1963).

Levine, Laura, *Men in Women's Clothing: Anti-theatricality and Effeminization 1579–1642* (Cambridge: Cambridge University Press, 1994).

Little, Arthur L., Jr, '"Transshaped" Women: Virginity and Hysteria in *The Changeling*', in James Redmond (ed.), *Madness in Drama* (Cambridge: Cambridge University Press, 1993), pp. 19–42.

Loomba, Ania, *Gender, Race, Renaissance Drama* (Manchester and New York: Manchester University Press, 1989).

——, '"Delicious traffick": Racial and Religious Difference on Early Modern Stages', in Catherine M.S. Alexander and Stanley Wells (eds), *Shakespeare and Race* (Cambridge: Cambridge University Press, 2000), pp. 203–24.

Lust's Dominion (London, 1657), Literature Online, University of Salerno, 16 June 2002, <http://lion.chadwyck.co.uk>.

Lyotard, Jean François, *Political Writings*, trans. by Bill Readings and Kevin Paul Geiman (Minneapolis: University of Minnesota Press, 1991).

McLuskie, Kathleen, 'Drama and Sexual Politics: The Case of Webster's Duchess', in James Redmond (ed.), *Drama, Sex, and Politics* (Cambridge: Cambridge University Press, 1985), pp. 77–91.

MacLean, Gerald, *Rise of Oriental Travel. English Visitors to the Ottoman Empire, 1580–1720* (Houndsmill and New York: Palgrave, 2004).

McMath, James, *The Expert Midwife: A Treatise of the Diseases of Women with Child and in Child-Bed* (Edinburgh, 1694).

McVicar, John, 'Performance Sex', *FHM*, 51 (March 1994), 43–7.

Marchitello, Howard, 'Vesalius' *Fabrica* and Shakespeare's *Othello*: Anatomy, Gender and the Narrative Production of Meaning', *Criticism*, 35 (1993), 529–58.

Marinelli, Giovanni, *Le medicine partenenti alle infermità delle donne* (Venice, 1563).

Marlowe, Christopher, *Edward II*, ed. Moelwyn Merchant (London, Ernest Benn, 1967).

Marshall, Cynthia, '*Coriolanus*, Gender, and the Theatrical Construction of Interiority', in Valerie Traub, M. Lindsay Kaplan and Dympna Callaghan (eds), *Feminist Readings of Early Modern Culture* (Cambridge: Cambridge University Press, 1996), pp. 93–118.

Marston, John, *Antonio's Revenge*, ed. G.K. Hunter (London: Edward Arnold, 1966).

Martin, Emily, *The Woman in the Body: A Cultural Analysis of Reproduction* (Milton Keynes: Open University Press, 1989 [1987]).

Massinger, Philip, *The Selected Plays of Philip Massinger* (Cambridge: Cambridge University Press, 1978).

——, *The Renegado*, in Daniel J. Viktus (ed.), *Three Turk Plays from Early Modern England* (New York: Columbia University Press, 2000).

Matar, Nabil, 'The Renegade in English Seventeenth-Century Imagination', *Studies in English Literature*, 33 (1993), 489–505.

——, *Turks, Moors, and Englishmen in the Age of Discovery* (New York: Columbia University Press, 1999).

Mauriceau François, *The Diseases of Women with Child, and in Child-Bed*, trans. Hugh Chamberlen (London, 1683).

Maus, Katharine E., 'Horns of Dilemma: Jealousy, Gender, and Spectatorship in English Renaissance Drama', *English Literary History*, 54 (1987), 561–83.

Mercurio, Scipione, *La Commare o riccoglitrice* (Venice, 1601).

Middleton, Thomas, *Women Beware Women*, ed. Roma Gill (London: Ernest Benn, 1968).

Middleton, Thomas and Rowley, William, *The Changeling*, ed. N.W. Bawcutt (London: Methuen, 1958).

Mitchell, Juliet and Rose, Jacqueline, *Feminine Sexuality: Jacques Lacan and the Ecole Freudienne* (London: Macmillan, 1982).

Montaigne, Michel de, *The Essayes of Michael Lord of Montaigne*, trans. by John Florio (1603) (London and New York: Routledge, 1885).

Montrose, Louis A., '"Shaping Fantasies": Figurations of Gender and Power in Elizabethan Culture', in Stephen Greenblatt (ed.), *Representing the English Renaissance* (Berkeley: University of California Press, 1988), pp. 31–64.

Moretti, Franco, 'The Great Eclipse: Tragic Form as the Deconsecration of Sovereignty', in *Signs Taken for Wonders: Essays in the Sociology of Literature*, trans. by Susan Fischer, David Forgacs and David Miller (London and New York: Verso, 1988 [1987]), pp. 42–82.

Muir, Edward and Ruggiero, Guido, eds, *Sex and Gender in Historical Perspective* (Baltimore MD: Johns Hopkins University Press, 1990).

Mullaney, Steven, *The Place of the Stage: Licence, Play, and Power in Renaissance England* (Chicago and London: Chicago University Press, 1988).

Neill, Michael, 'Changing Places in *Othello*', *Shakespeare Survey*, 37 (1984), 115–31.

——, 'Unproper Beds: Race, Adultery, and the Hideous in *Othello*', *Shakespeare Quarterly*, 40 (1989), 383–412.

——, '"Hidden malady": Death, Discovery, and Indistinction in *The Changeling*', *Renaissance Drama*, 22 (1991), 95–121.

Newman, Karen, *Fashioning Femininity and English Renaissance Drama* (Chicago and London: The University of Chicago Press, 1991).

Niccoli, Ottavia, '"Menstruum quasi monstruum": Monstruous Births and Menstrual Taboo in the Sixteenth Century', trans. by Mary M. Gallucci, in Edward Muir and Guido Ruggiero (eds), *Sex and Gender in Historical Perspective* (Baltimore MD: Johns Hopkins University Press, 1990), pp. 1–25.

Nietzsche, Friedrich, *On the Genealogy of Morals and Ecce Homo*, trans. by Walter Kaufmann (New York: Vintage Books, 1989).

O'Malley, C.D., 'Helkiah Crooke, MD, FRCP (1576–1648)', *Bulletin of the History of Medicine*, 42 (1968), 1–18.

Orgel, Stephen, 'Nobody's Perfect: Or Why Did the English Stage Take Boys for Women', *South Atlantic Quarterly*, 88 (1989), 7–29.

Orkin, Martin, '*Othello* and the "Plain Face" of Racism', *Shakespeare Quarterly*, 38 (1987), 166–88.

Paré, Ambroise, *The Workes*, trans. by Thomas Johnson (London, 1634 [1549]).

——, *On Monsters and Marvels*, ed. Janis L. Pallister (Chicago: University of Chicago Press, 1982).

Park, Katharine, 'The Rediscovery of the Clitoris: French Medicine and the Tribade, 1570–1620', in David Hillman and Carla Mazzio (eds), *The Body in Parts: Fantasies of Corporeality in Early Modern Europe* (New York and London: Routledge, 1997), pp. 171–93.

Park, Katharine and Daston, Lorraine J., 'Unnatural Conceptions: The Study of Monsters in France and England', *Past and Present*, 92 (1981), 20–54.

Park, Katharine and Nye, Robert A., 'Destiny Is Anatomy', *The New Republic* (18 February 1991), 53–7.

Parker, Patricia, '*Othello* and *Hamlet*: Dilation, Spying, and the "Secret Place" of Woman', *Representations*, 44 (1993), 60–95.

——, 'Gender Ideology, Gender Change: The Case of Marie Germain', *Critical Inquiry*, 19 (1993), 337–64.

Paster, Gail Kern, *The Body Embarrassed: Drama and the Disciplines of Shame in Early Modern England* (Ithaca and New York: Cornell University Press, 1993).

Perkins, William, *Christian Economy* (1609), trans. by Thomas Pickering, in Joan Larsen Klein (ed.), *Daughters, Wives and Widows: Writings by Men about Women and Marriage in England, 1500–1640* (Urbana and Chicago: University of Illinois Press, 1992), pp. 154–73.

Plato, *Timaeus*, trans. by R.G. Bury, in *Works*, VII, Loeb Classical Library (London: Heinemann, 1929).

Pouchelle, Marie-Christine, 'Espaces cosmiques et dispositifs mécaniques. Le Corps et les outils au XIIIe et XIVe siècles', in *Traverses* (Special issue: *Panoplies du corps*), 14–15 (1979), 93–104.

Prior, Mary, ed., *Women in English Society 1500–1800* (London and New York: Methuen, 1985).

Rackin, Phyllis, 'Historical Difference/Sexual Difference', in Jean R. Brink (ed.), *Privileging Gender in Early Modern England: Sixteenth Century Essays & Studies Vol. XXIII* (Ann Arbor: Michigan University Press, 1993), pp. 37–63.

Randall, Dale B.J., 'Some Observations on the Theme of Chastity in *The Changeling*', *English Literary Renaissance*, 14, 3 (1984), 347–66.

Redmond, James, ed., *Madness in Drama* (Cambridge: Cambridge University Press, 1993).

Roesslin, Eucharius, *The Birth of Man-Kinde; Otherwise named The Womans Book*, trans. Thomas Raynalde (London, 1626 [1545]).

Rose, Mary Beth, *The Expense of Spirit: Love and Sexuality in English Renaissance Drama* (Ithaca NY and London: Cornell University Press, 1988).

Rueff, Jakob, *The Expert Midwife, or an Excellent and Most Necessary Treatise of the Generation and Birth of Man* (London, 1637 [1554]).

Sadler, John, *The Sick Womans Private Looking-Glasse* (London, 1636) (repr. Amsterdam: Theatrum Orbis Terrarum, 1972).

Sawday, Jonathan, *The Body Emblazoned: Dissection and the Human Body in Renaissance Culture* (London and New York: Routledge, 1995).

Schor, Naomi, 'This Essentialism Which Is Not One: Coming to Grips with Irigaray', *Differences*, 2 (1989), 38–58.

Sedgwick, Eve Kosofsky, *Between Men: English Literature and Male Homosocial Desire* (New York: Columbia University Press, 1985).

——, *Tendencies* (London: Routledge, 1994).

Shakespeare, William, *The Complete Works*, ed. Peter Alexander (London and Glasgow: Collins, 1951).

——, *Antony and Cleopatra*, ed. M.R. Ridley (London: Methuen, 1954).

——, *Othello*, ed. M.R. Ridley (London and New York: Methuen, 1965).

——, *Coriolanus*, ed. Philip Brockbank (London: Methuen, 1976).

——, *Hamlet*, ed. Harold Jenkins (London: Methuen, 1982).

Sharp, Jane, *The Midwives Book* (London, 1671).

——, *The Midwives Book*, ed. Elaine Hobby (New York: Oxford University Press, 1999).

Sharrock, Cath, 'Hermaphroditism; or "The Erection of a New Doctrine": Theories of Female Sexuality in Eighteenth-Century England', *Paragraph*, 17 (1994), 38–48.

Shepherd, Simon and Wallis, Mick, eds, *Coming on Strong: Gay Politics and Culture* (London: Unwin Hyman, 1989).

Shirley, Thomas, *Discours of the Turkes*, ed. E. Denison Ross (London: Royal Historical Society, 1936).

Sinfield, Alan, *Faultlines: Cultural Materialism and the Politics of Dissident Reading* (Oxford: Clarendon Press, 1992).

——, 'How to Read *The Merchant of Venice* without Being Heterosexist', in Terence Hawkes (ed.), *Alternative Shakespeares: Vol. 2* (London and New York: Routledge, 1996), pp. 122–39.

Smith, Bruce R., *Homosexual Desire in Shakespeare's England* (Chicago: University of Chicago Press, 1991).

——, 'L[o]cating the Sexual Subject', in Terence Hawkes (ed.), *Alternative Shakespeares: Vol. 2* (London and New York: Routledge, 1996), pp. 95–121.

——, *Shakespeare and Masculinity* (Oxford: Oxford University Press, 2000).

Smith, Hilda, 'Gynecology and Ideology in Seventeenth-Century England', in Berenice A. Carroll (ed.), *Liberating Women's History. Theoretical and Critical Essays* (Urbana: University of Illinois Press, 1976), pp. 97–114.

Smith, Ian, 'Barbarian Errors: Performing Race in Early Modern England', *Shakespeare Quarterly*, 49 (1998), 168–86.

Spivak, Gayatri Chakravorty, *In Other Worlds: Essays in Cultural Politics* (London and New York: Methuen, 1987).

Stafford, Barbara Maria, *Body Criticism: Imagining the Unseen in Enlightenment Art and Medicine* (Cambridge MA: MIT Press, 1991).

Stallybrass, Peter, 'Patriarchal Territories: The Body Enclosed', in Margaret W. Ferguson, Maureen Quilligan, and Nancy J. Vickers (eds), *Rewriting the Renaissance: The Discourses of Sexual Difference in Early Modern Europe* (Chicago and London: Chicago University Press, 1986), pp. 123–42.

——, 'Reading the Body: *The Revenger's Tragedy* and the Jacobean Theater of Consumption', *Renaissance Drama*, 18 (1987), 121–48.

Stallybrass, Peter and White, Allon, *The Politics and Poetics of Transgression* (London: Methuen, 1986).

Stanton, Domna C., ed., *Discourses of Sexuality: From Aristotle to Aids* (Ann Arbor: The University of Michigan Press, 1992).

——, 'Introduction: The Subject of Sexuality', in *Discourses of Sexuality: From Aristotle to Aids*, ed. Domna C. Stanton (Ann Arbor: The University of Michigan Press, 1992), pp. 1–46.

Stone, Lawrence, *The Family, Sex and Marriage in England 1500–1800* (Harmondsworth: Penguin, 1979) (abr. ed.).

[T.E.], *The Law's Resolutions of Women's Rights* (1632), in Joan Larsen Klein (ed.), *Daughters, Wives and Widows: Writings by Men about Women and Marriage in England, 1500–1640* (Urbana and Chicago: University of Illinois Press, 1992), pp. 31–61.

Tennenhouse, Leonard, *Power On Display. The Politics of Shakespeare's Genres* (London and New York: Methuen, 1986).

——, 'Violence Done to Women on the Renaissance Stage', in Nancy Armstrong and Leonard Tennenhouse (eds), *The Violence of Representation: Literature and the History of Violence*, (London and New York: Routledge, 1989), pp. 77–97.

Todd, Barbara J., 'The Remarrying Widow: A Stereotype Reconsidered', in Mary Prior (ed.), *Women in English Society 1500–1800* (London and New York: Methuen, 1985), pp. 54–92.

Tourneur, Cyril, *The Atheist's Tragedy*, ed. Irving Ribner (London: Methuen, 1964).

Traub, Valerie, *Desire and Anxiety: Circulations of Sexuality in Shakespearean Drama* (London and New York: Routledge, 1992).

——, 'The (In)significance of "Lesbian" Desire in Early Modern England', in Susan Zimmerman (ed.), *Erotic Politics: Desire on the Renaissance Stage* (New York and London: Routledge, 1992), pp. 150–69.

——, 'The Psychomorphology of the Clitoris', *GLQ: A Journal of Lesbian and Gay Studies* (Special issue: *Pink Freud*, ed. Diana Fuss), 2, 1–2 (1995), 81–113.

Traverses (Special issue: *Panoplies du corps*), 14–15 (1979).

Treichler, Paula A., 'Feminism, Medicine, and the Meaning of Childbirth', in Mary Jacobus, Evelyn Fox Keller and Sally Shuttleworth (eds), *Body/Politics: Women and the Discourses of Science* (London and New York: Routledge, 1990), pp. 113–38.

Venette, Nicholas, *Conjugal Love; or, The Pleasures of the Marriage Bed* (London, 1750) (repr. New York and London: Garland, 1984).

Viardel, Cosme, *Observations sur la practique des accouchemens naturels, contre nature & monstreux* (Paris, 1671).

Vicary, Thomas, *A Profitable Treatise of the Anatomie of Mans Body* (London, 1577 [1548]) (repr. Amsterdam: Theatrum Orbis Terrarum, 1973).

Viktus, Daniel J., 'Turning Turk in *Othello*: The Conversion and Damnation of the Moor', *Shakespeare Quarterly*, 48, 2 (1997), 145–76.

——, 'Trafficking with the Turk: English Travelers in the Ottoman Empire During the Early Seventeenth Century', in Ivo Kamps and Jyotsna Singh (eds), *Travel Knowledge. European 'Discoveries' in the Early Modern Period* (Houndsmill and New York: Palgrave, 2001), pp. 35–52.

——, ed., *Three Turk Plays from Early Modern England* (New York: Columbia University Press, 2000).

Vives, Juan Luis, *The Instruction of a Christian Woman* (1523), in Joan Larsen Klein (ed.), *Daughters, Wives and Widows: Writings by Men about Women and Marriage in England, 1500–1640* (Urbana and Chicago: University of Illinois Press, 1992), pp. 100–22.

Webster, John, *The White Devil*, ed. Elizabeth M. Brennan (London: Ernest Benn, 1966).

——, *The Duchess of Malfi*, ed. John Russell Brown (Manchester: Manchester University Press, 1976).

Whigham, Frank, 'Sexual and Social Mobility in *The Duchess of Malfi*', *PMLA*, 100 (1985), 167–86.

——, 'Reading Social Conflict in the Alimentary Tract: More on the Body in Renaissance Drama', *English Literary History*, 55, 2 (1988), 333–50.

Whitford, Margaret, *Luce Irigaray: Philosophy in the Feminine* (London: Routledge, 1991).

Williams, Raymond, *Marxism and Literature* (Oxford: Oxford University Press, 1977).

Wilson, Luke, 'William Harvey's *Prelectiones*: The Performance of the Body in the Renaissance Theater of Anatomy', *Representations*, 17 (1987), 62–95.

Zimmerman, Susan, ed., *Erotic Politics: Desire on the Renaissance Stage* (New York and London: Routledge, 1992).

Žižek, Slavoj, *The Sublime Object of Ideology* (London and New York: Verso, 1989).

——, 'Looking Awry', *October*, 50 (1989), 31–55.

——, *Looking Awry: An Introduction to Jacques Lacan Through Popular Culture* (London and Cambridge MA: MIT Press, 1991).

——, 'Grimaces of the Real, or When the Phallus Appears', *October*, 58 (1991), 45–68.

——, *The Metastases of Enjoyment. Six Essays on Woman and Causality* (London and New York: Verso, 1994).

Index

Illustrations are indicated by the use of *italics*.